C++ Techniques and Applications Disk

Put C++ to work! The optional disk contains basic classes which can be used to create applications. Each class illustrates different facets of C++ programming and design. Classes developed include, List, Stack, Queue, BinaryTree, Bag, String, Window, Menu, TextWindow, and more. Available in MS/PC-DOS format.

To Order: Return this coupon with your payment to M&T Books, 501 Galveston Drive, Redwood City, CA 94063 or CALL TOLL-FREE 1-800-533-4372 (in CA 1-800-356-2002). Ask for Operator 7084.

YES! Please send me the C++ Techniques and Applications disk for $20.

CA residents add sales tax ___% _____

Total _____

_____ Check enclosed, payable to M&T Books.

Charge my _____ VISA _____ MC _____ AmEx

Card no. _____ Exp. Date _____

Signature _____

Name _____

Address _____

City _____ State _____ Zip _____

Note: Prices subject to change without notice. Disks may be returned for replacement only if damaged upon receipt.

7084

BUSINESS REPLY MAIL

FIRST CLASS PERMIT 871 REDWOOD CITY, CA

POSTAGE WILL BE PAID BY ADDRESSEE

M&T BOOKS

501 Galveston Drive
Redwood City, CA 94063-9702

PLEASE FOLD ALONG LINE AND STAPLE OR TAPE CLOSED

C++ Techniques and Applications

M&T BOOKS

C++ Techniques and Applications

Scott Robert Ladd

M&T Books
A Division of M&T Publishing, Inc.
501 Galveston Drive
Redwood City, CA 94063

© 1990 by M&T Publishing, Inc.

Printed in the United States of America
First Edition published 1990

Library of Congress Cataloging in Publication Data

Ladd, Scott.
    C++ techniques and applications / Scott Robert Ladd
        p.   cm.
    Includes index.
    ISBN 1-55851-075-3 : $29.95. -- ISBN 1-55851-076-1 (book/disk) :
$39.95. -- ISBN 1-55851-077-X : $20.00
    1. C++ (Computer program language)   I. Title. II. Title: C plus
    techniques and applications.
    QA76.73.C153L33   1990
    005.26'2--dc20
                                                        90-6392
                                                        CIP

93 92 91 90   4 3 2 1

Project Editor: David Rosenthal   **Cover Designer:** Michael Hollister

To my parents,
Robert and Janet Ladd,
who taught me I could accomplish
anything I set my mind to.

Contents

Why this Book Is for You

This book was written for the experienced C programmer interested in understanding C++. C++ is the object-oriented successor to C, developed at AT&T Bell Labs. Providing support for data abstraction, inheritance, and polymorphism, C++ offers significant software engineering benefits over C. While being nearly 100 percent compatible with ANSI C, C++ enhances C with non-object-oriented features like strong type-checking, inline functions, and function overloading.

C++ Techniques and Applications is the book for programmers who want to know the how, what, and why of C++ programming. The emphasis is on learning by doing, showing actual examples of practical C++ programming. All of the source code has been tested with the major C++ compilers for MS-DOS, including Zortech C++, the new Turbo C++, and ports of the AT&T *cfront* C++ translator for both MS-DOS and UNIX. No matter what your environment is, this book has something for you.

Subjects of particular interest include:

- Object-oriented programming design
- C++ programming tactics
- The "inside" story on how C++ works
- Examples of differences between C and C++
- Complete, object-oriented examples, such as windows and video screens; list, stacks, and queues; dynamic strings; and artificial life simulations

Introducing Object-Oriented Programming

Plunging into C++

I was introduced to the C++ programming language during the summer of 1988 by the good folks at *Micro Cornucopia Magazine* (a fine magazine which is, alas, now defunct). While I had heard of C++ before, it had never really caught my active attention.

As I began to investigate C++, I was a bit wary. I'm always skeptical of "the latest and greatest" innovations, both in and out of the computer world. Today's hot news is too often tomorrow's forgotten curiosity. While several people told me how wonderful and fantastic C++ is, I wanted to get to know it better before I made any personal judgments. C, Fortran, and Modula-2 provided everything I needed for my work as a consultant and writer. In addition, at that time C++ was implemented as a translator; it converted C++ to C which then needed to be compiled by a regular C compiler. This made developing with C++ a frustratingly slow task, and I had better things to do with my time.

In mid-1988, Zortech Inc. introduced a C++ compiler for MS-DOS computers. This was a momentous event for several reasons. To begin with, it was the first *true* C++ compiler -- it translated C++ source code directly into object form, without translating it to C first. Second, the compiler was inexpensive (an important consideration for a "starving writer" such as myself).

My first impression of C++ was that it was an attempt to "fix" C. This is how many books and periodicals have portrayed C++ -- as a "better" C. The additions of strong type-checking and data abstraction allowed me to do things in C++ which I had previously done in strongly-structured languages such as Modula-2. And, as many programmers have done, I learned C++ by writing C programs using C++'s advanced capabilities.

As I worked with C++, my opinion began to change. I had previously done some substantial work in Smalltalk, the premiere object-oriented programming language. I'd become disillusioned with Smalltalk because it suffered from severe performance penalties due to its interpreted nature and graphic interface. When I realized that C++ allowed me to do everything I had done previously in Smalltalk and C, it won my support completely.

I don't program much in C anymore; C++ has supplanted it. The power of object-oriented programming is addictive; I've becomes so accustomed to using encapsulation, inheritance, and polymorphism, that I find it unpleasant to program in a non-object-oriented language like C. While I still do some work in Smalltalk, C++ has many features its "purer" object-oriented cousins lack.

Most C programmers like the fact that C assumes they know what they're doing. They balk at languages like Pascal and Modula-2 that place straitjackets on them to prevent accidental mistakes. While straitjacket languages prevent simple mistakes, they also make creativity more difficult. I've always felt restrained by languages such as Modula-2 because I can't break the rules when I want to. C has never placed restrictions on the programmer, and so it tends to attract the mavericks; those highly creative individuals who create programs.

C++ continues the C tradition. It takes almost nothing away from C, and it adds a whole new realm of capabilities. C++ is, in my opinion, the most powerful general-purpose programming language in existence. It propels the already potent C language into the world of object-oriented programming.

However, this power comes without seat belts. Like C, C++ assumes that you know what you're doing; if you tell it to do something wrong, C++ merrily follows your commands without question. As an additional headache, C++ is a young language and its definitions are often imprecise. Learning C++ is often like taking a walk blindfolded through an Indiana Jones adventure -- you don't know a trap is there until it's sprung.

Current books on C++ take one of two approaches. Most C++ tomes offer simple introductions to the language, outlining the mechanics of C++ programming without filling in the details you need to make the language jump through hoops. The other books treat C++ as an improved C and fail to give you a full understanding of what object-oriented programming means to your work.

In many ways, I've written this book to save you from going through some of heartache and frustration I've experienced in learning C++. When I first started out, there were very few references on the language. Those references that did exist were already out-of-date or poorly written. So, I learned C++ by "playing" with it, designing projects and building them in C++. The result was that I uncovered many of the languages strengths and secrets. Until the publication of this book, these secrets have remained hidden for every programmer to find on his own.

You'll find that this book contains a number of personal comments, some anecdotes, and even a few jokes. Some people think programming is a serious subject deserving of a cold (and boring) academic treatment. Personally, I like books that are fun to read, and I hope that is what I've created in writing C++ *Techniques and Applications*. The programming examples are meant to be both educational and interesting. Heck, I wouldn't be a programmer if I didn't think it was something fun to do.

There are some prerequisites. This book assumes that you are already a proficient C programmer. I recommend that you wait to read this book if you're not comfortable with ANSI C; you don't need to be an expert C programmer, but you should understand the fundamentals. For example, this book doesn't give a description of how pointers work; it's assumed that you already know about pointers from having worked with C. As with all learning, it's best to understand the fundamentals before getting into the complexities.

What is Object-Oriented Programming?

The computer industry has a particular fascination with terminology. We can all fondly remember when terms like "ergonomics" and "user-friendly" were bandied about as if they were magic words. Unfortunately, those terms were also used in many inappropriate places and they subsequently became buzzwords. Once a term is overused enough to be called a buzzword, it is written off as meaningless. That same overuse seems to be happening to the phrase "object-oriented."

In some ways, you can draw a parallel between object-oriented and the current fascination for oat bran. Oat bran has been proven to reduce some forms of cholesterol in the bloodstream, and since that discovery every day sees new food product introduced that contain oat bran. Similarly, since it has been "proven" that object-oriented techniques make for better computer programs, everybody and his uncle is slapping the label "object-oriented" on hardware and software products. The result is the same: both oat bran and object-oriented are becoming the key terms in jokes.

Object-oriented programming isn't a joke (although oat bran may be). It's an important set of techniques that can be used to make program development more efficient while improving the reliability of the resulting computer programs. However, in order to understand what object-oriented programming is, it's necessary to understand its roots. So, let's begin by looking at the history of the programming process, examining how object-oriented programming evolved, and analyzing why it is important.

Linear Programming

Computer programming is a young discipline. The first programmable computers were only developed forty years ago. Over the last four decades, the evolution of programming has shown a clear trend; programming computers has become increasingly oriented towards the needs of the human programmer.

The first computers were programmed in binary; mechanical switches were used to load programs. With the advent of mass-storage devices and larger computer memories, the first high-level computer programming languages came into use. Instead of thinking in terms of bits and bytes, programmers could write a series of English-like instructions that a compiler could translate into the binary language of the computer.

These first programming languages were designed to develop programs that performed relatively simple tasks. These early programs were primarily concerned with doing calculations, and therefore were not very demanding on the programming language. What's more, most of these programs very short, often less than 100 lines of source code in length.

As the computers' capacity increased, so did the ability to develop more complex computer programs. Early programming languages were inadequate for these more involved programming tasks. The facilities needed to reuse existing program code were nearly nonexistent in linear programming languages. In fact, a piece of source was duplicated every time it was used in many programs. Programs tended to run on in one long sequence, making their logic difficult to understand. Program control was performed by jumping around in the program, often without any clear indication of how the program got where it was or why. To make matters worse, linear languages had no capability to control the visibility of data items. All data items in a program were global, meaning that they could be modified by any part of the program. Tracking down spurious changes to global data items in long, convoluted code sequences kept many programmers busy into the wee hours of the morning.

Structured Programming

It soon became apparent that new languages with new language features would have to be developed in order to create more sophisticated applications. The revolution occurred in the late 1960s and 1970s with the introduction of structured programming. Structured programs are organized according to the operations they perform. In essence, the program is broken up into individual procedures (also known functions) that perform discrete tasks in a larger, more complex process. These procedures are kept independent of each other as much as possible, each with its own data and logic. Information is passed between procedures using parameters, and procedures can have local data that cannot be accessed outside of the procedure's scope. In a way, functions can be thought of as miniature programs that are put together to build an application.

The goal was to make software development easier for the programmer while improving program reliability and maintainability. A structured program is built by breaking down the program's primary function into fundamental pieces which then become the functions within the program. By isolating processes within functions, a structured program minimizes the chance that one procedure will affect another. This also makes it easier to isolate problems. Compartmentalization allows you to write clearer code and maintain control over each function. Global variables disappear and have been replaced by parameters and local variables that have a smaller, more controllable scope. This better organization means that you have a fighting chance when it comes to understanding the logic of a structured program, making both development and maintenance faster and more efficient.

A powerful concept was introduced with structured programming: abstraction. Abstraction could be defined as the ability to look at something without being concerned with its internal details. In a structured program, it is sufficient to know that a given procedure performs a specific task. How that task is performed is unimportant; so long as the procedure is reliable, it can be used without having to know how it correctly completes its function. This is known as functional abstraction and is the cornerstone of structured programming.

Today, structured programming and design techniques are ubiquitous. Nearly every programming language has the facilities required to support structured programming. Even traditionally unstructured languages like Basic have begun to exploit structured programming constructs. The reason for this is simple. Structured programs have proven themselves to be easier to write and maintain than non-structured programs.

And these advances in the types of applications programmers write have continued. As the complexity of a program grows, so does its dependency on the fundamental data types that it processes. It has become apparent that the data structures in a program are just as important as the operations performed on them. This becomes more evident as a program grows in size. Data types are processed in many procedures within a structured program, and when changes occur in those data types, modifications must be made to every location that acts on those data types within the program. This can be a frustrating and time-consuming task in programs that contain thousands of line of code and hundreds of functions.

A further weakness of structured programming appears when multiple programmers work on an application as a team. In a structured program, each programmer is assigned to build a specific set of functions and data types. Since different programmers handle separate functions that relate to mutually-shared data types, the changes one programmer makes to data items must be reflected in the work of the rest of the team. While structured programs were easier to work with in a group situation, errors in communication between team members could lead to time spent rewriting.

Data Abstraction

Data abstraction does for data what functional abstraction does for operations. With data abstraction, data structures and items can be used without having to be concerned about the exact details of implementation. For instance, floating-point numbers are abstracted in all programming languages. You don't have to be concerned with the exact binary representation of a floating-point number when assigning it a value. It is not necessary to understand the vagaries of binary multiplication in order to multiply floating-point values. The important thing is that floating-point numbers act in a correct and understandable manner.

Data abstraction frees you from worrying about non-essential details. If a programmer had to be cognizant of every minute aspect of a program's function, few programs would ever be written. Fortunately, data abstraction exists in all programming languages for complicated elements such as floating-point numbers. It has only been recently, however, that languages have been developed that allow you to define your own abstract data types.

Object-Oriented Programming

The object-oriented paradigm is built on the foundation laid by structured programming concepts and data abstraction. The fundamental change is that an object-oriented program is designed around the data being operated upon, rather than upon the operations themselves. This is quite natural once you realize that the purpose of a program is manipulate data. After all, the work performed by computers is called data processing. Data and action are linked on a fundamental level; each requires the other to have purpose. Object-oriented programs make this relationship explicit.

Object-oriented programming associates data structures with operations, which is how we all think about the world. We associate a specific set of actions with a given type of object, and base assumptions on those associations. For example, we know that a car has wheels, moves, and has its direction changed by turning a steering wheel. Similarly, we know that a tree is a plant with a woody stem and leaves. A car is not a tree, and a tree is not a car, and we can assume that what can be done with a car cannot be done with a tree. For example, it is futile to try to steer a tree, while a car does not grow when we water it.

Object-oriented programming allows us to use these same mental processes with the abstract concepts used in computer programs. A personnel record can be read, changed, and saved, or a complex number can be used in calculations. Yet a complex number cannot be written to a file as a personnel record, and two personnel records cannot be added together (I should hope). An object-oriented program specifies the exact characteristics and behavior of its data types, which allows us to know exactly what to expect from various data types.

It's also possible to create relationships between similar, yet distinct data types in an object-oriented program. People naturally classify things. We constantly relate new concepts to existing ones, and are able to make deductions based on relationships between things. We like to conceptualize the world as a tree-like structure, with successive levels of detail building on earlier generalizations. This is an efficient method of organizing the world around us. Object-oriented programs work in the same natural manner in that they allow new data/operation frameworks to be built on existing frameworks, incorporating the features of the base framework while adding new features.

Let's look at this further on a non-programming level. When you hear the word "plant," you can immediately visualize a generic item of that type. You do not need to be told the exact species of plant, but you can generalize based on the characteristics shared by all plants. Every plant converts solar energy into food, and most plants are green because of the chlorophyll they use in the energy conversion process. These types of generalizations are useful, since, when discussing plants in general, we do not need to know the specifics of any one species of plant.

I'm sure many of you have seen a taxonomic chart which shows the relationships of various kinds of plants. For instance, blue-green algae and an oak tree are both plants, yet they are very different. Blue-green algae are tiny, single-celled plants that live in the water. An oak tree is a multi-cellular plant that is often large and has a woody trunk and leaves. Both are plants, and yet both are very different. Biologists thus define the algae and oak trees as members of the same family, but they belong to different sub-groups of that family.

Object-Oriented Terminology

Object-oriented programming lets you organize the data in your program the same way a biologist organizes different kinds of plants. In the parlance of object-oriented programming, cars, trees, inventory records, complex numbers, and books would all be known as classes. A class is a template that describes both the data structure and the valid actions for data items. When a data item is declared to be a member of a class, it is called an object. Those functions that are defined as valid for a class are known as methods, and they are the only functions that manipulate the data of that class's objects.

Each object has its own copies of the class data elements, which are called instance variables. The methods defined for the class can be invoked by objects of that class. This is called sending a message to the object. Messages are object-specific; only the object receiving the message acts upon that message. Objects are independent of each other, therefore changes to the instance variables of one object have no affect on the instance variables of other objects, and sending a message to one object has no affect on other objects.

The standard data types built into a programming language can be thought of as classes. When you declare an integer variable, you know that it can store non-fractional numbers between certain values. Integers can be manipulated using the standard numeric operations. However, you cannot assign a text value to an integer. What's more, changing one integer does not affect any other integers you may have declared. Object-oriented programming allows you to create your own data tightly controlled types, which are just like the types built into the language.

Unlike the built-in data types, classes can use other classes as building blocks. New classes can be built from old ones through inheritance. A new class, referred to as a derived class, can inherit the data structure and methods of the original, or base class. The new class can add data elements and methods to those it inherits from its base class. Any class (including a derived one) can have any number of derived classes. It is through the inheritance mechanism that hierarchies of classes are built. Class hierarchies often look similar to family trees, which is why a base class is called a parent class and a derived class is called a child class.

For example, we'll build a set of classes that describe a library of publications. There are two primary types of publications: periodicals and books. We can create a general publication class by defining data items for the number of pages, a library catalog number, the copyright date, and the publisher. Publications can be retrieved, stored, and read. These are the methods of a publication.

Next, we define two derived classes named periodical and book. A periodical has a volume and issue number and contains multiple pieces by different authors. Data items for these will be included in our definition of a periodical. The periodical will also need a unique method: subscribe. Data items specific to a book will include the names of its author(s), a cover type (hard or soft), and its ISBN number. As you can see, a book and a periodical share the characteristics of a publication while having their own unique attributes.

Our base class, publication, defines methods for storing and retrieving data. However, a periodical may be stored in a binder, while a book is placed on a shelf. Furthermore, the way to find a specific periodical to be retrieved is different from finding a book. Periodicals are located through a guide to periodical literature, while books are found using a card catalog system. We could make a "find through periodical guide" method for a periodical, and a "find through card catalog" method for a book. But is this the best way to handle this situation?

Object-oriented programming provides an elegant facility called polymorphism to handle these circumstances. When classes are derived from a base class, it may be necessary to change the way in which the base class methods work. In our example, we find that both periodicals and books can be retrieved. However, the retrieval method for a periodical is different from the retrieval method for book, even though the end result is the same. Polymorphism allows you to define a method for retrieving a publication that can work for both periodicals and books. When a periodical is retrieved, the retrieve method that is specific to a periodical is used, but when a book is retrieved, the retrieve method associated with a book is invoked. The end result is that a single method name can be used for the same operation performed on related derived classes, even if the implementation of that method varies from class to class.

Polymorphism depends on binding, which is the process whereby a method is associated with an actual function. When polymorphic methods are used, the compiler cannot determine which method function to call. The specific function called depends on the class of the item to which the message is being sent, therefore the function to be called is determined at run time. This is known as late binding, since it occurs when the program is executing. Early binding occurs in some object-oriented programming languages for non-polymorphic (also known as static) methods. The compiler knows exactly which method function is invoked so it can build a direct call at compile time. While early binding is very efficient, most object-oriented languages use late binding for all methods.

As you can see, object-oriented programming introduces several new terms and concepts to computer programming. While it all sounds interesting, what do all these things mean to you? Can object-oriented programs fulfill the promise of making software development faster while improving reliability? The answer is yes.

Object-oriented programs are built from reusable software components. Once a class is completed and tested, it can be used like a building block to construct the program. If new features or changes are required, new classes can be derived from existing ones; the tried-and-true capabilities of base classes do not need to be redeveloped. Programmers can get on with writing new code instead of writing something over. Software becomes easier to test since program errors can be isolated within the new code of derived classes.

As a collection of classes is created, it will become easier to develop new applications from those classes. Programmers who work in a group can build an application as a series of classes, which are then melded together to form a final program. You also can use and enhance classes developed by other project members, without making changes to the actual implementations of those classes, or even seeing them.

Another important use of classes is to hide implementation details. For example, a library of graphics classes could have different implementations for various types of video display. A program that uses graphics classes could be written in such a way that it is compilable, without change, on any computer to which the library's implementation has been ported.

15

From here, we move into looking at how C++ implements the object-oriented programming concepts discussed here. While you may still be somewhat confused by the quantity of new ideas, actually working with an object-oriented language like C++ should make your understanding complete.

CHAPTER

2

The Fundamentals of C++ for C Programmers

"What is C++?" "Why is it important?" "What can you do with C++ that you can't do with other programming languages?" "Is it really worth spending the time to learn one of the most complex computer programming languages ever designed?" "How can C++ really be used effectively?" "What are C++'s strengths and weaknesses?"

I've heard these questions from host of programmers over the last two years. This book will attempt to provide answers to these and related questions. But before we address the intricacies and inner workings of C++, let's lay some groundwork by discussing the basics of C++ in terms that C programmers will understand.

Developing Tools

Our ancestors started down the road to civilization by creating tools. Tying a sharpened stone to the end of a stick created a tool that could be used to kill large animals for food. A similar stone was used to skin animals, and the hides became clothes that protected humans from the environment. The discovery of methods to control fire provided light in the night, warmth from the cold, and a way to cook food.

Without tools such as these, the human race would never have progressed beyond the level of animals. It is our intelligence that allows us to identify and examine a problem, and then create a tool that provides a solution. As our understanding of the world and our needs grows, we expand and modify our arsenal of tools. We began with bonfires and have learned to build furnaces, internal combustion engines, and rockets to the moon. As our technology has advanced, we have learned to use tools to build other, more complicated tools.

A computer represents a pyramid of tools. The computer hardware itself is a tool. However, in order for the computer to accomplish a task, it must be given a set of step-by-step instructions that explain how that task is to be accomplished. To create the software, which are the tools that make the computer perform a task, we use other tools such as programming language compilers, text editors, and object-module linkers. As computers add capabilities, we demand more from our software. That demand, in turn, drives advances in software development tools.

The primary software development tool is the computer programming language itself. Every ten years or so, programming languages must be modified so they become better able to deal with the increasing complexity of the software applications they are meant to produce. Consider that we have evolved from programming computers in binary to using English-like text to describe how a process is to be performed. Today, computer applications have reached another plateau of intricacy, and we are now seeing new programming languages emerge that make solving these problems easier.

C++ as a Tool

C++ evolved from C, which in turn evolved from earlier programming languages.

C gained significant popularity in the 1980s, but its widespread use led to the recognition that C had flaws and limitations that made it unsuitable for complex programming projects. C++ is an attempt to improve upon C by expanding the programming language to support new software development concepts.

As I stated in the introduction, this book is meant to be used by a proficient C programmer who wishes to learn more about C++. This first step is to introduce the minor, yet significant, differences between the current ANSI definition of C and the definition of AT&T C++ 2.0. The next step is to examine how functions are used differently in C++. The chapters that follow describe how object-oriented programs can be designed and written in C++. This will not only show you how C++ differs from C, but why programmers like me believe that C++ is a major step forward in software engineering.

In the years to come, more and more C programmers will migrate to C++. They don't need to know that arrays and pointers in C++ are related, or how a function is declared. All they need to know is how C++ works in comparison to C.

While C++ attempts to be a superset of ANSI C, the compatibility between the two languages isn't perfect. This chapter documents many tricky areas of incompatibility which can cause hours of frustration for anyone who is unaware of them.

New Keywords

In order to add features to C, a number of new keywords were created for C++. Any C program that uses identifiers with the same name as these keywords will have to be changed before that program can be compiled with C++. These new keywords are:

asm	*catch*	*class*	*delete*	*friend*
inline	*new*	*operator*	*private*	*protected*
public	*template*	*this*	*virtual*	

The *catch* and *template* keywords are reserved by C++ 2.0, but have not yet been implemented.

// Comments

C++ supports two types of comments. C programmers will already be familiar with comments delimited by /* and */. The compiler ignores everything which comes after a /* until it finds a */. For instance, in this program:

```
1:  /*
2:      program: iterate
3:      purpose: prints integers 0 to 9
4:  */
5:
6:  #include "streams.hpp"
7:
8:  int main()
9:      {
10:     int i;
11:
12:        for (i = 0; i < 10; ++ i) // loop i from 0 to 9
13:            cout << i << "\n";     // display i
14:     }
```

everything between /* on line 1 and */ on line 4 is ignored by the compiler.

This program also demonstrates the second type of comment. Lines 12 and 13 show a comment that begins at a // and goes to the end of the current line.

In general, the /* ... */ comment style is used for large block commands and the // style is used for one-line comments.

Casts

C++ supports two different forms of explicit casts:

```
int  i = 0;
long l = (long)f; // traditional C-type cast
long m = long(f); // a new-style C++ cast
```

Some programmers consider the later form, which looks like a function call, easier to read. Since it's possible to create functions to perform casts involving user-defined types, the second form may be better to use under certain circumstances.

void

The type *void* represents the null set, i.e., an object of type *void* has no values. At first glance, it might seem senseless to have a type for which there are no defined values. In practice, however, *void* is very useful, so useful, in fact, that ANSI C incorporates it.

A function that does not have a meaningful return value can be declared to return a *void* value. This eliminates the possibility that such functions could return a useless *int* value.

void can be used to define a pointer to a generic item. Prior to the introduction of *void*, a pointer to a *char* or *int* would be used to refer to some part of memory without having to be concerned with the type of data stored there. The original Kernighan & Ritchie (K & R) version of the *malloc* memory allocation function returned a *char **. Under ANSI C and C++, *malloc* returns a *void **. Since a *void ** can be assigned to any pointer, you can avoid many useless casts. You can think of a *void ** as a pointer to any type.

Flexible Declarations

C demands that all declarations within a given scope occur at the beginning of that scope. Or to put it simply, all global declarations must appear before any functions, and any local declarations must be made before any executable statements. C++, on the other hand, allows you to mix data declarations with functions and executable code.

C++ Techniques and Applications

Consider this correct, if somewhat badly written, C function:

```
void makeit(void)
    {
    float i;
    char * cp;

    /* imagine 200 lines of code here! */

    /* allocate 100 bytes for cp */
    cp = malloc(100); /* 1st use of cp */

    for (i = 0; i < 100; ++i) /* 1st use of i */
        {
        /* do something in this loop */
        }

    /* more code */
    }
```

After 200 lines of code, space for *cp* is allocated, and *i* is finally used
in a loop. Unfortunately, by that time the programmer has forgotten
what *i* was declared as. So, since *i* is a *float*, the *for* loop is created
using a *float* for the iterator, which makes it slower than it should
be. Declarations that are made far away from the use of the data
item they declare can be confusing and lead to errors.

C++ allows declarations to be placed closer to their point of actual
usage. Let's rewrite *makeit* in C++.

```
void makeit()
    {
    // 200 lines of code

    // allocate 100 bytes for cp
    char * cp = new char[100];

    // do the loop
    for (int i = 1; i < 10; i++)
        {
        // do something in this loop
        }
    }
```

The C++ version is easier to follow by declaring *i* and *cp* when they are first used, rather than declaring them 200 lines earlier. This is another example of how C++ has made C less prone to errors.

const

While ANSI C borrowed the concept of *const* values from C++, it does not implement them in the same manner. In both C and C++, a value declared as *const* is inviolate; it may not be modified by the program in any way. The most common use of *const* values in C is to replace *#defined* literal constants.

In C++, *const* values can be considerably more flexible. To begin with, *const* values can be used in place of any literal constant. This is an immensely useful capability that allows you to create typed constants instead of having to use *#define* to create constants that have no type information.

The following code fragment is acceptable in C++, but would be flagged as an error by ANSI C:

```
const int ArraySize = 100
int Array[ArraySize];
```

The scoping of *const* values differs between ANSI C and C++, too. In ANSI C, *const* values have global scope, meaning that they are visible outside of the file in which they are declared unless they are also declared static. This can wreak havoc when placing *const* definitions in a header file that is included by more than one source module of a program. C++ solves this problem by making all *const* objects static by default.

Type Compatibilities

C is fairly flexible when it comes to type compatibility. C++, however, is far pickier. For example, C++ defines the types *short int*, *int*, and *long int* as different types. Even if a *short int* is identical in size and format to a plain *int*, C++ still considers them different types that must be cast when those types values are assigned to one another. This is a safety precaution — truly portable code must treat these types as different since different architectures may define the implementations of these types differently.

The character types are another example of types that the compiler sees as different, even though the programmer may think of them as the same. *unsigned char*, *char*, and *signed char* will each have a size equal to 1, but they are not considered identical by C++. Once again, this is match to promote portable code. In C++, the types of values must exactly match for complete compatibility. Otherwise, a cast is required.

sizeof(char)

In C, all *char* constants are stored as *int*s. This means that in C:

```
sizeof('1') == sizeof(int);
```

In C++, a single *char* is treated as a single byte, and it is not promoted to the size of an *int*. So, in C++:

```
sizeof('1') == 1;
```

When writing code in C++, be careful that your programs do not rely upon the C convention.

struct and *union* Tags

In C++, *struct*s and *union*s are actually types of classes; they can contain both data definition and functions. However, two changes have been made in C++ that are of interest to those of you with existing C programs.

To begin with, *struct* and *union* tags are considered to be type name, just as if they had been declared by the *typedef* statement. In C, we would have this code fragment:

```
struct foo { int a; float b};

struct foo f;
```

This declares a *struct* with the tag name *foo*, and then creates an instance of *foo* named *f*.

In C++, things are simpler:

```
struct foo { int a; float b};

foo f;
```

The same conventions apply to *unions*. However, to maintain compatibility with C, C++ still accepts the older syntax.

Anonymous unions

A special type of *union* has been added by C++. Called an *anonymous union*, it merely declares a set of items that share the same memory address. An *anonymous union* does not have a tag name, and the items can be directly accessed by name. This is an example of an anonymous union in C++:

```
union
    {
    int i;
    float f;
    }
```

Both *i* and *f* share the same memory location and data space. Unlike unions which have tags, however, *anonymous union* values are accessed directly. This code fragment could appear after the above anonymous *union* was declared, and it would be acceptable:

```
i = 10;
f = 2.2;
```

enum Types

Enumerated types are treated slightly differently in C++ than they are in ANSI C. For instance, the *enum* tag name is considered a type name, just as the *struct* and *union* tags previously discussed are considered type names.

C defines the type of *enum*s to be *int*. In C++, however, each enumerated type is its own, separate type. This means that C++ does not allow for an *int* value to be automatically converted to an *enum* value. However, an enumerated value can be used in place of an *int*. This C code fragment would be wrong in C++:

```
enum Place {First, Second, Third};

Place John = First;    // this if okay...
int Winner = John;     // ...and so is this...
Place Tom  = 1;        // ... but this is an ERROR!
Place Mark = Place(1); // ... using a cast fixes it
```

All four of these statements would have been acceptable in C. However, C++ flags the assignment to *Tom* because the constant *1* is not a value defined for *Place*.

The :: Operator

:: is the scope resolution operator, and is used to access an item hidden in the current scope. For example:

```
#include "stream.hpp"

int a;

int main()
    {
    float a;

    a   = 1.5;
    ::a = 2;

    cout << "local  a = " << a << "\n";
    cout << "global a = " << ::a << "\n";
    }
```

In essence, the *::* operator says, "Don't use the local a; use the one declared outside of this scope." Thus, the above program will display:

```
local  a = 1.5
global a = 2
```

The scoping operator is also used in class method function definitions to declare the class that owns a given method. The scope operator can also be used to differentiate between members of base classes with identical names. A later chapter will clarify many of these issues.

new and *delete*

In traditional C programs, all dynamic memory allocation is handled via library functions, such as *malloc* and *free*. C++ defines a new method of doing dynamic allocation using the *new* and *delete* operators.

Here's a traditional C function that uses dynamic memory:

```
void func(void)
    {
    int * i;

    i = malloc(sizeof(int));
    * i = 10;
    printf("%d",* i);
    free(i);
    }
```

In C++, the *new* operator replaces the C function *malloc*, and the *delete* operator takes the place of *free*. So in C++, we could rewrite the above function like this:

```
void func()
    {
    int * i = new int;
    i = 10;
    cout << i;
    delete i;
    }
```

I think you'll agree that the C++ syntax is much clearer and easier to use. To allocate an array of 10 *int*s, you'd use the following statement:

```
    int * i = new int[10];
```

By the way, if *new* cannot allocate the requested amount of memory, and a heap error handler has not been defined (see below), its return value is NULL. This is just like a *malloc* call, which also returns NULL when a heap error occurs.

You might wonder why *new* and *delete* were added to C++ when the existing C library functions work just as well. The answer is flexibility. Any class can use operator overloading to define its own versions of *new* and *delete*. If a class does not define *new* and/or *delete*, the default global versions of those operators are used. This allows a class to define its own memory allocation functions for special applications. In addition, the global *new* and *delete* operators also can be replaced. By defining memory allocation in terms of operators instead of functions, C++ gives the programmer flexibility in dynamic memory management.

The new operator can replace both the *malloc* and *calloc* functions from the standard C library. The only commonly used C library memory-allocation function that cannot be replaced by *new* is *realloc*, which changes the amount of memory allocated to a pointer. *realloc* can be simulated like this:

```
// change the space allocated to a char pointer

char * temp = new char[new_size]; // allocate new space

if (temp != NULL)  // if the space was allocated
    {
    // copy data from old location to new location
    if (new_size > old_size)
        memcpy(temp,cp,old_size);
    else
        memcpy(temp,cp,new_size);

    delete cp;  // delete old data
    cp = temp;  // cp now points to new data location
    }
```

This approach is considerably clumsier than *realloc*. It takes many more lines of source, and it requires knowledge of the original size of the space allocated through the pointer being changed. Luckily, there is no incompatibility between pointers whose memory was allocated via the default versions *new* and *dispose*, and the standard C library functions. Therefore, you can generally continue to use *realloc* to change the space allocated to pointers generated by *new*.

However, a problem can arise when mixing the function-based dynamic memory functions with *new* and *delete*. It's possible to create custom versions of *new* and *delete* on a global or class level. A custom memory allocator based on *new* and *delete* will probably not use the same memory management techniques as the C library functions.

Therefore, if *new* and *delete* are replaced, you won't be able to use *re-alloc*, *malloc*, or *free* with the C++ memory allocators.

In general, it's best to stay with either the C functions (*malloc*, etc.) or the C++ operators *new* and *delete*. Trying to use both dynamic memory management systems can lead to all sorts of problems and inconsistencies. Also, it tends to make the program confusing when, for example, both *malloc* and *new* are used to create objects on the heap. For the sake of consistency, I will use only the C++ system.

new has yet another advantage. Unlike *malloc*, any memory allocation errors can be caught with a user-defined handler. C++ defines a special function pointer; when *new* is used and a memory allocation error occurs, the function pointed to by that pointer is called. The definition of this pointer is:

```
void (* _new_handler)();
```

To put it in English, *_new_handler* is a pointer to function with an empty (*void*) argument list that does not return a value. By creating such a function and assigning its address to *_new_handler*, you can catch all memory allocation errors in your function. It works like this:

```
#include "new.h"          // defines _new_handler
#include "stream.hpp"

void heapProblem();

void heapProblem()
    {
    cout << "Heap failure!\n";
    }

int main()
    {
    // some code here

    // set _new_handler to point to heapProblem
    _new_handler = heapProblem;

    // and some code here!
    }
```

There is also a library function defined in *new.h* called *set_new_handler* which does assign a function to *_new_handler*. Frankly, I haven't seen any reason to use the function when direct assignment is available.

References

C can be clumsy at times. For example, if you want to write a function that swaps the values of a pair of integers, you could write it like this:

```
void swapint(int * a, int * b)
    {
    int temp;

    temp = *a;
    *a = *b;
    *b = temp;
    }
```

Calling the swap function would be done with this kind of statement in C:

```
swapint(&i1, &i2);
```

C++ supports a special type of identifier know as a reference. You can think of a reference as an alias for another identifier. References can make functions that change the values of their parameters much more elegant. A C++ version of *swapint* would be:

```
void swapint(int & a, int & b)
    {
    int temp = a;
    a = b;
    b = temp;
    }
```

A reference is indicated by using the *&* operator in the same way you use the * operator to indicate a pointer. The difference between a pointer to something and a reference to something is that the pointer needs to be dereferenced where the reference does not. Thus, the C++ version of *swapint* does not need to dereference the parameters a and b in order to change the values of the arguments.

The calling syntax is much simpler, too:

```
swapint(i1,i2);
```

C++ automatically passes the address information for *i1* and *i2* as arguments to the *swapint* function.

When used for function parameters, C++ references are similar to *VAR* parameters in Pascal and Modula-2. References are particularly useful when passing large structures and objects to a function. By using a reference for a parameter only the address is passed, not the entire structure or object. This not only saves time and stack space, it also makes using the structure/object parameters easier within the function itself.

Reference parameters are efficient, and should be used whenever large structures are being passed to functions. Sometimes, though, you'll want to pass something by reference for efficiency, even though you don't want the value to be changed. This can be done with the *const* qualifier, like this:

```
void yaba(const int & daba);
```

The *yaba* function will accept an integer value (*daba*) passed by reference, but *const* states that *daba* cannot be changed. The *const* qualifier allows you to use efficient references without sacrificing data integrity.

While references may seem similar to pointers, they are not pointers. They cannot be used to allocate dynamic memory, nor can they be manipulated mathematically. The purpose behind references was to make is possible to write functions that change their arguments, and those functions that accept structures and objects as parameters, in a clearer fashion.

Functions in C++

You may be surprised at the number of ways C++ has changed and improved the way C supports functions. Many of these changes are simple, while others require you to adopt a new way of thinking when organizing your program's code. In many cases, these modifications were driven by the requirements of object-oriented facilities in C++. They also were invented to make C++ programs "safer" and more readable than their C equivalents.

main()

C does not define a specific format for the *main()* function (other than its name). I often write the definition of main like this:

```
void main(void)
    {
    // main program code here
    }
```

In many programs, I don't care about returning any sort of status to the operating system. C++, however, explicitly defines *main* as matching one of the two following prototypes:

```
int main();
int main(int argc, char * argv[]);
```

In C++, any other header format for *main* will generate an error. Most C++ compilers will also give you an error or warning if you don't return a value from *main*. This can be done with a *return* statement or a call to the *exit* function.

Since C++ forces *main* to have a return value, it's a good programming practice to actually return a value from *main*. Just letting your program end by reaching the end of *main* will result in an unpredictable return value. Even if your program has no informative return value, having an explicit return 0 statement where your program exits *main* will indicate that your program was successful.

Function Prototypes

You may have encountered function prototypes in ANSI C. However, you may not know that ANSI C borrowed the concept of function prototypes from C++. A function prototype is a declaration that defines both the return type and the parameters of a function. In traditional C, functions are declared like this:

```
int something();
```

You'll notice that the above declaration says nothing about the types of parameters accepted by *something*. In pre-ANSI C, a function declaration merely defined the return value type for a function.

Under C++, *something* would be declared using a statement like this:

```
int something(char * str, unsigned int len);
```

This states that *something* is a function returning an *int* value with two parameters, a pointer to a character and an *unsigned int*. The compiler uses the prototype to ensure that the types of the arguments you pass in a function call are the same as the types of the corresponding parameters. This is known as strong type-checking, something which pre-ANSI C lacks.

Without strong type-checking, it's easier to pass illegal values to functions. A non-prototyped function will allow you to send an *int* argument to a pointer parameter, or use a float argument when a function expected a *long*. These kinds of errors result in invalid values for the function parameters. In addition, when improper types are passed to a function the compiler may not restore the correct amount of stack space and your stack may crash.

While ANSI C merely allows you to use prototypes, C++ requires them. In C++, prototypes do more than make sure that arguments and parameters match. As we'll discuss later in this chapter, C++ internally generates names for functions, including parameter type information. The parameter information is used when several functions have the same name.

In function prototype for *something*, the parameter tags *str* and *len* are not stored in the symbol table, nor do they need to match the names of the corresponding parameters in the function definition. They are present solely to document the purpose of the parameters; you can think of them as short "comments" describing what the function parameter is expecting for an argument. For the sake of clarity, I suggest the parameter tags you use in a function prototype be identical to the names of the corresponding parameters in the function definition.

You'll also need to change the way you declare and define functions that have a void (i.e. empty) argument list. Functions with an unspecified number of parameters of unknown types are also declared differently in C++.

To compare, let's consider these two C prototypes:

```
/* this is C */
int doit(void); /* function accepting no parameters */
int grok();     /* function w/ open parameter list */
```

In C++, you can leave out the void and use a set of empty parenthesis instead, as in this example:

```
// this is C++
int doit();    // function accepting no parameters
int grok(...); // function w/ open parameter list
```

A C++ function that has an empty parameter list cannot except arguments. In order to have an "open" parameter list, you need to use the ellipses.

Remember that all functions in C++ must be prototyped! That means every function must have its argument list declared, and the actual definition of a function must exactly match its prototype in the number and types of parameters.

Prototyping functions may mean a bit more work when you initially write a program, but prototypes can be invaluable tools in preventing hard-to-find errors. C++ was designed to prevent many of the problems caused by sloppy programmer passing the wrong type to methods. If you really need to pass a *long* as an *int*, you can do so using a cast. That way you have explicitly (rather than accidentally) passed a value of one type as an argument to a parameter of another type.

Prototype-like Function Headers

For those of you who began your C programming career working with K & R's C, you may be used to writing function definitions like this:

```
void widget(a, b)
int a;
double b;
        {
        // do whatever a widget does
        }
```

While C++ accepts this form, it's considered better programming practice to use a prototype-like format for the function header. In C++, the function above would be written like this:

```
void widget(int a, double b)
        {
        // do whatever a widget does
        }
```

The C++ style is easier to understand than the C style. In future versions of C++, beyond C++ 2.0, the C syntax may be dropped altogether.

"Name Mangling"

C++ does something referred to as "name mangling," which really sounds worse than it is. C++ uses name mangling to change the names of functions in order to incorporate information on the types of parameters associated with that function. These changes are all internal and consist of appending parameter information to the function identifier. Since several functions may have the same name, the C++ compiler differentiates between them by changing the names internally to reflect the differences in parameter types. Name mangling is necessary to support overloaded functions and operators (discussed below).

In most cases, you'll never see the mangled names. However, if you put C++ functions into object module libraries, or if you experience linkage errors during compilation, you may see these mangled names. Sometimes it's handy to be able to "decode" mangled names, as in the case of a linker error that results when a function was not found. Actually, name mangling is a very simple process. A sequence of codes is appended to the name of the function to indicate the types of parameters and the order in which they occur. (A more comprehensive discussion of name mangling system can be found in a later chapter.)

In the case of C++ translators, mangled names can cause problems for the underlying C compiler. The translator generates an intermediate C program that is compiled into object form by a C compiler. This makes C++ translators dependent upon the underlying C compiler. In the case of name mangling, C++ does not define a maximum identifier length, but all C compilers I've seen do set a maximum. The ANSI C standard says that all internal identifiers must be unique within the first 31 characters, and that identifiers with external linkage must be unique within 8 characters.

Unfortunately, the ANSI C limits on identifier length do not work well with C++. C++ translators will often create identifiers with 40 or more characters. Ignoring the fact that some identifiers will not be unique within 8 or 31 characters, most C compilers will complain about the long names with numerous warnings. Luckily, C++ compilers translate C++ directly to object code without using a C compiler, and don't have this problem.

Inline Functions

A well-structured program uses functions to break up code into logical, self-contained units. However, functions incur a certain amount of processing overhead: arguments must be pushed onto the stack, a call must be executed, and a return must be implemented followed by the removal of the parameters from the stack. At times, this function overhead forces the C programmer to duplicate code throughout a program to increase efficiency.

The designers of C++ recognized this problem and invented the inline function to solve it. When a function definition header line contains the word "inline," that function is not compiled as a separate piece of callable code. Instead, the function is inserted wherever a call to that function appears. This eliminates function overhead while still allowing a program to be organized in a structured manner.

For example, C++ compiles this function as inline code:

```
inline int addemup(int a, int b)
    {
    return a + b;
    }
```

This function would not actually exist as a callable subroutine. Instead, the compiler inserts the code to accomplish its task wherever a call to *addemup* appears in the program. C++ translators create macros for inline functions and insert those macros into resulting C program at points where the function is called. A C++ compiler precompiles the routine and inserts the precompiled instructions at the appropriate locations.

There are some rules for using inline functions. Inline functions must be defined before they can be used. This is because the code for the inline function must be precompiled (or turned into a macro in the case of a translator) before it can be inserted into the program. Therefore, the following code would not compile as expected:

```
#include "stdio.h"

int addemup(int a, int b);

int main()
    {
    int x = addemup(1,2);

    printf("%i\n",x);
    }

inline int addemup(int a, int b)
    {
    return a + b;
    }
```

Cfront, the standard AT&T C++ translator, will give you an error indicating that you've declared and used *addemup* as a real function, but have defined it as inline. Adding the keyword inline to the function prototype won't help; you must always define your inline functions before they are referenced.

Of course, the only consistency in life is inconsistency. The Zortech compiler for MS-DOS does not generate an error as docs cfront. Since the actual definition of *addemup* is after its use, it won't be compiled inline for *main*. Instead, *addemup* is compiled as a standard, callable function.

Things get even more complicated when you use the Zortech compiler to compile this program:

```
#include "stdio.h"

int addemup(int a, int b);
void func();

int main()
    {
    int x = addemup(1,2);

    printf("%i\n",x);

    func();
    }

inline int addemup(int a, int b)
    {
    return a + b;
    }

void func()
    {
    int x = addemup(3,4);

    printf("%i\n",x);
    }
```

Zortech generates a function body and a function call because of the call to *addemup* in *main*, which occurs before the compiler sees the inline specifier on the definition for *addemup*. However, when addemup is called from *func*, the code for *addemup* is generated inline.

These subtle differences between different implementations of C++ can hurt you if you're not careful. In this case, it's best not to rely upon Zortech's abilities to handle out-of-order, inline function definitions. Instead, you should assume that you're using AT&T's cfront, which requires that all inline functions be defined before they are used. Otherwise, your programs will not be portable to cfront implementations.

The major drawback to using inline functions is that, in most cases, they make your program larger. Simple functions, such as addemup, might actually be smaller than a real function, since each call sequence would be replaced by a set of add and assignment instructions. On the other hand, complex inline functions can contain a large amount of code. You'll have to watch the size of your functions to be sure that you aren't bloating your program's to improve performance by a few seconds.

If your inline function contains complex flow control statements, you may find that your C++ compiler ignores the inline specification. While the cfront translator generates macros for inline functions, which are then inserted into the C program wherever an inline function occurs, macros are severely limited in their ability to contain control structures such as loops and conditional statements. The limitations are stricter for cfront, which cannot handle any conditional or loop statements in an inline function. By contrast, the Zortech compiler can easily handle simple *if* statements as part of an inline function. In general, though, inline functions should consist only of assignments, expressions, and simple function calls.

The *inline* keyword serves as a suggestion to the compiler, not a command. As with the *register* keyword, the compiler is can ignore *inline* if it so chooses. For example, if you have too many inline functions, you may find that the compiler will stop inlining functions when it runs short on memory. Long *inline* functions, even those that lack control structures, also may be compiled as regular functions. In addition, recursive functions, i.e. functions that call themselves, cannot be made inline for obvious reasons.

There are a number of tricks and caveats that will help you make good use of inline functions. As you'll see in later chapters, inline functions are important when you're creating your own data types. Throughout the extended examples in the later part of this book, I'll demonstrate the judicious and efficient use of inline functions.

Default Argument Values

One of the most useful facilities in C++ is its ability to define default argument values for functions. Normally, when you call a function, you need to specify an argument for every parameter defined for that function. For example:

```
1:      void delay(int loops); // prototype
2:
3:      void delay(int loops) // function definition
4:           {
5:           if (loops == 0)
6:                return;
7:
8:           for (int i = 0; i < loops; ++i)
9:                ;
10:          }
```

Whenever the *delay* function is called, it must be passed a number of loops to determine how long it iterates. In many situations, however, you may find that you're almost always calling delay with the same value for *loops*. But there is a way to tell C++ that a parameter has a default value. Let's say that you want the default value of *loops* in the *delay* function to be 1000. A simple change to the prototype in line 1 will accomplish this:

```
void delay (int loops = 1000);
```

Whenever a call to *delay* is made without specifying an argument for *loops*, the program will automatically assign *loops* a value of 1000. For example,

```
delay(2500);    // loops will be set to 2500
delay();        // loops will default to 1000
```

One thing most C++ texts don't tell you is that the default value for a parameter can be a global constant, a global variable, or even a function call. For example, a function to set a clock could have a prototype like this:

```
int setclock(time_t start_time = time(NULL));
```

If *setclock* is called without an argument for *start_time*, a default value will be obtained by making a call to the standard library function *time*.

The default arguments are given only in the function prototype and should not be repeated in the function definition. The compiler uses the prototype information to build a call, not the function definition. Be careful to ensure that all of your program modules use the same prototype for a function.

A function may have more than one default parameter. The default parameters must be grouped consecutively as the last (or only) parameters for a function. When calling a function that has multiple default arguments, you can only leave out arguments from right to left, and you must leave them out consecutively. Some examples should clarify these rules:

```
// this prototype is an error!
void yucky(int a = 1, int b, int c = 3, int d = 4);

// and this one's okay!
void funky(int a, int b = 2, int c = 3, int d = 4);
```

The first prototype assigns default arguments to the first, third, and fourth parameters. Since arguments can only be consecutively dropped from right-to-left, there is no way to use the default argument for the first parameter, since the second parameter has not default. The second prototype is perfectly acceptable.

Let's use look at some good and some bad calls to the *funky* function:

```
// okay; args for every parameter
funky(10,15,20,25);

// bad! parameter a doesn't have a default arg!
funky();

// good; params c and d are assigned default args
funky(12,15);

// error! skipped parameters must be consecutive
funky(3,10,,12);
```

Default arguments can make programs easier to write and maintain. For example, if you have an existing function that needs to have new parameters added, you can use default arguments for these new parameters. This alleviates the need to change existing code. Default arguments can also be used to combine similar functions into one. As you'll see in the detailed examples in this book, default arguments can have a wide range of applications.

Type-Safe Linkage

In C, there are no provisions to handle linkage with object modules created by other programming languages. For example, Pascal and Fortran generally order parameters on the stack in the opposite order from that used by C. Most Pascal compilers convert all identifiers to uppercase, while C compilers allow both upper and lower case. In order to allow multi-language programming, C compiler designers have added several new keywords to identify the calling convention of a particular function or identifier. In most MS-DOS C compilers, the keyword pascal can be added to the declaration of a function to identify this function as one that uses the Pascal calling sequence. For example,

```
pascal int foobar(int a, int b);
```

is the prototype for a function, *foobar*, that uses the Pascal calling conventions. The biggest drawback to special language keywords such as *pascal* is that they aren't officially standardized.

Remember, too, that C++ does name mangling, while C does not. Therefore a mechanism called *type-safe linkage* was invented to specify a standard form of linkage specification. In C++, declarations of functions located in modules compiled by a C compiler would be written like this:

```
extern "C" {
    double sin(double x);
    double cos(double x);
    double tan(double x);
    }
```

The declarations for functions compiled by C are in a block that begins with the statement extern "C". This tells the C++ compiler not to mangle these function names.

The conventions of other languages also can be specified using this syntax; the C++ specification leaves room for C++ implementations to define linkages to other languages. Zortech C++, for example, supports Pascal linkages. It's even conceivable that someone will invent FORTRAN and COBOL linkages.

Let me offer a further hint to C++ programmers who use assembley language modules. Instead of worrying about name mangling, write your assembler language functions exactly as if they were to be linked with C. Then specify "C" linkage in the header included into your C++ programs.

Another hint for C programmers: Most C programmers will have a library of C functions. Linking these to C++ require the use of type-safe linkage. However, I don't know of any C compiler that will accept, or even ignore, the syntax for type-safe linkage from C++. Assuming you're a good C programmer, you have declarations for your library functions stored in one or more header (#include) files. Change these header files so they have this syntax:

```
#if defined(__cplusplus)
extern "C" {
#endif

// your declarations here

#if defined(__cplusplus)
    }
#endif
```

This will only include the C++ type-safe linkage statements when you're compiling a C++ program; all C++ compilers define the *__cplusplus* macro automatically. Or you can bracket the inclusion of C-language headers in C++ programs like this:

```
extern "C"
    {
    #include "stdio.h"
    #include "ctype.h"
    }
```

Making either of these minor changes to your C-language headers will make your C libraries usable for both C and C++ programs.

Overloading

C++ has made two more significant additions to the capabilities of function. You can have multiple functions with the same name through a process called overloading. In addition, C++ allows you to define your own functions for symbolic operators, such at +, —, or *.

Overloading is a two-fold concept. Its most obvious function is to allow the same function name to be used by different function implementations. Less obvious but equally important is its ability to overload operators by creating functions that are invoked when a symbolic operator is used. Both of these capabilities are powerful, and their effective use requires the programmer to be judicious and careful.

Function Overloading

In C, as in most computer languages, every function must have a unique name. At times this can be annoying. For instance, in C there are several functions that return the absolute value of a numeric argument. Since a unique name is required, there is a separate function for each numeric data type. Thus, there are three different functions that return the absolute value of an argument:

```
int abs(int i);
long labs(long l);
double fabs(double d);
```

All of these functions do the same thing, so it seems a bit silly to have three different function names. C++ solves this paradox by allowing you to create three different functions with the same name. This is called overloading. For example, in C++ you could define these three functions to replace those listed above:

```
int    abs(int i);
long   abs(long l);
double abs(double d);
```

Through name mangling (discussed previously), the C++ compiler can determine exactly which implementation of the *abs* function is appropriate for a given function call. For example:

```
abs(-10);      // calls int    abs(int i)
abs(-100000);  // calls long   abs(long l)
abs(-12.34);   // calls double abs(double d)
```

The process of picking which overloaded function to use is the same process used by C++ to resolve other ambiguities. If, for example, an implementation of an overloaded function exists that has identical parameter types to those of the arguments being passed in a call, that implementation is called. Otherwise, the C++ compiler calls the implementation that provides the easiest series of conversions. For instance:

```
abs('a');      // calls int abs(int i)
abs(3.1415F);  // calls double abs(double d);
```

Built-in conversions are favored over the conversions you've created. When we get into object-oriented programming later in the book, you'll see how to define conversions between your own data types and intrinsic types. In almost all cases, the choice of which overloaded function to use will be made based on the ease of fitting the arguments to the parameter lists available.

It's possible to take the address of an overloaded function, provided that you somehow make the compiler can determine from which version of the overloaded function you are taking the address. I suspect an example is needed to clarify this concept:

```
int foo(int i);
int foo(char c);

int (*ptr2foo)(int) = &foo;
int (*ptr2foo)(char) = &foo;
int (*ptr2foo)(double) = &foo;     // Error
int (*ptr2foo)(...) = &foo;        // Error
```

In the first two address assignments, the compiler can easily match up the type of the pointer to the type of a version of *foo*. The third assignment fails because there isn't a *void foo(double)*. The final assignment is ambiguous; without a detailed parameter list, the compiler has no way of knowing for which version of *foo* you want the address.

Overloaded Function Caveats

There are some restrictions on the use of overloaded functions. Like a C program, a C++ program can ignore a function's return value. Therefore, overloaded functions must differ in ways other than their return type. The following declarations would be illegal:

```
int process(int i);
void process(int i);
```

There would be no way for the compiler to know which implementation of the function was called if the return value was ignored. So, overloaded functions must at least differ in the type or number of parameters they accept.

Make sure the different types of your overloaded function parameters are actually different types. A *typedef* type is merely an alias for an existing type and does not constitute an original type of its own. So the following code fragment would be wrong:

```
typedef INT int;

// both prototypes are identical in use
void humbug(int x);
void humbug(INT x);
```

The example above would not compile correctly, because the compiler has no way of differentiating between the two versions of humbug. An *INT* is just another name for an *int*.

const and reference pointers in a function can differ by using a *const* qualifier, as in this code fragment:

```
void func(char * ch);
void func(const char * ch);

int main()
    {
    const char c1 = "a";
    char c2 = "b";

    func(&c1); // calls void func(const char * ch);
    func(&c2); // calls void func(char * ch);
    }
```

It's very bad programming form to have overloaded functions that perform different actions. Functions with the same name should have the same general purpose. To create an implementation of the *abs* function which returns the square root of a number would be both silly and confusing.

I also suggest that you use overloaded functions in moderation. Their purpose is to provide a mnemonic name for several similar but slightly divergent functions. Overusing overloaded functions can make a program unreadable.

Operator Overloading

When you create a new data type in C, you may find that operations involving that data type are clumsy. For instance, let's say that you've written this C program:

```
#include "stdio.h"

/* structure definition */
typedef struct
    {
    double real, imag;
    }
    complex;
```

```
/* prototypes */
int main(void);
complex cplx_set(double r, double i);
void cplx_print(complex c);
complex cplx_add(complex c1, complex c2);
complex cplx_sub(complex c1, complex c2);

/* main program */
int main(void)
    {
    complex a, b, c, d;

    a = cplx_set(1.0,1.0);
    b = cplx_set(2.0,2.0);

    c = cplx_add(a,b);
    d = cplx_add(b,cplx_sub(c,a)); /* clumsy! */

    printf("c = ");
    cplx_print(c);
    printf(" and ");

    printf("d = ");
    cplx_print(d);
    printf("\n");
    }

/* set the value of a complex */
complex cplx_set(double r, double i)
    {
    complex temp;

    temp.real = r;
    temp.imag = i;

    return temp;
    }

/* display a complex */
void cplx_print(complex c)
    {
    printf("(%g,%g)",c.real,c.imag);
    }

/* return the result of adding two complexs */
complex cplx_add(complex c1, complex c2)
    {
    complex temp;

    temp.real = c1.real + c2.real;
    temp.imag = c1.imag + c2.imag;
```

```
    return temp;
    }

/* return the value of subtracting two complexs */
complex cplx_sub(complex c1, complex c2)
    {
    complex temp;

    temp.real = c1.real - c2.real;
    temp.imag = c1.imag - c2.imag;

    return temp;
    }
```

This program creates a structure called *complex* that contains the two components (real and imaginary) of a complex number. Four functions are defined to manipulate *complex* values. *cplx_set* sets the value of a *complex*; *cplx_print* displays a *complex* value; *cplx_add* and *cplx_sub* allow *complex*s to be added and subtracted.

Using the tools presented so far in this book, we can create a better version of that program using C++:

```
#include "stdio.h"

// structure definition
struct complex
    {
    double real, imag;
    };

// prototypes
int main(void);
complex cplx_set(double r, double i);
void cplx_print(complex c);
complex operator + (complex c1, complex c2);
complex operator - (complex c1, complex c2);

// main program
int main(void)
    {
    complex a, b, c, d;

    a = cplx_set(1.0,1.0);
    b = cplx_set(2.0,2.0);
```

```
    c = a + b;
    d = b + c - a;

    printf("c = ");

    cplx_print(c);
    printf(" and ");

    printf("d = ");
    cplx_print(d);
    printf("\n");
    }
// set the value of a complex
complex cplx_set(double r, double i)
    {
    complex temp;

    temp.real = r;
    temp.imag = i;

    return temp;
    }

// display a complex
void cplx_print(complex c)
    {
    printf("(%g,%g)",c.real,c.imag);
    }

// return the result of adding two complexs
complex operator + (complex c1, complex c2)
    {
    complex temp;

    temp.real = c1.real + c2.real;
    temp.imag = c1.imag + c2.imag;

    return temp;
    }

// return the value of subtracting two complexs
complex operator - (complex c1, complex c2)
    {
    complex temp;

    temp.real = c1.real - c2.real;
    temp.imag = c1.imag - c2.imag;

    return temp;
    }
```

These two programs are very similar. However, in the C++ is version, operations on complex values are carried out using standard arithmetic notation, rather than using lengthy functions names. Where in the C program we had the statement:

```
d = cplx_add(b,cplx_sub(c,a));
```

we have this corresponding statement in the C++ program:

```
d = b + c - a;
```

Both statements produce the same result, but the C++ statement is easier to understand. I'll bet you can already see places where your own program can become clearer through the use of operator overloading.

C++ works by creating functions that define the actions performed on non-intrinsic types by an operator. An operator function is declared using the *operator* keyword and an operator symbol. In the preceding examples, the C function *cplx_add* is replaced by the C++ function operator + (complex *c1*, complex *c2*). C++ sees that + is a binary operator, and the compiler knows that the first parameter is to the left of the symbol, while the second parameter is to the right of the symbol. The program statements between the two programs that actually add two complex values are identical. All that differs is the syntax of addition.

The Most-Asked Questions About Operator Overloading

The following are some common questions about operator overloading;

Which operators can be overloaded?

Almost every C++ operator can be overloaded. The only operators that cannot be overloaded are:

```
.    .*    ::    ?:
```

If an operator has unary and binary forms (such as + or &), both forms can be overloaded. A unary operator has one parameter, while a binary operator has two parameters. The only trinary operator, ?:, cannot be overloaded. (See the section on Operator Function Details for explanations about overloading each type of operator.)

It may be important to note that the dynamic memory management operators *new* and *delete* can be overloaded. Replacing these operators with your own functions allows you to customize the memory allocation system.

You can overload the pointer, reference, and dereference operators, too. By overloading these in conjunction with creating your own *new* and *delete*, you can completely replace the entire memory allocation and pointer system in C++. C++'s built-in dynamic memory system is designed for general use.

new and *delete* aren't the only candidates for overloading that are less than obvious. The function call and subscript operators, *()* and *[]* respectively, can be overloaded, for instance.

How does the compiler know which operator function to use?

Overloaded operator functions are chosen by the compiler using the same mechanism that is used to choose from several overloaded functions. When a non-intrinsic operator is encountered, the compiler looks for an operator function that has parameters to match the operands that are found.

What is the precedence of operator functions?

The operator functions you've defined have the same precedence as the intrinsic operations that use the same operator. For example, the * operator always has precedence over the + operator. There is no way to change operator precedence.

Is it possible to redefine intrinsic operators?

What you are really asking is, is it possible to create your own operator for adding a pair of *ints*? The answer is no. Allowing you to change the behavior of intrinsic operations would make any program virtually unreadable. However, you can create operator functions that accept intrinsic types as parameters, but those functions must not have identical parameter types and return values to the standard definitions for those operators.

Can operator functions be made inline?

Yes. In fact, it's highly recommended that simple operations, such as + and –, are defined by inline functions. This makes your arithmetic statements very efficient. However, avoid inlining complex operator functions, particularly when those functions are more than a few lines in length. What you'll gain in code speed you'll lose in code size.

How do intrinsic and overloaded operators work differently?

There is no way to create different overloaded versions of operators like — and ++ for prefix and postfix notation. For example, if you define your own version of —, it will work in the same way when used in either prefix and postfix notations.

How do you explicitly call an operator?

Sometimes, you want to call a specific operator, usually to override a default operator function chosen by the compiler. The process isn't complicated, as this example shows:

```
complex operator + (complex c1, complex c2);

int main()
    {
    complex x, y;
    // several lines of code
    complex z = operator + (x,y);
    }
```

Operator functions expect a specific set of arguments. In most cases, operators with the same number of arguments can be grouped together.

Unary Operators

The unary operators are:

```
  *    &    ~    !    ++    -    sizeof    (type name)
```

Unary operators must be defined as having only one argument. There is no difference between postfix and prefix notation with unary operators; if you define your own routine for the increment operator (++), it will work the same way whether it is placed before or after its argument.

There are two exceptions. The unary operators should return a value of the same type as their argument. In the case of the sizeof operator, it should return a value of type *size_t* (defined in the header file *stddef.h*) The (*type name*) operator is used for conversions. It should return a value of the type listed in parenthesis, which is the converted equivalent of the value of its argument.

Binary Operators

The binary operators are:

```
  *    /    %    +    -    <<    >>    <    >    ,
  <=   >=   ==   !=   &    !=    ^     |    &&   ||
```

I guess it's obvious that functions for binary operators need to be defined with two arguments. These two arguments do not need to be identical types, although they should almost always be the same type.

Assignment Operators

The assignment operators are:

```
=    +=   -=   *=   /=   %=   >>=  <<=  &=   ^=   |=
```

Assignment operators are defined as having one argument, just as do unary operators have one argument. There are no restrictions on the argument or return types for an assignment operator.

Member Access Operator

This is the -> operator and it should only be overloaded with great care. It is normally used to access the members of a structure or class, and any other use is probably misleading. For all intents and purpose, you can define the member access operator the same way you would define a unary operator.

Subscript Operator

The subscript operator [] should be used to find a specific element within a data item. Normally, it is used with arrays, but you can define it to work with your own data types. The *String* data type (defined in a later chapter) defines the subscript operator to return the character at a given position within a *String*. The subscript operator has only one argument.

Function Call Operator

I've never overloaded the () operator, and I suspect I never will. I've seen some clever uses for defining a function call operator, but none seem to aid in program readability or functionality. I strongly urge caution in defining your own version of ().

The function call operator can have any number of arguments (including no arguments), and any type of return value.

Operator Function Tactics

While the principle of operator overloading is simple enough, the overloading of operators is not something that should be attempted without caution or forethought. A facility this powerful can easily be misused, making a program difficult to understand and possibly impossible to maintain.

First of all, make sure that your operators maintain the spirit of their original purpose. Don't define the + operator to subtract two values (unless, of course, you are trying to confuse yourself and others). Think about the logic of your operator definitions before you write code. I've seen many novice C++ programmers go wild with operator overloading, creating programs that look more like hieroglyphics than computer programs. While you may think that the circumflex (^) should be used for exponentiation, that isn't it's original use within C++ where it serves as the bitwise exclusive or operator.

That's not to say that there's anything wrong with being creative in your use of operators. It's possible to create arrays that have string or floating point subscripts by defining your own function for the subscript operator. That doesn't violate the spirit of array indexing, since you're using a value to find a specific element of an array. However, using the subscript operator to search for substrings within text is not in keeping with the original function of the *[]* operators.

Finally, make sure that you document your overloaded operators. Don't assume that what is obvious to you is obvious to another programmer. Consider my friend who defined the subscript operator to do substring searches on a string value when a string value was contained in the brackets. That same programmer also defined the binary *&* operator as a substring extractor. Personally, I think both cases were examples of poor judgment in overloading operators; neither of these operator uses was intuitive or logical to me.

Of course, there are better ways in C++ to build a data type for handling complex numbers. That involves object-oriented programming, the most powerful capability of C++. And that's the subject I'll discuss in the next several chapters.

Classes

Now that we have introduced several object-oriented programming concepts in a general sense, it's time to see how C++ implements those concepts. We'll begin by looking at the way C++ defines classes.

This program is taken from the C++ complex number example presented in Chapter 2:

```
#include "stdio.h"

// structure definition
struct complex
    {
    double real, imag;
    };

// prototypes
int main(void);
complex cplx_set(double r, double i);
void cplx_print(complex c);
complex operator + (complex c1, complex c2);
complex operator - (complex c1, complex c2);

// main program
int main(void)
    {
    complex a, b, c, d;

    a = cplx_set(1.0,1.0);
    b = cplx_set(2.0,2.0);

    c = a + b;
    d = b + c - a;
```

```
    printf("c = ");
    cplx_print(c);
    printf(" and ");

    printf("d = ");
    cplx_print(d);
    printf("\n");
    }

// set the value of a complex
complex cplx_set(double r, double i)
    {
    complex temp;

    temp.real = r;
    temp.imag = i;

    return temp;
    }

// display a complex
void cplx_print(complex c)
    {
    printf("(%g,%g)",c.real,c.imag);
    }

// return the result of adding two complexes
complex operator + (complex c1, complex c2)
    {
    complex temp;

    temp.real = c1.real + c2.real;
    temp.imag = c1.imag + c2.imag;

    return temp;
    }

// return the value of subtracting two complexes
complex operator - (complex c1, complex c2)
    {
    complex temp;

    temp.real = c1.real - c2.real;
    temp.imag = c1.imag - c2.imag;

    return temp;
    }
```

This program, called *cplx.cpp*, implements a structure and a simple set of associated functions to work with complex numbers. By defining operators to add and subtract, the program can manipulate complex values using the same familiar syntax that we use for the intrinsic mathematical types (*int*, *float*, etc.)

However, *cplx.cpp* is not an object-oriented program. An object-oriented program combines the data and functional definitions of a type and binds them together. To prevent inadvertent changes to itself, an object-oriented data type controls access to its components. *cplx.cpp* lacks both of these characteristics. The functions that can affect the complex structure are not bound to the structure, and there is nothing to prevent direct manipulation of the internal components of the complex structure.

Class Definitions

A *struct* in C contains one or more data items (called *members*), which are grouped together as a unit. C++ extends the syntax of *struct* to allow the inclusion of functions in structures. The functions defined within a *struct* have a special relationship to the *struct*'s data members and are called *methods*.

Here's a new version of *cplx.cpp* called *cplx2.cpp*:

```
extern "C" {
    #include "stdio.h"
    }

// class definition
class complex
    {
    private:
        double real, imag;

    public:
        // set complex value
        void set(double r, double i = 0.0);

        // output display
        void print();
```

```
        // arithmetic methods
        complex operator + (complex c);
        complex operator - (complex c);
    };

// prototypes
int main(void);

// constructor
void complex::set(double r, double i)
    {
    real = r;
    imag = i;
    }

// display a complex
void complex::print()
    {
    printf("(%g,%g)",real,imag);
    },

// return the result of adding two complexes
complex complex::operator + (complex c)
    {
    complex temp;

    temp.real = real + c.real;
    temp.imag = imag + c.imag;

    return temp;
    }

// return the value of subtracting two complexes
complex complex::operator - (complex c)
    {
    complex temp;

    temp.real = real - c.real;
    temp.imag = imag - c.imag;

    return temp;
    }

// main program
int main(void)
    {
    complex a, b, c, d;

    a.set(1.0,1.0);
    b.set(2.0,2.0);
```

```
c = a + b;
d = b + c - a;

printf("c = ");
c.print();
printf(" and ");

printf("d = ");
d.print();
printf("\n");
}
```

The first thing you'll notice is that *struct complex* in *cplx.cpp* has been changed to *class complex* in *cplx2.cpp*. In C++, a *class* is almost exactly the same thing as a struct in C. In fact, *cplx2.cpp* could have been written using the *struct* keyword instead of *class*. There is a subtle technical difference between *struct* and *class*, but we'll cover that a bit later in this chapter. For now, assume that *class* is better suited to the *cplx2.cpp*. Any general comments about classes also apply to structures; remarks specific to *class* or *struct* will be designated as such.

Objects

In C++, an object is an item declared to be of a class type. The variables a, b, c, and d in *cplx2.cpp* are all objects. An object is also called an instance of a class. A pointer or reference to an object provide indirect ways to access an object, but the pointer or the reference itself is not an instance of a class.

Data Members and Instance Variables

Data members cannot be declared to be *auto, register,* or *extern*. They can be *enums*, bit fields, and other intrinsic or user-defined types. Data members can be objects in their own right; however, only objects of previously declared or defined classes can be members. A class may not define data members which would be instances of itself. A class can, however, contain references and pointers to instances of itself.

Each object has a unique set of variables that correspond in name and type to the data elements defined for its class. A variable associated with an object is called an instance variable. As shown in *cplx2.cpp*, the same syntax is used to access an object's instance variables that is used to access the data members of a struct in C. Objects are self contained; the instance variables of one object have no affect on the instance variables of other objects.

Methods

A function declared within the definition of a class is called a member *function* or *method*. These two terms are interchangeable; member function is a C++ term and method is a general object-oriented programming term. The member functions provide controlled access to the data members of a class.

In *cplx2.cpp*, you'll note that the definition of class complex contains prototypes for its member functions. These prototypes follow the same syntax as the prototypes used to declare non-member functions. The definitions for these member functions are elsewhere — they can be in the same file or another source file.

Member function definitions have a slightly different header format than non-method functions. The name of the class with which a method is associated is added as a prefix to a method function's name. The scoping operator, ::, separates the class name from the function name. Several classes may have functions of the same name, and this syntax indicates the class associated with the method function definition.

The following program shows how this syntax is used to differentiate between methods of the same name that are declared in different classes.

```
extern "C" {
    #include "stdio.h"
    }

class C1
    {
    private:
        int i;
    public:
        void set(int x);
        void print();
    };

class C2
    {
    private:
        int j;
    public:
        void set(int x);
        void print();
    };

void C1:set(int x)
    {
    i = x;
    }

void C1::print()
    {
    printf("%d",j);
    }

void C2::set(int x)
    {
    j = x;
    }

void C2::print()
    {
    printf("%x",j);
    }

int main()
    {
    C1 a;
    C2 b;

    a.set(100);    // calls C1::set
    b.set(100);    // calls C2::set
```

```
a.print();    // calls C1::print
b.print();    // calls C2::print
}
```

The classes *C1* and *C2* both define the methods *set* and *print*. Implementations of these methods include the name of the proper class in the header to identify the class that includes them.

Non-operator methods are called using the same syntax you would use to access a data member of a class. In *cplx2.cpp* the methods *set* and *print* are called for a specific object by giving the name of the object, the member access operator (the period), and the name of the method.

The Implicit Object

A call to a method function is associated with a specific object via the member access operator. I refer to this object as the implicit object. A pointer to the implicit object is passed as a "hidden" first argument in the method call, and this pointer argument is named *this*. You don't need to declare the *this* argument. In fact, *this* is reserved in C++. The C++ compiler automatically generates a *this* pointer for every non-static member function.

There are two ways to access the members of the implicit object. Let's look at the most common form of access by examining the *set* method from *cplx2.cpp*:

```
void complex::set(double r, double i)
    {
    real = r;
    imag = i;
    }
```

The assignments to *real* and *imag* in the definition of *set* refer to the instance variables of those names that are part of the implicit object. No qualification is need; the compiler assumes that unqualified instance variable references are associated with the implicit object. I call this inferred member access, since the programmer does not specify the object with which the instance variables are associated.

The complement of inferred member access is direct member access. The *set* method could be changed to reference the instance variables of the implicit object via the *this* pointer. In that case, the definition of *set* would look something like this:

```
void complex::set(double r, double i)
    {
        this->real = r;
        this->imag = i;
    }
```

There isn't any functional difference between inferred and direct member access. In some cases, direct member access can be the clearer of the two, especially when there are many objects at work within a method function. Most C++ programmers use inferred syntax to access the instance variables of the implicit object since it saves them a few keystrokes. I'll follow that trend by using inferred member access in the C++ programs given in this book.

Since programmers tend to use inferred access, the *this* pointer is not often used. Its primary role is to return a pointer or reference to the implicit object. Classes offered later in this book use *this* for that purpose. Before Version 2.0 of C++, it was common to do direct assignments to *this* to control memory allocation for objects. By adding the ability to customize the *new* and *delete* operators for a class, it's no longer is necessary to make assignments to *this*, and the practice should be avoided.

Class Scope

The term scope refers to the area in a program where a given identifier is accessible. The two most common types of scope found in C are *global* and *local*. Identifiers declared outside of a function body have global scope, meaning that they can be accessed from anywhere within that program. Identifiers defined within a function or {} block are only accessible within that function or block and are said to have local scope.

The purpose of scope is to control access to identifiers. To control how members of classes are accessed, C++ has introduced the concept of class scope. All members of a class are said to be in the scope of that class; any member of a class can reference any other member of the same class. This is part of encapsulation, where C++ considers all members of a class to be related parts of a whole.

The member functions of a class have unrestricted access to the data members of that same class. Access to data and function members of a class outside of the class scope is controlled by the programmer. The idea is to encapsulate the data structure and functionality of a class so that access to the class's data structure from outside of the class's member functions is limited or unnecessary.

Access Specifiers

In a class definition, an access specifier is used to control the visibility of class members outside of the class scope. In *cplx2.cpp*, class *complex* is defined as having two data members and four function members. The data members are defined in a section labeled *private*, and the function members are declared in the section labeled *public*. *private* and *public* are access specifiers. Any member listed in a *public* section of a class can be accessed by any part of the program. Those members listed in a *private* section are only accessible within the scope of the class.

A class may have multiple *private* and *public* sections. Each access specifier is in effect until the next access specifier (or the end of the class) is encountered. For example:

```
class practice
    {
    private:
            int a;          // a is private
    public:
            float b;        // b is public
    private:
            char c;         // c is private
    };
```

An access specifier is not required within a class definition. When you create a *struct* in C, all members are public. Unless you use an access specifier to indicate otherwise, the same holds true for C++. The *a* and *b* of the members of this *struct* default to public access, while the *c* and *d* members are private:

```
struct xyz
    {
    // these members default to public access
            int a, b;
    private:
            int c, d;
    }
```

The only functional difference between a *struct* and a *class* is that *class* members default to private access. So, changing the *struct* to *class* in the example above would change the access of the *a* and *b* members to private.

If *class* and *struct* are nearly identical, why would anyone use *class* instead of *struct*? There's no technical reason to choosing *class* instead of *struct*. The choice is based on fitting the keyword to the use. When encapsulating data and function, we are creating a class in object-oriented programming terms. Therefore, it seems logical to use the *class* syntax to accurately describe what our program is doing. When working strictly with data structures that don't have methods, it's better to use the *struct* keyword. I'll be following this convention throughout this book.

In designing class *complex*, I've made all of the data members private and all of the functional members public. By making the data members private, I have restricted access to those members to the methods defined for the class. The methods are then made public, and they provide the interface to work with complex objects. As a general rule, data members are always private and methods are always public.

Operator Methods

There are two operators defined for class *complex*: + and -. They are member functions,which provides them with an implicit first argument. This implicit object becomes the argument to the left of the operator symbol. So, the operators only need to define one explicit argument, which is the object to the right of the operator symbol. In other words, the implicit object replaces the first argument normally defined for any operator function.

Let's see how that works by dissecting what's happening in the following statement taken from *cplx2.cpp*'s main function:

```
c = a + b;
```

The complex variable *a* is the implicit object in the call to *complex::operator* +. The explicit argument is *b*, which is assigned to the parameter *x* in the operator function. Inside *complex::operator* +, a local complex value named *temp* is assigned the value of adding the implicit object and *x*. *temp* is returned and assigned to *c* back in *main*.

Inline Methods

Like any other C++ function, member functions can be made *inline* (as discussed in Chapter 2). There are two ways to make a member function inline: by applying the *inline* keyword to the function definition, or by defining it within the class definition.

The definition of class *complex* in *cplx2.cpp* declares all of its methods using prototypes. The definitions of these functions are provided elsewhere in the program. And because they are defined outside of the class definition, the member function definitions have the *complex::* prefix to indicate that they are members of class *complex*.
These functions could be made inline by adding the *inline* keyword to their definitions. For instance, changing the definition of *set* to:

```
inline void complex::set(double r, double i)
     {
     real = r;
     imag = i;
     }
```

would make it an inline function.

Another way to make a function inline is to combine the prototype in the function definition with a function body. For example:

```
class whatsis
     {
     private:
             int i;
     public:
             void set(int x)
                     {
                     i = x;
                     }

             int get();
     };

inline int whatsis::get()
     {
     return i;
     }
```

Both member functions of class *whatsis* are inline. The *set* function defines the function inside of the class definition, making it inline. The definition of *get* is qualified by the *inline* keyword.

All of the caveats and restrictions on inline functions discussed in Chapter Two apply to inline member functions.

Constructors

A constructor is a special member function that literally builds objects. A constructor is called to allocate space for itself, assign values to its data members, and perform other housekeeping tasks for a new object. Nearly every class you create will have one or more constructors. To choose which constructor to call, the compiler compares the arguments used in an object's declaration to the constructors' parameter lists. This process is identical to that used to choose between other overloaded functions.

A constructor is a member function with the same name as the class with which it is associated. It may have parameters like any other function, but it cannot have a return value. This restriction is imposed because constructors are usually called when defining a new object when there's no way to retrieve or examine any return value from a constructor. This can be a problem when a constructor needs to return an error status. Future classes in this book will show ways to get around this restriction.

If you don't define any constructors for a class, the compiler will generate a default constructor. The default constructor has no arguments and simply places zeros in every byte of the instance variables of an object. Very few real-world programs use the default constructor because an all-zero initialization usually will not prepare an object for use.

If you do define constructors for a class, the default constructor is not generated. Here's an example of a class that has constructors:

```
class circle
        {
        private:
                int    center_x, center_y;
                double radius;
        public:
                circle(int x, int y, double r)
                        {
                        radius   = r;
                        center_x = x;
                        center_y = y;
                        }

                // other methods...
        };
```

When a *circle* object is declared, it must have three arguments following its name in order to provide parameters for the constructor. Without a default constructor, it's an error to declare a *circle* object without a complete set of arguments. For example:

```
circle c1(10,15,5.5);    // correct declaration
circle c2;               // error! needs arguments
circle c3(25,20);        // error! too few arguments
```

It's possible to make the declaration of *c3* legal by defining a default argument for the *r* parameter for the constructor. In some cases, this eliminates the need to create multiple constructors.

In the case of class *complex* in *cplx2.cpp*, the method *set* should be rewritten as a constructor. Once rewritten, the definitions of class *complex*, *set*, and *main* would look like this:

```
// class definition
class complex
        {
        private:
                double real, imag;

        public:
                // set complex value
```

```
                Complex(double r = 0.0, double i = 0.0);

                // output display
                 void print();

                // arithmetic methods
                 complex operator + (complex c);
                 complex operator - (complex c);
        };

// constructor for class complex
complex::complex(double r, double i)
        {
        real = r;
        real = i;
        }

// other parts of the program

// main program
int main(void)
        {
        complex a(1.0,1.0), b(2.0), c, d;

        c = a + b;
        d = b + c - a;

        printf("c = ");
        c.print();
        printf(" and d = ");
        d.print();

        printf("\n");
        }
```

Direct calls are no longer needed to assign values to the instance variables of a *complex* object. As you can see, the default arguments make it possible to declare a *complex* object with two, one, or no arguments.

The Copy Constructor

A constructor that creates a new object from an existing one is called a copy constructor. The copy constructor has only one argument: a reference to an object of the same class. A copy constructor for complex *class* would look like this:

```
complex::complex(const complex & source)
        {
        real = source.real;
        imag = source.imag;
        }
```

A default copy constructor is created by the compiler if you don't define one for a class. The default copy constructor copies the source object bit by bit to the new object. In many classes, particularly those that do not have pointers or references as data members, the default copy constructor is adequate.

Destructors

A destructor is a member function with the same name as the class, plus a leading tilde (~). A class will have only one destructor function, which will have no arguments and no return type. A destructor performs the opposite function of a constructor, cleaning up after an object is no longer needed (such as freeing up dynamic memory allocated by the object). Some objects may need to do some final housekeeping. For example, a display window object would probably erase itself from the screen when it is destroyed.

Here's an example of a class with a destructor:

```
class chunk
        {
        private:
                void * p;
        public:
                chunk(unsigned int alloc)
```

```
                        {
                        p = new char [alloc];
                        }

            ~chunk()
                        {
                        delete p;
                        }
        }
```

The destructor could also be defined outside of the class definition using this syntax:

```
chunk::~chunk()
        {
        delete p;
        }
```

If a destructor is not defined for a class, a default destructor will be created that does nothing. For many classes, such as the *complex*, a do-nothing default destructor is all that's required.

The Assignment Operator

The assignment operator for a class is slightly different from other operators. If you don't define an assignment operator in one of your classes, an assignment operator will be generated for you by the compiler, just as a default constructor is generated if you fail to define a constructor. In the *complex* class, a default assignment function is created to assign the value of one complex value to another. The default assignment operator copies the source bit by bit copy to the destination. For many simple classes, like *complex*, the default assignment function works fine.

It may seem strange to have both a copy constructor and an assignment operator, since both copy the data members of one object to another. The difference is that a copy constructor creates a new object, while the assignment operator changes the value of an existing object.

The default assignment operator is inadequate for most non-trivial classes. An alternative assignment constructor for class *complex* would be defined like this:

```
complex::operator = (const complex & source)
        {
        real = source.real;
        imag = source.imag;
        }
```

Conversions

Intrinsic types have a predefined set of conversions. You can assign an *int* value to a *long* variable, or add a *long* value to a *float*. There are two types of conversions: implicit and explicit. An implicit cast is made by the compiler, such as when an *int* value is assigned to a *long* variable. Explicit casts occur when a cast is used to force a specific conversion. Explicit casts are often used in function calls to pass arguments that have different types than the corresponding parameters.

The class types you define don't magically acquire conversions to other types; that's something you need to do yourself. C++ provides ways to define both implicit and explicit conversions. An implicit conversion is defined by a conversion constructor, and an explicit conversion is defined by a conversion operator or cast operator.

An implicit conversion is defined by providing a conversion constructor for a class. The conversion constructor accepts an argument of the type being converted into an object of that class. For example, the following conversion constructor would convert an *int* value into a *complex* value:

```
complex::complex(int i)
        {
        real = (double)i;
        imag = 0.0;
        }
```

This is a one-way conversion, which takes a value or object of one type and converts it to an object of the class. Conversion constructors cannot be used to convert class objects to other types, and they can only be used in assignments and initializations.

However, conversion operators can be used to convert objects to other types, and can also be used for purposes other than assignments and initializations. A conversion operator cannot have parameters or a return type. It's name is given in the following format:

```
operator type ();
```

type represents the name of the type to which an object will be converted. The following code fragment shows how a conversion operator works:

```
class integer
    {
    private:
            int value;
    public:
            // combined regular & conversion constructor
            integer(int i = 0)
                    {
                    value = i;
                    }

            // conversion operator
            operator int()
                    {
                    return value;
                    }

            // assignment operator
            void operator = (const integer & source)
                    {
                    value = source.value;
                    }
    };
```

Using that class definition, this next code fragment explains which method is called for different statements:

```
// this statement   calls this set of methods
---------------     ------------------------------------
integer z;          // integer(0)
integer y = 25;     // integer(25)
integer x(10);      // integer(10)
int a = int(x);     // operator int()
z = a;              // temp = integer(a); operator = (temp)
x = z;              // operator = (z);
```

Temporary Objects and "Hidden" Method Calls

C++ creates temporary objects. In the above example, the line that reads

```
z = a;      // temp = integer(a); operator = (temp)
```

creates a temporary object. The class integer defines only one assignment operator, which assigns one integer to another. The variable *a*, however, is of type *int*. So, the compiler notices the conversion constructor which creates an *integer* from an *int*. The conversion constructor is used to create a hidden, "temporary" integer, which is then passed to the assignment operator function as an argument. If a destructor had been defined by class *integer*, it would be called for the temporary object immediately after the call to the assignment operator.

Conversion constructors can make a class like *integer* simpler to use by having the compiler automatically perform conversions. This prevents classes like *integer* from having to define multiple methods for similar processes. However, overhead is incurred by forcing a "hidden" constructor call and a possible "hidden" destructor call. For example, the assignment of an *int* value to an *integer* would be accomplished far more efficiently if the following assignment operator were defined for integers:

```
void integer::operator = (int source)
        {
        value = source;
        }
```

The tradeoff is in increased class complexity and decreased code speed. On one hand, relying upon conversion constructors cuts down on the number of member functions defined for a class. For a complicated class with many methods, conversion constructors can greatly simplify things. On the other hand, defining methods for each type can reduce code size and increase program speed by eliminating "hidden" constructor and destructor calls.

Another Example

To wrap up this discussion of "special" member functions, I've created a simple example. The following class definition demonstrates all of the various types of constructors, destructors, conversions, and the assignment operator, as discussed above.

```
class whole
        {
        private:
                long * value; // current length of the string

        public:
                // combined regular & conversion constructor
                whole(long l = 0L)
                        {
                        value = new long;
                        *value = l;
                        }

                // conversion constructor
                whole(int i)
                        {
                        value  = new long;
                        *value = i;
                        }
```

```
                        // destructor
                        ~whole()
                                {
                                delete value;
                                }

                        // conversion operator
                        operator long()
                                {
                                return *value;
                                }

                        // assignment operator
                        void operator = (const & whole source)
                                {
                                *value = source.*value;
                                }
                };
```

Constructors and Member Objects

A class that has member objects is called an enclosing class. Member objects need to be constructed when an object of the class enclosing them is constructed. This is done by specifying a member initialization list for object members in the definition of the constructor for the enclosing class. This may sound complicated, but it really isn't. This example should clarify things:

```
class foo
    {
    private:
        int i;
    public:
        foo() { i = 0; }
    };

class bar
    {
    private:
        int i;
    public:
        bar(int x) { i = x; }
    };
```

```
class snafu
    {
    private:
        foo f;
        bar b1;
            bar b2;
    public:
        snafu() : b1(1), b2(2) {}
    };
```

A colon separates the member initialization list from the function header in the definition of *snafu*'s constructor. The member initialization list comes after the colon and before the actual function statements. Each object that requires initialization has its name listed along with a list of arguments for the object's constructor. If multiple member objects exist, their initializations can be listed in any order, separated by commas (as shown above).

When an object of class *snafu* is instantiated, constructors are called for its three member objects. Since the constructor class *foo* does not have arguments, there is no need for *f* to be in the member initialization list. *b1* and *b2* both require an argument for their constructor, so they are listed. C++ does not guarantee the order in which member objects are constructed.

It's important to remember that an enclosing class must have a constructor if there are any object members that require constructor arguments. Even though *snafu*'s constructor contains no statements of its own, it must still be defined so that a member initialization list can be provided. This means that a class like *snafu* could not rely upon a default constructor.

static **Members**

A member of a class can be declared *static*. For a data member, the *static* designation means that there is only one instance of that member. A *static* data member is shared by all objects of that class and exists even if no objects of that class exist. For instance:

```
#include "stdio.h"

class pumpkin
        {
        private:
                int weight;
                static int total_weight;
                static int total_number;

        public:
                pumpkin(int w)
                        {
                        weight = w;
                        total_weight += w;
                        total_number++;
                        }

                ~pumpkin()
                        {
                        total_weight -= weight;
                        total_number--;
                        }

                void display()
                        {
                        printf("The pumpkin weighs %d pounds\n",
                                weight);
                        }
        };

// initialization of static members
int pumpkin::total_weight = 0;
int pumpkin::total_number = 0;

int main()
        {
        pumpkin p1(15), p2(20), p3(12);

        p1.display();
        p2.display();
        p3.display();
        }
```

When a *pumpkin* object is created, its weight is added to *total_weight*, which is a static member of the *pumpkin* class. Another static member, *total_number*, is incremented as a count of the number of *pumpkin* objects in existence. Both static members of *pumpkin* are initialized outside of the class definition; C++ does not consider initialization to be violation of their private status. Note that the name of the class and the scoping operator are required to designate members of the *pumpkin* class are initialized.

When called, a *static* member function is not associated with a specific object. Since an object is not required, a *static* member function does not have a *this* pointer. The *static* member functions for a class can be called whether or not an object of that class has been instantiated. Usually, *static* member functions are used to act globally on all objects of a class. To display the two *static* members of the *pumpkin* class, the following function could be added to the class definition:

```
static void total_display()
      {
      printf("%d pumpkins weigh %d pounds\n",
             total_number, total_weight);
      }
```

total_display could be called using either of the following statements:

```
pumpkin::total_display();
p1.total_display();
```

In the second statement, *total_display* is called as if it were a regular method. The first statement is considered the better form; remember that *static* methods are not associated with a specific object, so using the first form is a more direct approach than the second form.

Dynamic Objects

Objects can be allocated on the heap, just like any other data elements. Dynamic objects use the same syntax for member access as do dynamic structures. This function creates and uses a dynamic *pumpkin* object:

```
void dynapump()
      {
      pumpkin *p = new pumpkin (20);

      p->display;

      delete p;
      }
```

The constructor arguments for a dynamic object are listed in parenthesis just before the semicolon in a call to *new*.

Redefining *new* and *delete*

A class may define its own versions of the *new* and *delete* operators. If a dynamic object is created and the class has defined the *new* and *delete* operators, those operator functions will be called in place of the default global *new* and *delete* functions. This means that you define your own memory allocation schemes on a class-by-class basis. Chapter 6 gives complete examples of implementing class-specific *new* and *delete*.

Class-specific dynamic memory management is tricky, and should only be attempted when you feel comfortable with C++, and when you have a complete understanding of how a class allocates memory. For instance, a class could allocate a private static pool of memory to be used by a class that fragments memory due to small allocations and deallocations. In my work, I have yet to need class-specific memory dynamic management, but your programming problems may be just waiting for this solution.

Arrays of Objects

You can create arrays of objects in the same manner that you create arrays for intrinsic types. The program offered here demonstrates arrays of objects:

```
class ant()
        {
        public:
                seek_food()
                        {
                        // perform food search operations
                        }
        };

int main()
        {
        ant colony_members[100]; // array of 100 ants

        for (int i = 0; i < 100; ++i)
                colony_members[i].seek_food();

        // do some more!
        }
```

In the case of the *ant* class the default constructor is called for every *ant* object in the array. In the case of the *pumpkin* class, which doesn't have a no-argument constructor, an initializer list would have to be given for an array. This, for instance, is the declaration for an array of *pumpkin* objects called *patch*:

```
pumpkin patch[5] =
        { pumpkin(10), pumpkin(30),
          pumpkin(25), pumpkin(12) };
```

An explicit constructor call is provided for every object in the array, and must be done when creating arrays of objects that do not have a constructor without arguments.

const Objects

Like other data items, an object can be declared *const* (constant). Unless otherwise specified, the only methods that can be used on a *const* object are constructors and destructors. The theory is that *const* objects are not supposed to be modified, only created or destroyed. However, you may want other methods (like a *print* method) to be able to manipulate *const* objects. Any member function that has the keyword *const* immediately following the parameter list in its prototype can be used with *const* objects of that class.

In the *pumpkin* class, if the definition of the *display* method were changed to work with *const* objects, it would look like this:

```
void display() const // note const keyword!
        {
        printf("The pumpkin weighs %d pounds\n",
                weight);
        }
```

The *const* keyword indicates that the *display* method can be used with *const* objects.

Friends

A class can give another function or class privileged access to its private areas. Such access must be explicitly given by declaring the other class or non-member function to be a *friend*. *friend*s are treated as if they were members of the class, and have unrestricted access to the public areas of objects. For example:

```
class thing
     {
     private:
            int data;
     public:
            friend void loadup(thing t, int x);
     };
```

```
void loadup(thing t, int x)
        {
        t.data = x;
        }
```

The definition of class *thing* contains the prototype for the *loadup* function and designates it as a *friend. loadup* is not a member of class *thing,* but a regular function that has been granted special access to the private members of a *thing* object. There isn't an implicit object for *loadup* either. However, because it is a *friend* of class *thing, loadup* can directly access the private data member *data* of its *thing* parameter.

An entire class can be made a *friend* of another class like this:

```
class rooster;

class chicken
        {
        public:
                friend class rooster;
        };
class rooster
        {
        // whatever
        };
```

A friend class must be declared before it can be designated as a friend, as shown in the first line of the example which is a simply says "yes, class rooster exists." Every member function of *rooster* is a friend of class *chicken.* The designation of a friend can be in a *private* or *public* section of a class. Often, two classes are so closely related that it only makes sense to give them open access to each other.

Friends are also useful to avoid some limitations in C++. Examine this simplified form of an earlier example:

```
class integer
      {
      private:
              int value;
      public:
              integer(int i = 0)
                      {
                      value = i;
                      }

              integer operator + (integer i)
                      {
                      value += i.value;
                      }
      };

int main()
      {
      integer i1 = 10;

      integer i2 = i1 + 5; // okay!
      integer i3 = 3 + i2; // Error!
      }
```

Here we see that binary operator functions have a problem when they are members of a class. The operator + member of class *integer* can handle expressions in which both operands are *integers*, or when the left operand is an *integer* and the right operand is an *int*. In the later case, the conversion constructor is used to convert the *int* to a temporary *integer*.

Alas, as the example shows, this won't work if the left operand is an *int*. The operator + method needs to be associated with an *integer* object, which must be the left operand. In other words, automatic conversions via conversion constructors can only take place in the right operand for any binary operator that is a member of a class.

The solution is to change the operator + method function to a friend function. The example would then look like this:

```
class integer
  {
  private:
    int value;
  public:
    integer(int i = 0)
      {
      value = i;
      }

    friend integer operator + (integer i1, integer i2);
    };

integer operator + (integer i1, integer i2)
        {
        integer temp = i1.value + i2.value;
        return temp;
        }

int main()
        {
        integer i1 = 10;

        integer i2 = i1 + 5; // okay!
        integer i3 = 3 + i2; // Now this is fine!
        }
```

The new version explicitly defines both operands of the operator + function, and the conversion constructor now works on both operands. You'll find that most binary operators for classes are defined as friends to gain this capability.

unions as Classes

*union*s in C++ are another form of class. Non-anonymous *union*s can have member functions. Even constructors and destructors can be defined for a *union*. There are two differences between using the *class* keyword and the *union* keyword, however. First, a *union*'s members are automatically public (like a *struct*) unless another access mode is designated by an access specifier. Second, the data members of a *union* all begin at the same memory location, just as the do in C *union*s.

This facility of C++ is rarely used. Most *union*s contain only data members.

A Complex Class

Some C++ compilers provide a class to handle complex numbers. Others, such as the MS-DOS Zortech compiler, do not. In any case, building a complete class for handling complex numbers has its advantages. Many C++ programmers elect to build a complex number class as the first class in their repertoire. Complex numbers are narrowly defined and relatively simple in nature, and this lack of ambiguity makes them perfect candidates for encapsulation in a C++ class.

Personally, I like to have complete source code for the classes and function libraries I use. Most C++ classes are provided in pre-compiled form with a compiler, which leaves you somewhat in doubt as to exactly what's going on.

Those of you who have not spent much time with mathematics might ask, "What is a complex number?" Most people never encounter complex numbers outside of school. So, some explanation as to what complex numbers are and how they are useful is in order before we proceed.

Complex numbers contain both a "real" and an "imaginary" component, represented by the form $a + bi$. The real component is a, and the imaginary part is b multiplied by the constant i, which will be explained in a moment. The familiar real numbers are represented by the standard C and C++ types *float* and *double*, and are actually the subset of complex numbers for which the value of b is 0.

Complex numbers were created to solve a special class of mathematical problems. For instance, it is impossible to solve the equation $X^2 = -1$, since no real number could be the square root of -1. Therefore, mathematicians created a new constant called i to represent the square root of negative one. This means that the square root of -4 is 2i, or 2 times the square root of -1.

The choice of the terms "real" and "imaginary" is, perhaps, unfortunate, but the terms have stuck for primarily historical reasons — a common practice in science. An imaginary number is no less real than a "real" number. Both are abstract concepts used by humans to do calculations. In fact, recent research into fractal geometry indicates that complex numbers have a valid representation in the real world, despite their imaginary component. Physics and theoretical mathematics also rely upon complex numbers.

The syntax of FORTRAN, a commonly used scientific programming language, directly incorporates complex numbers. Using C++'s classes, we should be able to create a complex number class that allows us to use complex numbers as naturally as we use doubles and *int*s.

Designing the Class

We now know that complex numbers have two data components to represent the number's real and imaginary parts. For simplicity, we'll make these two values *double*s, but a "single precision" complex number class could be created using *float*s. With a data structure in hand, we need to figure out what kinds of methods we'll need.

Any operation you might carry out on a floating-point number can be done with complex numbers. That means addition, subtract, multiplication, division, logarithmic, trigonometric, and comparison operations should all be defined for complex numbers. Since real numbers are a subset of complex numbers, we need to be able to perform calculations that use a mix of complex, *double*, and *float* values.

We also need to handle any errors that may occur. The best way I've found is to use an exception handler, which is a function called whenever an error (also called an exception) occurs. Some programming languages, such as Cobol and Ada, have exception handlers built into the language syntax. In the case of C++, the exception handlers have to be managed manually.

C++ Identifiers

Most C programmers use lower case letters in their identifiers. Since all of the keywords in C and C++ are lower case, programmers don't have to use the shift key. To minimize keystrokes, many C programmers prefer short identifiers that are not very descriptive; the notational simplicity of the language has led them to try and be as brief as possible.

Brevity may make programming quick and easy, but it does not make a program easy to understand *ff* even to its original author. I believe in programs that are self-documenting. That means defining easily readable identifiers that describe their purpose. Quite often, properly named identifiers and clearly written statements can eliminate the need to embed literal comments in a program.

However, some people go a bit far to make their identifiers comment-like. The use of Hungarian Notation (their term, not mine!) has become popular in some circles, particularly among Microsoft Windows and OS/2 programmers. In Hungarian Notation, an identifier has a prefix that identifies its type and scope. For example, a global *int* variable could have the name *giVariable*. This is a nice idea that falls flat in the real world. C++, for instance, defines several intrinsic types that begin with the letter 's,' but how do you tell several 's' types apart, short of using more than one character to represent a type? In addition, user-defined types don't work well in this system.

Here's the system I use. All global identifiers such as class and function names, are written in mixed-case, beginning with an upper case letter. All identifiers local to a function are written in mixed case, beginning with a lower case letter. #*defined* constants are in all upper case; enumeration constants are in mixed case. This system is used for all of the source listings in this book — you can take it, leave it, or cuss at it.

Some programmers love mixed-case; other hate it. I learned mixed-case when I was writing Modula-2 programs. To me, it's easier to read than using all-lower case or lower case with underscores. The only caution I have about mixed case identifiers is that they should only differ in their spelling. For example, having the names *identifier*, *Identifier*, and *IDENTIFIER* in a program is both confusing and foolish.

The long-term goal is to create programs that are easy to read, and therefore to maintain. If you have a different system from mine, and it works well, then more power to you.

Organizing Files

The definition of a class is generally placed in a C++ header file, which is #*included* into any other C++ source file that will use objects of that class. As a rule, only one class should be defined per header. The inline functions of the class also should be defined in the class header. The remaining member initializations and function definitions should be placed in a separate source file or files. Of course, the class header will need to be *included* in the other source files.

This organization reflects how the different parts of a class are used. The definition of the class, which consists of the class statement (containing a list of members), is required by any reference to the class. Thus, placing the definition of the class in a header file allows the file to be inserted wherever it is needed. Of course, inline functions must also be completely defined before they are used, and the best way to do that is to include them in the header with the class definition.

There can be problems when #*include*d files contain #*include* directives. The preprocessor pass of the C++ compiler creates a new source file that contains embedded copies of all of the files which were #*include*d. It's possible to have the same file #*include*d more than once, possibly duplicating the definitions of classes and inline functions; duplicate definitions will generate compile errors. To avoid this problem, every header file should contain the following preprocessor statements:

```
// beginning of header
#if !defined(__????????_HPP)
#define __????????_HPP 1

// header contents

#endif
// end of header
```

???????? represents the file name of the header file. When the header is first #*include*d, the symbol __*????????*_HPP is not defined. The preprocessor then defines the symbol, and processes the remaining header contents. If subsequent copies of the header are then #*include*d, the symbol for that header file is defined and the contents of the duplicate header are ignored. In essence, the #*include*d file is telling itself that it's already there.

File names should be mnemonic. Assuming you're working with an operating system like MS-DOS or Unix, file names can have different parts. A C++ file name should identify the class to which the file belongs, as well as the type of file it is. As a rule, the names of C++ header files end in the characters *.hpp*, and C++ source files end in *.cpp*. Sometimes the extensions *.hxx* and *.cxx* are used, but these are relatively rare and I don't use them in this book. The most common file organization for a C++ class will include one header file and one or more source files. Since file names in MS-DOS format are valid under OS/2 and Unix, I've used that format for all file names in this book. The class header for a complex number class would be *complex.hpp*, while the source files will have names in the format *cplx_???.cpp*.

A simple class may have only one source file that contains definitions of all static members that are non-inline functions. In fact, a class that consists of only inline functions may well be contained within a header file! Most classes, however, are complicated enough to require at least one source file in addition to the class header.

If a class has a large number of functions, it's a good idea to create several source files that contain related groups of functions. The source files for the complex number class will be broken up so that constructors and destructors are in one file and trigonometric functions are together in another. All told, the complex class has one header file and eight source files.

Building the Class Definition

With a general design in hand, it's time to build a class definition:

```
#if !defined(__COMPLEX_HPP)
#define __COMPLEX_HPP 1

class Complex
    {
    private:
        double Real; // Real part
        double Imag; // Imaginary part

        static void (* ErrorHandler)();
```

```
public:
    // constructors
    Complex (void);
    Complex (const Complex & c);
    Complex (const double & r, const double & i );
    Complex (const double & r);

    // method to set error handler function
    static void SetErrorHandler(
                        void (* userHandler)());

    // value extraction methods
    friend double real(const Complex & c);
    friend double imag(const Complex & c);

    // assignment methods
    void operator = (const Complex & c);

    // utility methods
    friend double abs(const Complex & c);
    friend double norm(const Complex & c);
    friend double arg(const Complex & c);

    // unary minus method
    Complex operator - ();

    // calculation methods
    friend Complex operator + (const Complex & c1,
                        const Complex & c2);

    friend Complex operator - (const Complex & c1,
                        const Complex & c2);

    friend Complex operator * (const Complex & c1,
                        const Complex & c2);

    friend Complex operator / (const Complex & c1,
                        const Complex & c2);

    Complex operator += (const Complex & c);
    Complex operator -= (const Complex & c);
    Complex operator *= (const Complex & c);
    Complex operator /= (const Complex & c);

    // comparison methods
    friend int operator == (const Complex & c1,
                        const Complex & c2);

    friend int operator != (const Complex & c1,
                        const Complex & c2);
```

```
        friend int operator <  (const Complex & c1,
                                const Complex & c2);

        friend int operator <= (const Complex & c1,
                                const Complex & c2);

        friend int operator >  (const Complex & c1,
                                const Complex & c2);

        friend int operator >= (const Complex & c1,
                                const Complex & c2);

        // polar coordinate methods
        friend Complex polar(const double radius,
                             const double theta = 0.0);

        friend Complex conj(const Complex & c);

        // trigonometric methods
        friend Complex cos(const Complex & c);
        friend Complex sin(const Complex & c);
        friend Complex tan(const Complex & c);

        friend Complex cosh(const Complex & c);
        friend Complex sinh(const Complex & c);
        friend Complex tanh(const Complex & c);

        // logarithmic methods
        friend Complex exp(const Complex & c);
        friend Complex log(const Complex & c);

        // "power" methods
        friend Complex pow(const Complex & c,
                           const Complex & power);

        friend Complex sqrt(const Complex & c);

        // output method
        int Print() const;
    };

#endif
```

This is *complex.hpp*, a C++ header file that should be *#include*d at the beginning of any source file containing *Complex* values. It contains the class definition.

Data Members

There are only two data members defined for *Complex: Real* and *Imag*, which are a pair of *double*s representing the real and imaginary components of the number, respectively. They are listed using a private access specifier to protect them from being modified outside of the class scope.

The Exception Handler

Also included in the private section is a static data member, *ErrorHandler*. *ErrorHandler* is a pointer to a function that is called whenever an error occurs while processing *Complex* objects. Initially, *ErrorHandler* is assigned the address of a default error handler defined in one of the source modules. The static member function, called *SetErrorHandler*, can be used to change the value of *ErrorHandler* to point to a function of the programmer's own design.

The definition of the default exception handler function and *SetErrorHandler* look like this:

```
// prototype for default error handler
static void DefaultHandler();

// assignment of default handler address to error function pointer
void (* Complex::ErrorHandler)() = DefaultHandler;

// default error handler
static void DefaultHandler()
    {
    puts("\aERROR in complex object:"
            "DIVIDE BY ZERO\n");

    exit(1);
    }

// method to set error handler function
void Complex::SetErrorHandler(void (* userHandler)())
    {
    ErrorHandler = userHandler;
    }
```

Constructors

There are four constructors for the *Complex* class. *Complex()* is a null constructor, which assigns 0 to both components of a complex value:

```
// constructors
Complex::Complex (void)
    {
    Real = 0.0;
    Imag = 0.0;
    }
```

The copy constructor creates new *Complex* objects based on existing ones:

```
Complex::Complex (const Complex & c)
    {
    Real = c.Real;
    Imag = c.Imag;
    }
```

While the default versions of the default and copy constructors would work for the *Complex* class, I prefer to define them explicitly to maintain control over exactly how objects are created and copied.

The next two constructors convert *double* values to *Complex* values. The first constructor accepts two *double* values, which are assigned to the *Real* and *Imag* members of a *Complex* value:

```
Complex::Complex (const double & r, const double & i)
    {
    Real = r;
    Imag = i;
    }
```

The second constructor is a conversion constructor. It changes a single *double* into a *Complex* value by assigning the *double* to the *Real* member of the *Complex* and 0 to the *Imag* member:

```
Complex::Complex (const double & r)
    {
    Real = r;
    Imag = 0.0;
    }
```

You might wonder why I haven't combined the *Complex(const double & r, const double & i)* constructor with the copy constructor by providing a default argument of 0.0 for *i* in the former. In C++, a conversion constructor must have only one argument of the type being converted. So, two constructors are required where it would seem that only one would do.

Complex doesn't need a destructor, since there's nothing to be cleaned up when a *Complex* object is destroyed. The compiler defines an empty default destructor.

The Assignment Operator

This is the definition of the assignment operator:

```
// assignment method
void Complex::operator = (const Complex & c)
    {
    Real = c.Real;
    Imag = c.Imag;
    }
```

Utility Methods

The methods *real* and *imag* return the *Real* and *Imag* members of a *Complex* object.

```
// value extraction methods
double real (const Complex & c)
    {
    return c.Real;
    }

double imag (const Complex & c)
    {
    return c.Imag;
    }
```

These methods are *friend* functions, so their syntax will resemble that used in FORTRAN. They would be called like this:

```
int main()
    {
    Complex c(10.0,3.5);

    double r = real(c);
    double i = imag(c);
    }
```

If they were defined as actual member functions with an implicit first argument, they would called like this:

```
int main()
    {
    Complex c(10.0,3.5);

    double r = c.real();
    double i = c.imag();
    }
```

Either syntax is acceptable. The advantage of the first approach is that it is more familiar to programmers who have worked with complex numbers in languages such as FORTRAN.

Methods like *real* and *imag* are required because *Complex* makes its
data elements private. I don't make *Real* and *Imag* public members of
Complex because that would eliminate the need for the *real* and *imag*
functions, simplifying the class. However, making the data components of a *Complex* public would allow direct assignment to them. To
protect the integrity of objects, data members should only be accessible
through the methods of a class.

abs and *conj* are utilitarian functions. *abs* returns the absolute value of
a *Complex*:

```
// utility methods
double abs(const Complex & c)
    {
    double result = sqrt(c.Real * c.Real + c.Imag * c.Imag);

    return result;
    }
conj returns a Complex's conjugate:
Complex conj(const Complex & c)
    {
    Complex result;

    result.Real =  c.Real;
    result.Imag = -c.Imag;

    return result;
    }
```

These methods are defined as *friend*s, so their syntax resembles that
used with other numeric functions.

The *Print* method is used to write a *Complex* to the standard output
device in a common format. *Print* returns the number of characters displayed and is specified with the *const* qualifier so that it can be used
on constant *Complex* values.

```
// output method
int Complex::Print() const
    {
    int out_len;

    out_len = printf("(%g", Real);
```

```
if (Imag >= 0.0)
    {
    ++out_len;
    putchar('+');
    }

out_len += printf("%g)", Imag);

return out_len;
}
```

Operators

The unary *minus* function has no arguments other than the intrinsic object:

```
// unary minus method
Complex Complex::operator - ()
    {
    Complex result;

    result.Real = -Real;
    result.Imag = -Imag;

    return result;
    }
```

The compiler differentiates between the binary and unary forms of an operator function by examining the number of parameters defined for it.

These four methods implement the basic arithmetic operators for *Complex*:

```
// calculation methods
Complex operator + (const Complex & c1,
                    const Complex & c2)
    {
    Complex result;

    result.Real = c1.Real + c2.Real;
    result.Imag = c1.Imag + c2.Imag;

    return result;
    }
```

```
Complex operator - (const Complex & c1,
                    const Complex & c2)
    {
    Complex result;

    result.Real = c1.Real - c2.Real;
    result.Imag = c1.Imag - c2.Imag;

    return result;
    }

Complex operator * (const Complex & c1,
                    const Complex & c2)
    {
    Complex result;

    result.Real = (c1.Real * c2.Real) -
                  (c1.Imag * c2.Imag);

    result.Imag = (c1.Real * c2.Imag) +
                  (c1.Imag * c2.Real);

    return result;
    }

Complex operator / (const Complex & c1,
                    const Complex & c2)
    {
    Complex result;
    double den;

    den = norm(c2);

    if (den != 0.0)
        {
        result.Real = (c1.Real * c2.Real +
                       c1.Imag * c2.Imag) / den;

        result.Imag = (c1.Imag * c2.Real -
                       c1.Real * c2.Imag) / den;
        }
    else
        Complex::ErrorHandler();

    return result;
    }
```

All of the binary operators are defined as *friend*s. As discussed earlier, this allows the conversion constructor to work with both

operands. In this case, either argument in a *Complex* binary operation may be a *Complex* or *double*. If both arguments are *doubles*, the calculation takes place using *double* operations. The result is then converted to a *Complex* via the conversion constructor.

The combined calculation/assignment operators have only one argument and are best defined as true member functions. They return the value of the implicit object so that they can be used in a chain of operations like the standard operators:

```
Complex Complex::operator += (const Complex & c)
    {
    Real += c.Real;
    Imag += c.Imag;

    return *this;
    }

Complex Complex::operator -= (const Complex & c)
    {
    Real -= c.Real;
    Imag -= c.Imag;

    return *this;
    }

Complex Complex::operator *= (const Complex & c)
    {
    double OldReal = Real; // save old Real value

    Real = (Real * c.Real) - (Imag * c.Imag);
    Imag = (OldReal * c.Imag) + (Imag * c.Real);

    return *this;
    }

Complex Complex::operator /= (const Complex & c)
    {
    double den = norm(c);

    if (den != 0.0)
        {
        double OldReal = Real;

        Real = (Real * c.Real + Imag * c.Imag) / den;
        Imag = (Imag * c.Real - OldReal * c.Imag) /den;
        }
```

```
else
    Complex::ErrorHandler();

return *this;
}
```

Comparison Operators

The next step is to define a group of comparison operators. Two *Complex* values are related by comparing their absolute values;

```
// comparison methods
int operator == (const Complex & c1, const Complex & c2)
    {
    return (c1.Real == c2.Real) && (c1.Imag == c2.Imag);
    }

int operator != (const Complex & c1, const Complex & c2)
    {
    return (c1.Real != c2.Real) || (c1.Imag != c2.Imag);
    }

int operator <  (const Complex & c1, const Complex & c2)
    {
    return abs(c1) < abs(c2);
    }

int operator <= (const Complex & c1, const Complex & c2)
    {
    return abs(c1) <= abs(c2);
    }

int operator >  (const Complex & c1, const Complex & c2)
    {
    return abs(c1) > abs(c2);
    }

int operator >= (const Complex & c1, const Complex & c2)
    {
    return abs(c1) >= abs(c2);
    }
```

Trigonometric and Logarithmic Methods

These are the implementations of trigonometric methods for *Complex* values:

```
// trigonometric methods
Complex cos(const Complex & c)
    {
    Complex result;

    result.Real =  cos(c.Real) * cosh(c.Imag);
    result.Imag = -sin(c.Real) * sinh(c.Imag);

    return result;
    }

Complex sin(const Complex & c)
    {
    Complex result;

    result.Real = sin(c.Real) * cosh(c.Imag);
    result.Imag = cos(c.Real) * sinh(c.Imag);

    return result;
    }

Complex tan(const Complex & c)
    {
    Complex result = sin(c) / cos(c);

    return result;
    }

Complex cosh(const Complex & c)
    {
    Complex result;

    result.Real = cos(c.Imag) * cosh(c.Real);
    result.Imag = sin(c.Imag) * sinh(c.Real);

    return result;
    }

Complex sinh(const Complex & c)
    {
    Complex result;

    result.Real = cos(c.Imag) * sinh(c.Real);
    result.Imag = sin(c.Imag) * cosh(c.Real);
```

```
    return result;
    }

Complex tanh(const Complex & c)
    {
    Complex result = sinh(c) / cosh(c);

    return result;
    }
```

The polar function is somewhat trigonometric. It converts a polar co-ordinate, which is specified as a length and angle, into a *Complex* number:

```
// polar coordinate methods
Complex polar(const double radius, const double theta)
    {
    Complex result;

    result.Real = radius * cos(theta);
    result.Imag = radius * sin(theta);

    return result;
    }
```

The natural logarithmic functions are implemented like this:

```
// logarithmic methods
Complex exp(const Complex & c)
    {
    double X = exp(c.Real);

    Complex result;

    result.Real = X * cos(c.Imag);
    result.Imag = X * sin(c.Imag);

    return result;
    }

Complex log(const Complex & c)
    {
    double hypot = abs(c);

    Complex result;

    if (hypot > 0.0)
        {
```

```
        result.Real = log(hypot);
        result.Imag = atan2(c.Imag, c.Real);
        }
    else
        Complex::ErrorHandler();

    return result;
    }
```

"Power" functions are actually logarithmic functions. The *sqrt* function is implemented as a simple call to the *pow* function. Their implementations are:

```
// "power" methods
Complex pow(const Complex & c, const Complex & power)
    {
    Complex result;

    if (power.Real == 0.0 && power.Imag == 0.0)
        {
        result.Real = 1.0;
        result.Imag = 0.0;
        }
    else
        {
        if (c.Real != 0.0 || c.Imag != 0.0)
            result = exp(log(c) * power);
        else
            Complex::ErrorHandler();
        }

    return result;
    }

Complex sqrt(const Complex & c)
    {
    return pow(c,Complex(0.5,0.0));
    }
```

All of the trigonometric and logarithmic functions are defined as *friend*s so their syntax parallels the syntax used for intrinsic types, like *double*. This is primarily a cosmetic decision to make programs look consistent. The names of these functions are in lower case — another concession to consistency. The equivalent functions for *double*s are all in lower case.

Examining the Implementations

None of the methods for class *Complex* are inline. Many of the methods are simple enough to make inline, including the constructors and other utility functions. In this case, I had problems with one of my C++ translators which were unable to process a long class definition with several inline functions. Often, MS-DOS ports of AT&T's *cfront* translator run out of memory.

In the long run, I have found that making the methods callable functions increases run time by about 5 percent while decreasing code size by 50 percent. That seems to be a fair tradeoff. If your application needs that extra 5 percent speed, and your compiler or translator is not limited in capacity, you could take some methods and make them inline.

The *Complex* class has eight implementation files that group the class's methods into categories. *complex.hpp* is the header file that must be #*include*d into any program source file using *Complex* values. *cp_util.cpp* contains the implementations of the constructors, *cp_ops.cpp* defines the binary operator methods, and *cp_asop.cpp* contains the assignment operator implementations. The comparison operators are defined in *cp_comp.cpp*. Trigonometric methods are implemented in *cp_trig.cpp*. Logarithmic and power method definitions are located in the files *cp_log.cpp* and *cp_pow.cpp*, respectively. Any other method definitions are contained in the file *cp_misc.cpp*. The complete implementation files for *Complex* are provided in Appendix A.

Breaking a large class like *Complex* into several implementation files makes maintenance and compilation faster. With all of the functions in one implementation file, it took nearly twenty minutes to recompile after a minor change. Using a *make* facility to manage the compilation of the multiple modules, I was able to recompile only the part of the class that had been changed.

In addition, most linkers build programs from entire object modules without eliminating the routines from an object module that is referenced. If only one function in an object module is referenced in a program, the entire object module is linked in, leaving large amounts of "dead" code in your final executable code. The smaller an object file, and the more closely related its functions, the less space is wasted. So, multiple object modules can make a program smaller if only part of a class is used.

It may be hard to see how to use *Complex* objects by examining just the class definition. Appendix A contains a program named *compdemo.cpp* that demonstrates the *Complex* class. By examining *compdemo.cpp*, you will see that using *Complex*es is just as natural and easy as working with *int*s or *double*s.

Examine the listings, and reread this chapter if something doesn't quite make sense. I'd suggest trying to build some simple classes of your own incorporating the items we've discussed so far. The *Complex* class may seem a bit overwhelming right now, but thoroughly understanding how is works and why works is important in comprehending the more advanced subjects discussed later in this book.

4

Inheritance and Polymorphism in C++

As discussed in Chapter 1, there are two concepts that are important to realizing the full power of object-oriented programming: inheritance and polymorphism. Inheritance allows classes to build upon existing classes. Polymorphism treats objects of related classes in a generic manner. We have already covered stand-alone classes, which provide for programmer-designed data abstraction. Now let's look at how C++ implements inheritance and polymorphism.

Simple Inheritance

First, a quick terminology refresher is in order. Recall that one class which inherits from another class is called a derived class. The class from which it inherits is known as a base class.

Any class may be a base class. What's more, a class may be a base class for more than one derived class. A derived class can, in turn, be a base class for another class.

A derived class lists the name of its base class in its definition. It looks something like this:

```
enum BugColor {Red, Green, Blue, Yellow, Black};

class Bug
    {
      private:
           int Legs;
           BugColor Color;
      public:
           Bug(int numLegs, BugColor c);

           void Draw();
    }

class HumBug : public Bug
    {
      private:
           int Frequency;
      public:
           HumBug(int numLegs, BugColor c, int Freq);

           void Hum();
    }
```

The inclusion of *public Bug* in the definition of *HumBug* says that *HumBug* is derived from *Bug*. The use of the *public* keyword indicates that all *public members* of *Bug* are also public members of *HumBug*.

Any *HumBug* objects will have the three data members: *Legs*, *Color*, and *Frequency*. While *HumBug* defines a method of its own, it also inherits the methods defined for *Bug*. Therefore the following function is valid:

```
void func()
    {
    Bug b(6,Blue);
    Humbug h(10,Green,1000);

    b.Draw();
    h.Draw();
    h.Hum();
    }
```

As you can see, the object *h* can use the methods defined for HumBug's base class *Bug*. It works as if the definitions for the two classes were combined. And, as you'll see, a base class is often treated like an object member.

Constructors and Destructors in Inheritance

Constructors and destructors are not inherited by derived classes. Instead, the constructors for derived classes must contain parameter information for the constructors of the base class. In the case of *HumBug*, the definition of its constructor must pass values to the constructor for *Bug*. The definition of *HumBug*'s constructor would look like this:

```
Humbug::Humbug(int numLegs, BugColor c, int freq)
    : Bug(numLegs, c)
    {
    Frequency = freq
    }
```

In other words, calls to a base class constructor are made in the same fashion as calls to the constructors for object members. Basically, the name of the base class is given, followed by the parameter list for the constructor. Here's another example:

```
class Bed
    {
    private:
        int Length;
        int Width;
    public:
        Bed(int l, int w)
            {
            Length = l;
            Width  = w;
            }
    };

class BedBug : public Bug
    {
    private:
        Bed Home;
    public:
        BedBug(int numLegs, BugColor c, int l, int w)
```

117

```
                    : Bug(numLegs, c), Home(1, w)
                    { /* empty */ }
        };
```

The class *BedBug* is derived from *Bug* and contains the member *Home* which is a *Bed* class object. The constructor for *BedBug* must have an initialization list that provides constructor arguments for both the base class and the member object. The constructor for the base class is identified by its name. The constructor for the object member is identified by the object's name.

The existence of a base class or object member that requires constructor arguments means you must define a constructor for a class. In the case of *BedBug*, for example, its constructor exists only to define the constructor arguments for its base class and object member.

Base Member References and Access

A derived class cannot access private members of a base class. This is a deliberate control mechanism to prevent deriving a new class in order to circumvent the private status of the members of a given class.

All public base class members are accessible inside of the scope of a derived class. Access to base members from outside the scope of the derived class is controlled by an access specifier that is applied to the name of the base class. If a derived class declares a base class to be public, all public members of the base class become public members of the derived class. If the derived class declares a base class to be private, then all public members of the base class become private members of the derived class. Again, this only affects access to public base class members from outside of the scope of the derived class, as the following example shows:

```
extern "C"
    {
    #include "stdio.h"
    }
```

```
class Base
    {
    private:
        int base_private;
    public:
        void Set(int i)
            {
            ·base_private = i;
            }

        void Print()
            {
            printf("%d",base_private);
            }
    };

class Derived1 : public Base
    {
    public:
        void PrintHex()
            {
            // ** Error! **
            // No access to private base members!
            printf("%x",base_private);
            }
    };

class Derived2 : private Base
    {
    // Derived2 members
    };

int main()
    {
    Derived1 d1;
    Derived2 d2;

    // these two lines work
    d1.Set(1);
    d1.Print();

    // these two lines FAIL!
    d2.Set(2);
    d2.Print();

    return 0;
    }
```

The definition of the *PrintHex* method in *Derived1* generates an error because *base_no* is a private member of *Base*. So in this case, a derived class is prevented from referencing the private members of its base class.

It's not necessary to use an access qualifier to specify a base class. If the qualifier is omitted, a base class, which is defined with the class keyword, will be assumed to be a private base class, while a base class declared with the struct keyword will be assumed to be a public base class. Most of the time, you'll want to use an access qualifier on base classes to explicitly declare your intentions.

The Protected Access Qualifier

Sometimes, you may want a derived class to access members of a base class, yet you don't want those base class members to be declared public. The best approach is to use the protected access specifier in the base class definition. Any members defined in a protected section of base class are treated as public inside the scope of its derived classes, while they are still considered private by everything else. For instance:

```
extern "C"
    {
    #include "stdio.h"
    }

class Base
    {
    protected:
        int base_no;
    public:
        void Set(int i)
            {
            base_private = i;
            }

        void Print()
            {
            printf("%d",base_private);
            }
    };

class Derived1 : public Base
    {
```

```
        public:
            void PrintHex()
            {
                // Now this works!
                printf("%x",base_private);
            }
        };
int main()
    {
    Base b;
    Derived1 d;

    // these two lines work
    d.Set(1);
    d.Print();

    b.Set(2);

    // Error! base_no is protected
    int i = b.base_no;

    return 0;
    }
```

While Derived1 can now access the protected *base_no* member of its base class, the rest of the program treats *base_no* as a private member of *Base*. The function *main* cannot reference *base_no* because of its protected status.

A protected member of a public base class is considered to be a protected member of the derived class. If a base class is declared private, its protected members become private members of the derived class.

The protected access qualifier is meant to give programmers more flexibility in controlling how class members are accessed when inheritance is involved. Members declared as private are protected from all access outside the scope of the class; protected members are protected from any access outside the scope of the class or its derived classes; public members can be accessed from any scope.

Class Conversions

An object of a derived class can automatically be used as if it were an object of its base class. This is because the derived class is a superset of the base class and contains all of the members of the base class. The reverse is not true, however; you cannot treat an object of a base class as if it were a member of a derived class. The base class object doesn't have all of the members required for it to be a derived class object.

This program shows how the conversion of a derived class object to a base class object works:

```
class Base
    {
    // various members
    };

class Derived : public Base
    {
    // various members
    };

int main()
    {
    Derived d;
    Base b;

    b = d; // class conversion
    }
```

Ambiguities

A derived class can define a member with the same name as a base class member. This is called overriding. When an overridden name is referenced, the compiler will assume that you wish to access the member in the derived class. Examine this program fragment to gain a better understanding of overriding:

```
class Base
    {
    private:
        int i;
    public:
        Base(int x)
            {
            i = x; // loads x into Base::i
            }
    };

class Derived : public Base
    {
    private:
        int i;
    public:
        Derived(int x)
            {
            i = x; // loads x into Derived::i
            }

        void PrintTotal()
            {
            int total = i + Base::i;

            printf("%d", total);
            }
    };
```

When the identifier *i* is used in the derived class methods, it references the *i* defined for *Derived*. However, when the name of the base class and the scope qualifier are used in the reference *Base::i*, the *i* member of *Base* is actually referenced.

Multiple Inheritance

A class can have more than one base class. This is known as multiple inheritance, since the derived class is inheriting from more than one base class. For example:

```
class Base1
    {
    protected:
        int b1;
    public:
        void Set(int i)
            {
            b1 = i;
            }
    };

class Base2
    {
    private:
        int b2;
    public:
        void Set(int i)
            {
            b2 = i;
            }

        int Get()
            {
            return b2;
            }
    };

class Derived : public Base1, private Base2
    {
    public:
        void Print()
            {
            printf("b1 = %d and b2 = %d",b1,Get());
            }
    };
```

Derived inherits from both *Base1* and *Base2*. *Base1* is declared as a public base class of *Derived*, while *Base2* is declared as a private base class. *Derived* can therefore directly access the protected and public data members of *Base1*, but it can only access the public members of *Base2*. In addition, the public members of *Base1* can be accessed as public members of *Derived*, but none of the members inherited from *Base2* can be accessed from outside the scope of *Derived*.

More Ambiguities

Applying multiple base classes introduces another set of ambiguities to our C++ programs. Given the above classes, which *Set* function would be called in this code fragment:

```
Derived d;

d.Set(10);
```

Derived inherits two different functions named *Set* from its two base classes. *Base1::Set* is a public member of a public base class, which makes it a public member of *Derived*. *Base2::Set* is a public member of a private base class, which makes it a private member of *Derived*. Therefore, it might seem logical that the compiler would select the version of *Set* defined for *Base1*, which is public.

Actually, the compiler complains that the reference to *Set* is ambiguous. The compiler can't determine which access mode to apply to the function until after it knows which specific function it is dealing with. Therefore, the statement *d.Set(10)* is wrong. In order to specify which Set function is being called, the statement would have to read:

```
d.Base1::Set(10);
// or
d.Base2::Set(10); // although this is an error!
```

Again, we use the name of the base class and the scope operator to indicate the base class from to invoke *Set*. The second invocation of *Set* above is actually wrong since *Base2::Set* is not publicly accessible from objects of the *Derived* class.

Let's look at another example:

```
class Int1
    {
    public:
        int i;
    };

class Int2
    {
    public:
        int i;
    };

class TwoInts : public Int1, public Int2
    {
    // no members of its own!
    };

int main()
    {
    TwoInts d;

    d.i = 10; // ambiguous!

    d.Int1::i = 12;
    d.Int2::i = 5;
    }
```

In effect, the *TwoInts* class defines two public *int* members named *i*. The compiler must be told which *i* is being referenced by explicitly stating the name of the base class for that *i*. If the base class in a reference to *i* isn't given, the compiler will complain that the reference is ambiguous.

Constructing Multiple Base Classes

If a class has multiple base classes, constructor arguments for all the base classes can be given in the constructor for the derived class. For instance:

```
class Base1
    {
    private:
        int i;
```

```
       public:
              Base1(int x)
                     {
                     i = x;
                     }
       };

class Base2
       {
       private:
              int j;
       public:
              Base2(int x)
                     {
                     j = x;
                     }
       };

class Derived : public Base1, public Base2
       {
       public:
              Derived(int x) : Base1(x), Base2(0)
                     { /* empty */ }
       };
```

Remember, if a base class does not define a default (no argument) constructor, any class derived from it must define a constructor that calls the base class constructor with the required arguments. For example, this set of classes are valid:

```
class Base1
       {
       private:
              int i;
       public:
              Base1(int x)
                     {
                     i = x;
                     }
       };

class Base2
       {
       private:
              int j;
       public:
              Base2()
                     {
```

```
                    j = 0;
                    }

            Base2(int x)
                    {
                    j = x;
                    }
        };
    class Derived : public Base1, public Base2
        {
        public:
            Derived(int x) : Base1(x)
                { /* empty */ }
        };
```

While *Base2* defines a pair of constructors, one of them is a default
constructor that doesn't have parameters. This means that the constructor for *Derived* doesn't have to call a destructor for its *Base2* base
class. However, *Base1* only defines one constructor which must have
an argument. So, *Derived*'s constructor is forced to call the constructor
for *Base1*.

Virtual Base Classes

You cannot declare the same class twice in a list of base classes for a
derived class. However, it is possible for the same base class to show
up more than once in the ancestry of a derived class. This generates
errors, since there is no way to distinguish between two ancestor base
classes. The following code fragment demonstrates the problem:

```
    class A
        {
        public:
            int v1;
        };

    class B : public A
        {
        public:
            double v2;
        };
```

```
class C : public A
    {
    public:
        float v3;
    };

class D : public B, public C
    {
    public:
        char v4;
    };

int main{}
    {
    D obj;

    obj.v4 = 'a';
    obj.v3 = 3.14159F;
    obj.v2 = 1.5;
    obj.v1 = 0;        // very ambiguous!
    }
```

Everything here is fine until the reference to *v1* member of *obj* in *main*. *v1* is a member of *A*, which is a base class for both base classes of *D*. In other words, there are two *A* base classes for *D*, and the compiler has no way to know whether to make the assignment to the *v1* inherited via *A* or the *v1* inherited through *B*.

The solution is to declare *A* as a virtual base class of both *B* and *C*. The definitions of classes *B* and *C* would then look like this:

```
class B : virtual public A
    {
    public:
        double v2;
    };

class C : virtual public A
    {
    public:
        float v3;
    };
```

Virtual base classes, which are the same class type, are combined to provide only one base class of that type for any derived class that inherits them. Both A base classes will become only one *A* base class in any class derived from both *B* and *C*. This means that *D* will have only one base of class *A*, thus eliminating the ambiguities.

The virtual base class concept is hard to understand and complicated to use. You need to plan ahead and think in terms of how multiple classes will be combined, then consider which base classes need to be made virtual. In the example above, *B* and *C* both have unique *A* base classes and so do not suffer from ambiguity. Ambiguities will only exist if *D* or some other entity needs to directly access the *A* base classes inherited by *D*.

Even with virtual base classes, it's possible for a class with multiple bases to have more than one ancestor of the same class. For example:

```
class A
    {
    public:
        int v1;
    };

class B : virtual public A
    {
    public:
        float v2;
    };

class C : virtual public A
    {
    public:
        float v3;
    };

class X : public A
    {
    public:
        double v5;
    }

class D : public B, public C, public X
    {
    public:
        char v4;
    }
```

Here, *D* inherits a combined *A* base class from *C* and *D*, and inherits a second *A* base class from *X*. Again, we have an ambiguity, since *X* doesn't declare its base class as virtual. This is perhaps one of the darker corners of C++.

Polymorphism

To explore polymorphism, let's begin a different kind of example. Suzy owns a kennel where she boards pets. The kennel building contains 20 stalls, and she usually has cats in half the stalls and dogs in the other half. Let's develop a simple C++ program to manage the kennel.

Four classes will define the kennel and its residents. Let's begin by defining a base class for animal types:

```
class Animal
    {
    protected:
        char * Name;

    public:
        Animal()
            {
            Name = NULL;
            }

        Animal(char * n)
            {
            Name = strdup(n);
            }

        ~Animal()
            {
            delete Name;
            }

        void WhoAmI()
            {
            printf("generic animal");
            }
    };
```

Animal is the base class from which the *Dog* and *Cat* classes are derived. When an *Animal* is constructed, it is given a name that is stored in the object. The *Animal* class only defines the common data element (a pointer to the name string), and constructors and destructors for the two classes derived from it (*Cat* and *Dog*). Note that the *Name* data member is declared as protected, so that it can be accessed by derived classes without being public.

Now, classes for specific *Animal* types can be derived from *Animal*. For now, let's define two classes for cats and dogs:

```
class Cat : public Animal
    {
    public:
        Cat() : Animal() { /* empty */ }

        Cat(char * n)
            : Animal(n)
            { /* empty */ }

        void WhoAmI()
            {
            printf("I am a cat named %s\n",Name);
            }
    };
class Dog : public Animal
    {
    public:
        Dog() : Animal() { /* empty */ }

        Dog(char * n)
            : Animal(n)
            { /* empty */ }

        void WhoAmI()
            {
            printf("I am a dog named %s\n",Name);
            }
    };
```

The *Cat* and *Dog* classes are very similar. Each defines constructors that merely send arguments on the base class (*Animal*) constructors.

What's more, both classes have a method called *WhoAmI*, which displays a string that gives the type and name of this object.

With a set of classes describing animals, it's now time to define a kennel as a class:

```
class Kennel
    {
    private:
        unsigned int MaxCats;
        unsigned int NumCats;
        Cat ** Kitties;

        unsigned int MaxDogs;
        unsigned int NumDogs;
        Dog ** Doggies;

    public:
        Kennel(unsigned int maxc, unsigned int maxd);

        ~Kennel();

        unsigned int Accept(Dog * d);
        unsigned int Accept(Cat * c);

        Dog * ReleaseDog(unsigned int pen);
        Cat * ReleaseCat(unsigned int pen);

        void ListAnimals();
    };
```

The methods for a *Kennel* are too complex to be made inline, so they are defined outside of the class definition. Basically, a *Kennel* object contains pointers to two arrays, one containing pointers to *Dogs* and the other containing pointers to *Cats*. Data members track the size each array, and how many spots in the arrays contain actual animals. These arrays are dynamically allocated based on the maximum size arguments proven in *Kennel*'s constructor:

```
Kennel::Kennel(unsigned int maxc, unsigned int maxd)
    {
    MaxCats = maxc;
    MaxDogs = maxd;
```

```
    NumCats = 0;
    NumDogs = 0;

    Kitties = new Cat * [MaxCats];
    Doggies = new Dog * [MaxDogs];

    for (int i = 0; i < MaxCats; ++i)
        Kitties[i] = NULL;

    for (i = 0; i < MaxDogs; ++i)
        Doggies[i] = NULL;
    }
```

The constructor for the *Kennel* class accepts two parameters that define the maximum number of dogs and cats the kennel can hold. It then dynamically allocates the *Doggies* and *Kitties* array to have the corresponding number of elements. The constructor also saves these maximum values, and sets the number of *Dogs* and *Cats* held to 0.

Since the *Kennel* object allocates dynamic memory, a destructor is required to free the allocated memory:

```
Kennel::~Kennel()
    {
    delete Kitties;
    delete Doggies;
    }
```

Two methods named *Accept* are declared. One accepts an argument that is a pointer to a *Dog,* and the other's argument is a pointer to a *Cat.* This is an example of overloading a function within a class:

```
unsigned int Kennel::Accept(Dog * d)
    {
    if (NumDogs == MaxDogs)
        return 0;

    ++NumDogs;

    int i = 0;

    while (Doggies[i] != NULL)
        ++i;

    Doggies[i] = d;
```

```
        return i + 1;
        }

unsigned int Kennel::Accept(Cat * c)
    {
    if (NumCats == MaxCats)
        return 0;

    ++NumCats;

    int i = 0;

    while (Kitties[i] != NULL)
        ++i;

    Kitties[i] = c;

    return i + 1;
    }
```

The Accept method stores its pointer argument in the array for the appropriate type of animal, if there's a space open. If space is available, it returns the number of "pen" into which the "animal" was stored. In there is no space, Accept returns a 0.

The *ReleaseDog* and *ReleaseCat* methods retrieve an animal from its pen. Basically, they accept an argument that tells them which pen to empty. If the pen is already empty, these methods return a *NULL* pointer. Otherwise, they "empty" the pen by assigning it the *NULL* pointer, and return the pointer to the animal which was stored there. *ReleaseDog* returns a pointer to a *Dog*, and *ReleaseCat* returns a pointer to a *Cat*. These methods differ only in their return type, so they must have unique names and cannot be overloaded. Here are their implementations:

```
Dog * Kennel::ReleaseDog(unsigned int pen)
    {
    if (pen > MaxDogs)
        return NULL;

    --pen;
```

```
    if (Doggies[pen] != NULL)
        {
        Dog * temp = Doggies[pen];
        Doggies[pen] = NULL;
        --NumDogs;
        return temp;
        }
    else
        return NULL;
    }

Cat * Kennel::ReleaseCat(unsigned int pen)
    {
    if (pen > MaxCats)
        return NULL;

    --pen;

    if (Kitties[pen] != NULL)
        {
        Cat * temp = Kitties[pen];
        Kitties[pen] = NULL;
        --NumCats;
        return temp;
        }
    else
        return NULL;
    }
```

Finally, the *ListAnimals* method displays a list of all of the animals stored in a *Kennel*. It does this by calling the *WhoAmI* method for each non-*NULL* pointer in the *Doggies* and *Kitties* arrays.

```
void Kennel::ListAnimals()
    {
    if (NumDogs > 0)
        for (int i = 0; i < MaxDogs; ++i)
            if (Doggies[i] != NULL)
                {
                printf("The dog in pen %d says: ",i);
                Doggies[i]->WhoAmI();
                }

    if (NumCats > 0)
        for (i = 0; i < MaxCats; ++i)
            if (Kitties[i] != NULL)
```

```
        {
        printf("The cat in pen %d says: ",i);
        Kitties[i]->WhoAmI();
        }
    }
```

Assuming that the class definitions and method implementations shown above are included, this program demonstrates how these classes work:

```
Dog d1("Rover");
Dog d2("Spot");
Dog d3("Chip");
Dog d4("Buddy");
Dog d5("Butch");

Cat c1("Tinkerbell");
Cat c2("Inky");
Cat c3("Fluffy");
Cat c4("Princess");
Cat c5("Sylvester");

int main()
    {
    Kennel K(10,10); // max of ten cats and dogs

    // animals are brought in and taken out
    K.Accept(&d1);

    unsigned int c2pen = K.Accept(&c2);

    K.Accept(&d3);
    K.Accept(&c1);

    unsigned int d4pen = K.Accept(&d4);

    K.Accept(&d5);
    K.Accept(&c5);

    K.ReleaseCat(c2pen);

    K.Accept(&c4);
    K.Accept(&c3);

    K.ReleaseDog(d4pen);

    K.Accept(&d2);

    K.ListAnimals();
    }
```

Ten global *Cats* and *Dogs* are declared. Then, a *Kennel* object is declared in *main*; the global *Dogs* and *Cats* are used in a series of *Kennel* method calls. Finally, the *ListAnimals* method is called to display the names of the animals still in the Kennel when the program ends.

Analyzing animals.cpp

This program works, but if could be redesigned for interactive input, which would allow Suzy to track exactly which animals reside in which cages. However, the program has some limitations that may make interactive input impractical.

For instance, what happens if Suzy has fifteen customers with dogs, and five customers with cats? She would need to change the program so that it defines fifteen of the cages for cats and five for dogs. Every time the mix of cats and dogs changes, Suzy has to change the definition of the *Kennel* object *K* to match the mix. Clearly, this is not ideal. What happens if halfway through the day, Suzy finds that her original mix of animals doesn't fit the number of animals she has actually received? Obviously, Suzy needs some way to dynamically choose whether a cage contains a cat or a dog.

Suzy lives in a trendy town, and the current rage among many yuppies is pet miniature pigs. Suddenly, she needs to add a new class to cover these miniature pigs. Of course, this also means that she has to change the *Kennel* class to reflect the new class. She'll have to add a new set of data members to control the array of mini-pigs, changing the constructor to match. Following that, she'll need to add a new pair of methods to store and retrieve mini-pigs from a *Kennel*. Finally, Suzy will need to modify the *ListAnimals* method so that it displays the mini-pigs along with the cats and dogs.

If Suzy has to go through this process every time a new type of animal shows up at her kennel, she'll quickly stop using this computer program. In addition, a new animal adds to her earlier problem of predefining space allotments by animal type. Is there no hope?

Enter Polymorphism

Of course there's hope! The designers of C++ anticipated these kinds of problems and incorporated polymorphism into the language. I have already described polymorphism as the ability to treat related classes of objects in a generic manner. Let's see how C++ implements polymorphism in this situation to help solve Suzy's dilemmas.

This is a new version of *animals.cpp* that uses some improved C++ programming techniques:

```
extern "C"
    {
    #include "stdio.h"
    #include "stdlib.h"
    #include "string.h"
    }

class Animal
    {
    protected:
        char * Name;

    public:
        Animal()
            {
            Name = NULL;
            }

        Animal(char * n)
            {
            Name = strdup(n);
            }

        ~Animal()
            {
            delete Name;
            }
```

```
            virtual void WhoAmI()
                {
                printf("generic animal");
                }
    };

class Cat : public Animal
    {
    public:
        Cat() : Animal() { /* empty */ }

        Cat(char * n)
            : Animal(n)
            { /* empty */ }

        virtual void WhoAmI()
            {
            printf("I am a cat named %s\n",Name);
            }
    };

class Dog : public Animal
    {
    public:
        Dog() : Animal() { /* empty */ }

        Dog(char * n)
            : Animal(n)
            { /* empty */ }

        virtual void WhoAmI()
            {
            printf("I am a dog named %s\n",Name);
            }
    };

class Kennel
    {
    private:
        unsigned int MaxAnimals;
        unsigned int NumAnimals;
        Animal ** Residents;

    public:
        Kennel(unsigned int max);

        ~Kennel();

        unsigned int Accept(Animal * d);

        Animal * Release(unsigned int pen);
```

```
        void ListAnimals();
    };

Kennel::Kennel(unsigned int max)
    {
    MaxAnimals = max;

    NumAnimals = 0;

    Residents = new Animal * [MaxAnimals];

    for (int i = 0; i < MaxAnimals; ++i)
        Residents[i] = NULL;
    }

Kennel::~Kennel()
    {
    delete Residents;
    }

unsigned int Kennel::Accept(Animal * d)
    {
    if (NumAnimals == MaxAnimals)
        return 0;

    ++NumAnimals;

    int i = 0;

    while (Residents[i] != NULL)
        ++i;

    Residents[i] = d;

    return i + 1;
    }

Animal * Kennel::Release(unsigned int pen)
    {
    if (pen > MaxAnimals)
        return NULL;

    --pen;

    if (Residents[pen] != NULL)
        {
        Animal * temp = Residents[pen];
        Residents[pen] = NULL;
        --NumAnimals;
        return temp;
```

```
        }
    else
        return NULL;
    }

void Kennel::ListAnimals()
    {
    if (NumAnimals > 0)
        for (int i = 0; i < MaxAnimals; ++i)
            if (Residents[i] != NULL)
                {
                printf("The animal in pen %d says: ",i
+ 1);

                Residents[i]->WhoAmI();
                }
        }

Dog d1("Rover");
Dog d2("Spot");
Dog d3("Chip");
Dog d4("Buddy");
Dog d5("Butch");

Cat c1("Tinkerbell");
Cat c2("Inky");
Cat c3("Fluffy");
Cat c4("Princess");
Cat c5("Sylvester");

int main()
    {
    Kennel K(20); // max of ten cats and dogs

    // animals are brought in and taken out
    K.Accept(&d1);

    unsigned int c2pen = K.Accept(&c2);

    K.Accept(&d3);
    K.Accept(&c1);

    unsigned int d4pen = K.Accept(&d4);

    K.Accept(&d5);
    K.Accept(&c5);

    K.Release(c2pen);

    K.Accept(&c4);
    K.Accept(&c3);
```

```
K.Release(d4pen);

K.Accept(&d2);

K.ListAnimals();
}
```

There are two modifications you should notice immediately. The *WhoAmI* function definitions have been changed, and the program is now considerably shorter.

Most of the problems in the original version of the program stemmed from treating the *Cat* and *Dog* objects separately. The new version redefines the *Cat* and *Dog* classes so that they can be treated as if they are related. After all, they are related because they share the same base class, *Animal*.

A pointer to a derived class object can be assigned to a pointer to a base class object. In other words, a pointer to a *Cat* or *Dog* object can be assigned to a pointer to an *Animal* object. This means that we can change the definition of *Kennel* to work with pointers to *Animals* instead of pointers to objects of classes derived from *Animal*. In this case, *Animal* provides a common foundation and unifying force for classes derived from it.

So, *Kennel* was redefined with only one array of pointers, i.e., an array pointing to generic *Animal* objects. This simplifies all of the methods. The constructor now accepts only one argument representing the total size of the *Kennel*. Only one *Accept* and *Release* method is needed, since only *Animal* pointers are being stored and retrieved. *ListAnimals*, however, presents a problem.

ListAnimals needs to call the *WhoAmI* method for each animal in the *Kennel*. The original definition of the *Animal* class doesn't define a *WhoAmI* method. Even if it did, calls to *WhoAmI* made through an *Animal* pointer would invoke *Animal::WhoAmI* instead of *Dog::WhoAmI* or *Cat::WhoAmI*. How do you get the program to determine that an *Animal* is actually a *Cat* or a *Dog*?

The solution is to use a virtual method. When a base class defines a method as virtual, and a derived class also defines a method of the same type, the compiler can distinguish the correct function (even through a base class pointer) to be called for the actual class type of the object.

In the example, a *WhoAmI* method is defined for the *Animal* class with the keyword *virtual*. The *virtual* keyword is also added to the definitions of *WhoAmI* in the *Dog* and *Cat* classes. Now, if a pointer is assigned to a *Dog* to a pointer to an *Animal*, then the *WhoAmI* method is called through the *Animal* pointer, the *WhoAmI* method for the *Dog* class will be called. The *WhoAmI* method for the *Cat* class will be called if a pointer to a *Cat* is assigned to an *Animal* pointer through which *WhoAmI* is called.

In essence, you can assign either a *Cat* or a *Dog* pointer to an *Animal* pointer, and any calls to the *virtual* function *WhoAmI* using the *Animal* pointer will invoke the proper method. The *ListAnimals* method is now rewritten to simply call *WhoAmI* for each assigned pointer in the *Residents* array. The *Animal* pointers in the array will contain pointers to both *Dogs* and *Cats*, and the proper *WhoAmI* function for each *Animal* will be called.

Adding Mini-Pigs

Polymorphism also solves Suzy's problem with adding the mini-pigs. Simply add a new class with the definition to the program:

```
class MiniPig : public Animal
    {
    public:
        MiniPig() : Animal() { /* empty */ }

        MiniPig(char * n)
            : Animal(n)
            { /* empty */ }

        virtual void WhoAmI()
            {
            printf("I'm a MiniPig named %s\n",Name);
            }
    };
```

MiniPig objects can now be created and used with the *Kennel* class. Since the *MiniPig* class is a polymorphic brother of the *Dog* and *Cat* classes, it can be used polymorphically wherever the other classes have been used. No changes to any other class are required. Suzy can now add as many new pet types as she likes (as long as they are derived from *Animal*), and store any combination of *Animal*s in a *Kennel* object.

In fact, Suzy could even derive a class from one of *Animal*'s child classes. Let's say that she wants to track Siamese cats separately from other cats. This class would do the trick:

```
class Siamese : public Cat
    {
    public:
        Siamese() : Cat() { /* empty */ }

        Siamese(char * n)
            : Cat(n)
            { /* empty */ }

        virtual void WhoAmI()
            {
            printf("I'm a Siamese named %s\n",Name);
            }
    };
```

She could use *Siamese* objects in the same way she uses *Cat*, *Dog*, and *MiniPig* objects. The virtual function *WhoAmI* still works, and it is polymorphic when accessed through either a pointer to an *Animal* or a pointer to a *Cat*.

The power of polymorphism is two-fold. First, it can let you treat related concepts in a similar fashion, making programs more abstract and easier to understand. Second, polymorphism can be used to make programs more extensible. When a new type is added that relates to existing types, its polymorphic nature lets it fit right in without having to change the rest of the program.

How Polymorphic Magic Works

The compiler makes virtual functions work by creating a hidden data member of the class for each virtual function. These hidden members are pointers to the correct virtual function for the actual class of the object. This means that a *Dog* object has a hidden data member that is a pointer to its *WhoAmI* method. The *Animal* class also has a hidden member pointing to its version of *WhoAmI*.

The compiler uses this hidden pointer to call the virtual function. When a pointer to an Animal contains a pointer to a *Dog*, a call to the *WhoAmI* function is done via the pointer in the *Dog* object. In this manner, the correct virtual method is invoked.

Virtual Function Specifics

The definitions of virtual functions between the base and derived classes need to be identical. This means that all versions of a virtual function are defined with the same return type, name, and parameter list. If the types of the functions are different, the *virtual* keyword is ignored and the compiler considers the function to be overridden by the derived class.

Since virtual functions rely upon the original class of the object for which they are called, they must have an implicit object and therefore must be true members of a class. This means *friend* functions cannot by virtual. However, a virtual function of one class may be declared as a *friend* in another class.

It's not necessary to explicitly include the *virtual* keyword for the definition of a virtual function in a derived class. Nevertheless, I like to include the keyword in derived classes because I think it clarifies the intent.

You don't have to redefine a virtual function inherited from a base class. If a derived class does not define its own version of a polymorphic method inherited from its base class, the function defined for the base class is used.

Abstract Base Classes

An abstract base class is a class that is only used as a base class for other classes. No objects of an abstract class will every be created, since it is used solely to define some general concept common to other classes. An example of an abstract class from our previous example is *Animal*.

In C++, the term "abstract class" specifically applies to classes that contain pure virtual methods. A pure virtual method is a virtual method whose implementation is defined as "nothing" in the class definition. This class, for example, is an abstract base class:

```
class Abstract
    {
    public:
        void Print() = 0;
        void Process() = 0;
        int Status();
    };
```

Print and *Process* are declared as pure virtual methods by = 0, which replaces the implementation of the function. *Status* is a normal member function and will need to have a definition somewhere.

No objects of an abstract class type can be instantiated. However, pointers and references to abstract class objects are valid. Any class that is derived from an abstract base class must redeclare all of the pure virtual methods it inherits. A derived class must define all of the pure virtual methods it inherits, either as pure virtual methods or with actual function definitions. For example:

```
class Derived : public Abstract
    {
    public:
        void Print() = 0;

        void Process()
            {
            // Derived's definition of Process
            }
    };
```

It's possible to create an abstract class, in an object-oriented sense, without it having to contain pure virtual methods. The *Animal* class defined in the second version of *animal.cpp* is an abstract class in an object-oriented sense. Changing the *WhoAmI* function in *Animal* to a pure virtual method would make *Animal* a C++ abstract base class.

Unfortunately, the C++ reference documentation only uses the term "abstract class" to refer to those classes that contain pure virtual methods. In general, any class used only as the basis for other classes can be called an abstract class. An easy way to identify abstract classes is to look for classes for which no objects are defined.

Using Polymorphism

I'm sure that polymorphism is a bit confusing. It is one of the more difficult object-oriented concepts to understand. Another example may help to clarify things. Let's begin by defining a simple class that describes a graphic point on the screen:

```
class Point
    {
    private:
        int X, Y;
    public:
        Point()
            {
            X = 0;
```

```
            Y = 0;
            }

        Point(int x_pos, int y_pos)
            {
            X = x_pos;
            Y = y_pos;
            }

        Point(const Point & p)
            {
            X = p.X;
            Y = p.Y;
            }

        void operator = (const Point & p)
            {
            X = p.X;
            Y = p.Y;
            }

        int GetX()
            {
            return X;
            }

        int GetY()
            {
            return Y;
            }
    };
```

Point is a simple class used to indicate a specific pixel location on a graphics screen. There's nothing particularly interesting about *Point* in and of itself; its primary purpose is to be used by other classes.

With *Point* ready, an abstract base class for graphic shapes can be created:

```
enum ColorType {White, Black, Red, Green, Blue,
                Yellow, Magenta, Cyan};

class Shape
    {
    private:
        ColorType Color;
    public:
        Shape(ColorType c)
```

```
        {
        Color = c;
        }

    virtual void Draw() = 0;
};
```

Shape is an abstract base class. It provides a simple basis for the
other graphic objects defined later. It defines a single data member
that contains the color of a *Shape*, a constructor that sets the color,
and a pure virtual method called *Draw* that displays a shape.

Line is a class derived from *Shape*:

```
class Line : public Shape
    {
    private:
        Point Start, End;
    public:
        Line(Point s, Point e, ColorType c)
            : Shape(c), Start(s), End(e)
            { /* empty */ }

        virtual void Draw();
    };
```

Line contains two data members that define the starting and ending
Points of a line. Its constructor accepts a pair of *Points* that are assigned to the *Start* and *End* members, along with a color value that is
passed to the constructor for the base class *Shape*. *Line* also declares
its own version of the Draw method, which is stored in another file.

Circle and *Rectangle* are similar to *Line* in that they define a few
data members, a constructor (which provides arguments for base class
and member constructors), and a unique version of *Draw*.

```
class Rectangle : public Shape
    {
    private:
        Point UpperLeft;
        Point LowerRight;
    public:
        Rectangle(Point ul, Point lr, ColorType c)
```

```
                    : Shape(c), UpperLeft(ul), LowerRight(lr)
                    { /* empty */ }

            virtual void Draw();
        };

    class Circle : public Shape
        {
        private:
            Point Center;
            int   Radius;
        public:
            Circle(Point ctr, int r, ColorType c)
                : Shape(c), Center(ctr)
                {
                Radius = r;
                }

            virtual void Draw();
        };
```

Square is somewhat different. It is derived from *Rectangle* and does not define any data members or a version of *Draw*.

```
    class Square : public Rectangle
        {
        public:
            Square(Point ul, int l, ColorType c)
                : Rectangle(ul, Point(ul.GetX()+l,
                            ul.GetY()+l), c)
                { /* empty */ }
        };
```

A *Square* is actually a *Rectangle* with sides of the same length. So, *Square* only requires a constructor, which accepts the starting point of the *Square*, the length of its sides, and its color. It then calls the constructor for *Rectangle*, using the starting point as the rectangle's upper-left corner and a calculated *Point* for the lower right corner.

Note how the call to the *Rectangle* constructor is done in the constructor for *Square*. The second argument is a temporary *Point* object, which is constructed from two arguments to *Square*'s constructor. This shows that you can use functions like *Point::GetX* and calculations in a base constructor call. Basically, to get the lower-right corner of the rectangle, the elements of the *ul* argument are extracted by methods, added to the provided *length l,* and then converted back to a temporary *Point.*

Picture is the last class we'll define in this example.

```
class Picture
    {
    private:
        Shape * s[6];
    public:
        Picture(Shape * s1, Shape * s2, Shape * s3,
                Shape * s4, Shape * s5, Shape * s6)
            {
            s[1] = s1; s[2] = s2; s[3] = s3;
            s[4] = s4; s[5] = s5; s[6] = s6;
            }

        void Paint()
            {
            for (int i = 0; i < 6; ++i)
                s[i]->Draw();
            }
    };
```

Picture contains an array of six *Shape* pointers, a constructor that loads the array, and a function that draws the six shape pointers. Notice how the Paint method calls the *Draw* method for each shape. It doesn't care what kind of shape is being drawn; it assumes that each *Shape* object knows which *Draw* method it needs to call based on its actual type.

Now we can put all of the above class and method definitions into a header file named *shapes.hpp* so that they can be #*included* into any program.

This short program shows how these classes work:

```
#include "Shapes.hpp"

int main()
    {
    Line        l1(Point(1,1), Point(250,300), Red);
```

```
Circle    c1(Point(100,75), 50, Blue);
Circle    c2(Point(50,200), 20, Green);

Rectangle r1(Point(10,10), Point(225,150), Yellow);
Rectangle r2(Point(300,30),Point(30,125), Magenta);

Square    s1(Point(150,150), 50, White);

Picture   p(&l1, &c1, &r1, &s1, &c2, &r2);
p.Paint();

return 0;
}
```

This program creates six objects from classes derived from *Shape*. Note how the constructor for the *Point* class is used to create temporary *Point* objects to construct the *Shape* objects. When the *Picture* object *p* is created, it's constructor is passed the addresses of the *Shape* objects. These are assigned by the constructor to the elements of the array in the *Picture*. Then, the *Paint* method is invoked for the *p*, which calls the *Draw* method for each of the shapes.

Pointers to the shapes are stored in a *Picture*. Even though the pointers point to objects of different classes, all of the pointers can be assigned to *Shape* pointers since the ultimate ancestor class of the *Line*, *Circle*, *Rectangle*, and *Square* classes is *Shape*. The *Draw* method for this class family is virtual, so the *Paint* method can merrily go ahead and draw every object pointed to by the *p* array without having to care about the specific class of the object to which it is pointing.

Learning Inheritance

Without inheritance and polymorphism C++ would be a simpler language to learn and to apply. It would also be less powerful. As I've become accustomed to having inheritance and polymorphism available when I write programs, it has become easier to use them effectively. It's often hard for the beginning C++ programmer to recognize just how classes fit together into a hierarchy. As I've stated previously, it's best to start slowly with simple programs and build up to a big C++ project.

Strategy

Strategy is defined as the art of devising a plan to reach a goal. Before we write a complex program, we need to develop a strategy to get that idea into software. Good software is not built by accident. In terms of software development, strategy refers to the act of defining, designing, and finally developing an application. Planning ahead makes it possible to reach the goal, which is to create reliable, usable software.

Understanding the syntax that C++ uses to create class hierarchies does not mean you have an equal understanding of how to put that syntax to work. The examples presented so far have been fairly simple, but when you get into a real-world development project, you'll need to be able to identify the parts of your program that can be encapsulated, and how those parts should be interrelated using inheritance and polymorphism.

Object-oriented programs require more planning than other types of computer programs. Class types and their relationships cannot be defined unless the application is thoroughly understood first. An unplanned object-oriented program quickly becomes a swamp of illogical classes tangled with thickets of poorly-designed class hierarchies. This chapter will show you how to design an object-oriented program.

Design

Classes define abstract data types. This means that classes encapsulate both the data definition and the functional capabilities of a type into an integrated package. If you've thoroughly done your initial analysis, your classes should become obvious. You need to know what kind of data your application processes, what those processes are, and how the data in your program is interrelated. The advantages of object-oriented programming can't be realized before you build a solid design.

Don't forget the techniques you've learned in the past. You shouldn't abandon the design practices you've used elsewhere just because you've changed paradigms. Object-oriented concepts are built upon the same ideas developed for structured programming. In a structured program, up-front analysis is important if you are to organize the application's functions effectively. You can use the same techniques to do an object-oriented analysis of a project. You can't design classes unless you know the details about how the program's data is organized and processed.

Unlike Smalltalk, C++ doesn't implement a standard hierarchy of classes. In Smalltalk, every data type in the language is defined by a class. C++ retains C's intrinsic types, and assumes that classes are used for user-defined data types. Smalltalk was built from the ground up as an object-oriented language; C++ adds object-oriented facilities to an existing structured programming language. The advantage of the approach used in Smalltalk is that all data types are classes, which makes for a more homogeneous language. The value of the hybrid C++ type system is that its C-like syntax is familiar, and in the speed of intrinsic types.

Some programmers have attempted to build Smalltalk-like class hierarchies to replace the built-in types provided by C++. I've seen *Integer* and *Float* classes written for C++ with object-oriented overlays for the *int* and *float* types that are intrinsic to the language. At the root of all classes is a generic ancestor class, usually named *Object*.

With a single class tree like this *ff* where all classes are related *ff* it's very easy to design generic data structures to handle a variety of objects.

In my view, replacing intrinsic data types with classes adds overhead and complicates use of the language. While having all of a program's data types members of the same class can make a program more homogeneous, it incurs a significant loss of program efficiency at run time. Replacing *int*s with a class called *Integer* will make every reference to an integer value slower in C++, even if inline functions are used.

I'm a firm believer in the old adage, "Don't reinvent the wheel." If, by creating a new wheel, you make it better, you've accomplished something. If your new wheel isn't any better than the original one, you've just wasted your time.

Building Hierarchies

Building a class hierarchy depends on your program design. Begin by determining the nature of the data structures used in the project. Find the similarities and differences between the data structures, and group similarities together to form the building blocks of base classes. Instead of building a function flow chart, design a class hierarchy chart showing the various data types and their relationship(s) to each other. Similar data structures are virtually guaranteed to have similar processing requirements, and recognizing those requirements will help you design polymorphic methods.

Obviously, you'll need to look for commonalities in your program's data types. Let's say you're working with a database application and you're processing information from a central data file. Build a *Database* class that incorporates all of the facilities for opening, reading, writing, and closing the database. That class reads and writes objects of a different base class that is designed to contain all of the common characteristics of your database records. You can then build a hierarchy of database record types from your base class.

Creative Classes

Most object-oriented gurus will refer to classes as abstract data types. It's a good term, but it tends to close a programmer's mind to other possibilities. Too many beginning object-oriented programmers see only how classes can define simple types, like complex numbers and containers. Classes are extremely flexible, and can be used to encapsulate processes, propagate standards and changes throughout class hierarchies, and conceal implementation details.

Classes as Processes

Don't overlook C++'s ability to encapsulate processes as classes. You can think of a class not only as the thing that defines an abstract data type, but also as a miniature "program" with encapsulated data and function definitions. Classes that define processes within a program provide both scope control and the ability to configure a program for specific tasks.

Programs often need to sort data stored in an array. Sometimes, one sorting algorithm is better than another, depending on the nature and organization of the data being sorted. A generalized, customizable sorting system can be created using C++ classes.

There are several design goals. One, the sort routines must be able to handle any type of array. This means that *void* pointers must be used to point to the data items being sorted. Two, the programmer must have complete control over ordering the elements of the array to allow for special sorting orders. Three, the different types of sort algorithms must be polymorphic so they can be interchangeable. The other advantage of polymorphic sorting is that the compiler can choose the algorithm that best suits the data to be sorted at run time.

The following example shows the abstract base class for all array-sorting classes:

```
#if !defined(__SORT_HPP)
#define __SORT_HPP 1

class SortArray
    {
    protected:
        void * Array;
        int    Size;

        int (* Compare)(void *, void *);

        void * ItemPtr(int item)
            {
            return (void *)((char *)Array +
                (Size * (item - 1)));
            }

    public:
        virtual void Sort(void * arrayPtr,
                int arrayLen, int itemSize,
                int (* CompareFunc) (void * item1, void * item2))
            {
            Array = arrayPtr;
            Size  = itemSize;

            Compare = CompareFunc;
            }
    };

#endif
```

SortArray is an abstract base class in the sense that it defines the common elements and interface for its derived classes; it does not define any pure virtual methods. A separate implementation file isn't required for *SortArray*, since its implementation is completely contained in its definition. The *Array*, *Size*, and *Compare* data members store global data that is used by the methods of a sort. *ItemPtr* is a protected method that returns a pointer to any member of the array.

The only public method for any array sort is *Sort*. This function has four parameters: a pointer to the first element of the array, the number of elements in the array, the size (in bytes) of those elements, and a pointer to a function that compares elements. The *CompareFunc* function must take two void pointer references to elements of the array. If the element pointed to by *item1* is less than the element pointed to by *item2*, *CompareFunc* returns a non-zero value. Otherwise, it returns 0.

QuickSortArray is derived from *SortArray*. It's definition is:

```
#if !defined(__QSORT_HPP)
#define __QSORT_HPP 1

#include "Sort.hpp"

class QuickSortArray : public SortArray
    {
    private:
        void * temp;

        void QSRecursive(int l, int r);

    public:
        virtual void Sort(void * arrayPtr,
                        int arrayLen, int itemSize,
                        int (* CompareFunc) (void * item1, void * item2));
    };

#endif
```

The *QuickSortArray* class implements the *QuickSort* algorithm for sorting an array. The implementation of *QuickSortArray* is:

```
#include "QSort.hpp"

extern "C"
    {
    #include "string.h"
    }

void QuickSortArray::Sort(
        void * arrayPtr,
        int arrayLen, int itemSize,
        int (* CompareFunc) (void * item1, void * item2))
    {
    SortArray::Sort(arrayPtr, arrayLen,
                    itemSize, CompareFunc);

    temp = new char [Size];
```

```
    QSRecursive(1,arrayLen);

    delete temp;
    }

void QuickSortArray::QSRecursive(int l, int r)
    {
    int i, j;
    void * x, * y;

    i = l;
    j = r;
    x = ItemPtr((l + r) / 2);

    do  {
        while (Compare(ItemPtr(i), x))
            ++i;

        while (Compare(x, ItemPtr(j)))
            --j;

        if (i <= j)
            {
            x = ItemPtr(i);
            y = ItemPtr(j);

            memcpy(temp,x,Size);
            memcpy(x,y,Size);
            memcpy(y,temp,Size);

            ++i;
            --j;
            }

        if (l < j)
            QSRecursive(l,j);

        if (i < r)
            QSRecursive(i,r);
        }
    while (i <= j);
    }
```

QuickSortArray defines one data member, called *temp*, which is used when exchanging items in the array. *temp* is shared by the two member functions: *Sort* allocates space through *temp* that is equal to the size of one array element. *QSRecursive* actually uses *temp* when it performs exchanges.

The *Sort* method for *QuickSortArray* begins by calling the *Sort* method that is defined in the base class *SortArray*. Even when a function is virtual, the original method inherited from the base class can be invoked using the scoping operator. *SortArray*'s *Sort* method is meant to handle the initialization of those data elements shared by all of its derived classes. This is a valuable use of base classes, since they can define the functional characteristics shared by classes that are derived from them.

The *QuickSort* algorithm is most easily programmed using a recursive function. Once the *QuickSortArray::Sort* method has called the base class *Sort* function, it allocates memory to *temp*, then calls *QSRecursive*, which is a private method that does all of the work. *QSRecursive* is a private recursive method that sorts the array. Once *QSRecursive* is finished, *Sort* deallocates the space pointed to *temp* and exits.

Under some circumstances, a *QuickSort* may not be the best solution. Another common sorting algorithm is called *Heap Sort*. We can create a *HeapSortArray* class by deriving it from *SortArray*:

```cpp
#if !defined(__HSORT_HPP)
#define __HSORT_HPP 1

#include "Sort.hpp"

class HeapSortArray : public SortArray
    {
    private:
        int  l, r;
        void * temp, * src, * dest;

        void Sift();

    public:
        virtual void Sort(void * arrayPtr,
                        int arrayLen, int itemSize,
```

```
                int (* CompareFunc) (void * item1, void * item2));
    };

#endif
```

The implementation of *HeapSortArray* is:

```cpp
#include "HSort.hpp"

extern "C"
    {
    #include "string.h"
    }

void HeapSortArray::Sift()
    {
    int i, j;

    i = 1;
    j = 2 * 1;

    src = ItemPtr(i);
    memcpy(temp,src,Size);

    while (j <= r)
        {
        if (j < r)
            if (Compare(ItemPtr(j),ItemPtr(j + 1)))
                ++j;

        if (Compare(ItemPtr(j),temp))
            goto done;

        src  = ItemPtr(j);
        dest = ItemPtr(i);

        memcpy(dest,src,Size);

        i = j;
        j = 2 * i;
        }

    done:

    dest = ItemPtr(i);

    memcpy(dest,temp,Size);
    }
```

```
void HeapSortArray::Sort(void * arrayPtr,
                         int arrayLen, int itemSize,
                         int (* CompareFunc)(void * item1, void * item2))
    {
    SortArray::Sort(arrayPtr, arrayLen,
                              itemSize, CompareFunc);

    temp = new char [Size];

    l = (arrayLen / 2) + 1;
    r = arrayLen;

    while (l > 1)
        {
        --l;
        Sift();
        }

    while (r > 1)
        {
        src  = ItemPtr(1);
        dest = ItemPtr(r);

        memcpy(temp,src,Size);
        memcpy(src,dest,Size);
        memcpy(dest,temp,Size);

        --r;
        Sift();
        }

    delete temp;
    }
```

The *HeapSortArray* class has several more data elements than
QuickSortArray. All of the data elements are shared between the
Sift and *Sort* methods. The *Sift* method is defined with private ac-
cess, and is used by the *Sort* method. The implementation of
HeapSortArray's Sort method follows the same general pattern as
QuickSortArray::Sort, it calls *SortArray::Sort*, assigns values to the
object's member data elements, and then performs the sort.

Here's an sample program, *sorttest.cpp,* which demonstrates how the sort classes are used:

```cpp
#include "HSort.hpp"
#include "QSort.hpp"

extern "C"
    {
    #include "stdio.h"
    #include "stdlib.h"
    #include "time.h"
    }

int comp(void * i1, void * i2)
    {
    return *((int *)i1) < *((int *)i2);
    }

int main()
    {
    int i, array[200];

    //-------------------------------
    // first sort will be a quicksort
    //-------------------------------

    printf("QuickSort of Array!\n");

    SortArray * sa = new QuickSortArray;

    srand((unsigned int)time(NULL));

    for (i = 0; i < 200; ++i)
        array[i] = rand();

    sa->Sort(array,200,sizeof(int),comp);

    for (i = 0; i < 200; ++i)
        printf("%8d",array[i]);

    delete sa;

    //--------------------------
    // now let's use a heap sort!
    //--------------------------

    printf("\n\nHeapSort of Array!\n");

    sa = new HeapSortArray;
```

```
srand((unsigned int)time(NULL));

for (i = 0; i < 200; ++i)
    array[i] = rand();

sa->Sort(array,200,sizeof(int),comp);

for (i = 0; i < 200; ++i)
    printf("%8d",array[i]);
}
```

An array of 200 integers is assigned a random series of values, and then it's sorted by a *SortArray* object named *sa*. *sa* is assigned the address of a dynamically allocated sort object of either the *QuickSortArray* or *HeapSortArray* classes. Because the classes derived from *QuickSortArray* are polymorphic, the call through *sa* to the *Sort* method calls the correct *Sort* method for the actual type of object to which *sa* points.

Why are polymorphic sorts so important? The amount and ordering of the original data can affect the performance of sorting algorithms. *QuickSort* works best with small-to-medium amounts of relatively unordered data. In particular, *QuickSort* performs poorly when sorting nearly-ordered data. *HeapSort* is slower than *QuickSort*, but it is not affected by the original order of the data. By using polymorphic sorting, a program could dynamically choose between *QuickSort* and *HeapSort* based on the nature of the data.

The data members of these classes are only used and set when the *Sort* method is called. In fact, for the purposes of the *sorttest.cpp* program, the data members could be redefined as static global data items in the implementation files for these classes. This would have no affect on how *sorttest.cpp* runs, and has the added advantage of making the arraysorting objects smaller.

Making the data members global, however, could present a problem. What would happen if we were working in a multiprocessing environment? If more than one sort object could be operating at the same time, sharing these data items could be disastrous. While one sort is running, another sort could start up, change the global values, and cause both sorts to fail.

One goal of object-oriented programming is to encapsulate all of the data and functions required by an object. One advantage that C++ has over C is that C++ provides a more flexible form of scoping. In C, a variable can either be local to a function or global to a program. C++ provides for an intermediate form of access, where data items are only accessible from a specified group of functions.

Derivation

Encapsulation of processes can be taken even further. Let's say that you need to design a report-generator class in C++. A derivational approach would design an abstract report class, with derived classes for each type of report. We would end up with a series of class definitions similar to this:

```
class Report
        {
        private:
                int PageNo;
                int LineNo;
        public:
                virtual void ObtainData();
                virtual void FormatReport();
                virtual void PrintReport();
        };

class DerivedReport
        {
        public:
                virtual void ObtainData();
                virtual void FormatReport();
                virtual void PrintReport();
        };
```

For every specific report type, we can generate a new class derived from *Report*. The class hierarchy above follows a standard derivational approach to class design. This system works well, but perhaps the report system can be improved by designing the classes differently.

Composition

Classes can be used to define reusable and customizable program components. This is where the compositional system of class design comes into play. Begin the design process by asking the question, "What is a report made of?" A simple answer would be that a report consists of a data retriever, a formatter, and an output processor. By considering the composition of a report, it's possible to develop a series of classes like these:

```
class ReportReader
        {
        // members needed to read data into a report
        };

class ReportFormatter
        {
        // members needed to format a report
        };

class ReportEmitter
        {
        // members needed to emit a report
        };

class Report
        {
        private:
                ReportReader * Reader;
                ReportFormatter * Formatter;
                ReportEmitter * Emitter;

        public:
                Report(ReportReader * r,
                        ReportFormatter * f,
                        ReportEmitter * e);

                void Make();
        };
```

By using objects as data members, we have created a modular report class. We can create derived classes for different purposes based on the component classes of a *Report*. Think of the abstract base classes *ReportReader*, *ReportFormatter*, and *ReportEmitter* as definitions of individual processes, each with its own unique purpose. When a *Report* object is created, it is given pointers to the *Reader*, *Formatter*, and *Emitter* objects that it is to use. The classes of these "process" objects will be derived from the appropriate *ReportReader*, *ReportFormatter*, or *ReportEmitter* classes.

To change how a *Report* object works, simply change the set of "processes" to be used when the object is created. The *ReportEmitter* class could have derived classes for handling different printers or for "printing" the report to a file. Classes derived from the *ReportReader* class could be created to obtain data for a report from diverse sources, such as on-line services or disk files. The variables are endless.

Compositional design makes it easy to customize a class like *Report* for specific situations. A program that uses the *Report* class can even change its behavior at run time by dynamically selecting the processes for a given report. Any one of the major actions of the report can be "plugged in," which allows one function of a report to be changed without affecting the other functions. This accomplishes one of the primary goals of object-oriented programming, to create modular components that can be assembled to build programs.

Propagation

A carefully-designed hierarchy of classes can simplify maintenance. For example, if you're designing a hierarchy of classes to handle the customer, client, and shipping records for a company, propagation can be a powerful tool. All of those record types have things in common: a phone number, an address, and a name. A common base class for these record types can contain this information.

That base class can do more than provide a common format for other types. Remember that changes to a base class are immediately propagated throughout the hierarchy of the classes derived from it. A skillful programmer can use propagation to allow common changes to filter through an entire class hierarchy. In our customer records example, the change from a five-digit to a nine-digit zip code would only need to be made in the base class. Immediately, all of the derived classes for customers, clients, and shippers would support nine-digit zips.

Propagation can work against you, too. If you make a mistake when modifying a base class, that mistake will be reflected throughout its class hierarchy. Changes to a root class become more difficult, and potentially more disastrous, as the tree of classes derived from it grows. Build your base classes so they can be changed internally, without having to change their interface. Carefully choose what goes into a base class, and think about the consequences of future modifications to the entire class hierarchy.

Concealment

I often use classes to conceal implementation-specific details. If a class is properly designed, all access to that class is through its public methods. As long as the public interface to a class remains unchanged, the details to implement that class can be modified without affecting the existing program code that uses objects of that class. Classes provide an excellent way to improve portability by hiding those details that change when software is moved to a new platform.

An excellent example of this will be offered in a later chapter that presents a general-purpose, text-based window class. This *Window* class knows nothing about the video display; all access to the display is performed through a class called *Screen*. In the form presented in this book, *Screen* is designed to work with standard MS-DOS video displays in text mode. However, the internal workings of the *Screen* class could be rewritten to work with any type of computer display.

Changes to the *Screen* class automatically change the capabilities provided to classes that use *Screen* for display access. Rewriting *Screen* to work on a graphic display would allow *Window* objects to work on the graphic display, too. No changes to the *Window* class would be required so long as the interface to *Screen* remained unchanged. By encapsulating dependencies in basic classes, you can improve the portability of entire class hierarchies and applications.

In general, applying creative thinking to encapsulate, propagate, and conceal you classes will make your programs easier to maintain and port.

Making Changes

Let's say that you've developed a string class that has been in use for some time. For a new project, you need to convert the first letter of every word in a string to uppercase (say for a proper name). The only problem is, you didn't build that capability into your string class in the first place. So do you change the base string class, or do you derive a new class that adds this new feature?

This kind of problem can be even more subtle. For instance, a class may contain a method that does almost what you want, but not exactly. Again, you can choose between modifying the existing class, or deriving a new class that provides slight changes in capabilities.

In the purest sense, you can apply the adage, "If it ain't broke, don't fix it." If the existing class is working, you should derive a new class that does what you want. That way, you don't risk accidentally "breaking" any software that uses the original class.

Unfortunately, the world is not pure. Deriving new classes to implement minor changes has its own set of demons. In a group situation, for example, where programmers are working on different segments of a specific project, you may find yourself with dozens of classes derived from the same base class. Every programmer may find a way to modify a given base class to fit his or her specific requirements. Instead of a nice, neat class tree, you have a thorn bush of derived classes tailored to the needs of individual programmers. Proper management of a project can alleviate this problem.

Deriving a new class should only be done when the alternative would mean making significant changes to the base class. For example, deriving a string class to allow for a foreign language would probably be a good move. But when the changes are small or mere enhancements, it is often better to just change the original class. It makes no sense to derive a new class when you want to add one or two simple methods.

Adding to a class is much easier than changing how it works. Changing the data structure or actions of an existing class's methods can be as dangerous as taking a stroll through a mine field. In particular, if the way in which a class object will act changes, it's best to build a new class. If the changes can be transparent, such as improving an algorithm, then you can safely modify the original class.

A balance must be struck between run-away class hierarchies and the integrity of your classes. Every case is a judgment call. There are no absolute rules to determine whether or not you should modify or derive.

In almost all cases, object-oriented design techniques are no different that structured design techniques. There are no hard and fast rules; the process of software design revolves around your skill at picking the right design concept for the job. The most important component in software design (and in life, for that matter) is common sense.

CHAPTER

6

Tactics

This chapter contains solutions to problems I've encountered while using C++ to develop programs as part of my work. The techniques presented here should be mastered by anyone who is considering doing serious software development in C++. In most cases, the solutions have been developed through trial and error while putting C++ to work. C++ is so new that few people have had the time to learn and document its darkest corners.

It's easy to teach people the basic syntax of a complex programming language like C++. What isn't easy is explaining all of the nuances to make that syntax generate a working, efficient program. I hope this chapter sheds some light on the specific problems you're likely to encounter.

Exceptions

Constructors and destructors (discussed in Chapter 3) provide ways to create and delete objects in a manner that gives the programmer complete control. Nearly every class will have at least one constructor, and most will have a destructor. However, constructors and destructors cannot have return values. So what do you do when something goes wrong during the construction of an object?

Let's say that you have a class that allocates dynamic memory in its constructor. When an object of that class is created and there isn't enough dynamic memory available, how does the program know there's a problem?

The answer is to use an exception handler. The *Complex* class and the *Container* family of classes both use exception handlers. Some programming languages, like Ada and COBOL, implement exception handlers directly in the language syntax. While the designers of C++ are working on adding exception handling, we are forced to implement "do it ourselves" for the time being.

The simplest and most effective way to implement an exception handler in a C++ class is as a pointer to a function. The function pointer can either be a static or a regular class member. When the pointer is a static member, the same exception handler is shared by all objects created from that class. If the exception handler pointer is a regular member, each object will have it's own exception handler.

Shared and private exception handlers are used for different types of classes. In the case of the *Complex* class, the exception handler traps calculation errors. For example, a division by zero in a *Complex* method causes the exception handler to be called. This is how the intrinsic numeric types work: If a *double* is divided by 0.0, an exception is generated. In general, shared exception handlers are used for errors that are not object-specific.

The *Container* family of classes (see Chapter 8) uses the private type of exception handler because each container object will be allocate and deallocate dynamic memory a number of times. *Container* objects are completely separate of each other, and errors in one *Container* do not affect other *Container*s. Therefore, each *Container* should have its own exception handler to manage its own errors. In most cases, private exception handlers are used for errors that are object-specific.

Both the *Complex* and *Container* classes define a default exception handler. For the *Complex* class, which has a shared exception handler, the assignment of the default handler occurs at program start-up. For the *Container* class, the default constructor is assigned when the object is created. Both classes define methods that can assign a user-defined function to exception handlers.

Some classes will need exception handlers; others won't. You'll need to determine which type of exception handler is appropriate for a given class. By the way, there's no reason that a class can't implement both types of exception handlers. After all, the exception handler's purpose is to provide a controlled method of handling errors in objects.

One-Instance Objects

Occasionally, you'll want to define a class for an object that has only one instance. Based on how one-instance *struct*s were defined in C, the traditional way to do this looks like this:

```
class
        {
        private:
                int Value;
        public:
                void Set(int i)
                        {
                        Value = i;
                        }

                int Get()
                        {
                        return Value;
                        }
        }
        OnlyOne;
```

This approach works quite well. It creates an object called *OnlyOne*, and no other objects of the same type can be created.

There is one problem with this scheme, however. Since no class type name is defined, no constructors and destructors can be defined. After all, a constructor or destructor has the same name as the class, and this class has no name! So, there's no way to automatically initialize *OnlyOne*. If you use *OnlyOne* before invoking its *Set* method, the value of *Value* is undefined.

There's another way to create a one-instance class: define all of the members as static. Here's how this technique would look:

```
class OnlyOneClass
      {
      private:
            static int Value;
      public:
            static void Set(int i)
                  {
                  Value = i;
                  }

            static int Get()
                  {
                  return Value;
                  }
      }
      OnlyOne;

int OnlyOneClass::Value = 0;
```

Now the *OnlyOne* object is automatically initialized by the assignment to its static member. The drawback to this approach is that it's now possible to declare more objects of the *OnlyOneClass* type. On the positive side, all of the objects of the *OnlyOneClass* will share the same exact value since they share the static variables and methods.

In the case of a one-instance class, you don't need to define a copy constructor or assignment operator. After all, there should be no other objects of that type to be copied or assigned. You should also avoid having virtual methods in the class.

We will examine one-instance objects more closely later in this book when we present the *Screen* class.

Global Class Initialization

Static data members can be initialized by placing their definition in an implementation file. However, static member initialization only takes place at compile time. In some cases the values of a static member can only be determined at run time. Some programs, for example, need to know the hardware and software environment in which they are running before they can initialize their static members.

You can create a static method that must be called before any objects are created in order to initialize the class's static members. This works, but it prevents you from having global objects that are constructed before any function calls can be made. Additionally, you mist call the initialization method only once. If you forget to call it at all, the class's static members won't be initialized; if you call it more than once, changes in the values of static members may be lost.

There are two other ways to implement class-wide initialization: you can use an initialization object, or an initialization class. An initialization object is a static global object whose sole purpose is to invoke a constructor that sets up the static members of the class:

```
extern "C"
    {
    #include "stdio.h"
    }

class Example
    {
    private:
        int Value;

        static int MinValue;

    public:
        friend class ExampleInit;
```

```
        Example(void * nada)
            {
            printf("Enter minimum value: ");
            scanf("%i",&Example::MinValue);
            }

        Example()
            {
            Value = MinValue;
            }

        static void Print()
            {
            printf("Min Value = %d",MinValue);
            }
    };

int Example::MinValue = 0;

Example E(NULL);

int main()
    {
    Example::Print();
    }
```

The initialization object must be defined in such a way that it calls a special initialization constructor for the class. This will usually require the creation of a constructor with a unique set of parameters by which it can be identified. In the case of *Example*, the initialization constructor is identified as taking a *void ** parameter, which it ignores.

Using an initialization object is clumsy and prone to errors. There's nothing to prevent another *Example* object from being created that would call the initialization constructor. And, of course, the initialization object takes up space.

The other method of performing class-wide initialization is to use an initialization class. Such a class is a friend of the class being initialize, and has only one method — a constructor. Changing the example above to use a initialization class would look like this:

```
extern "C"
    {
    #include "stdio.h"
    }

class Example
    {
    private:
        int Value;

        static int MinValue;

    public:
        friend class ExampleInit;

        Example()
            {
            Value = MinValue;
            }

        static void Print()
            {
            printf("Min Value = %d",MinValue);
            }
    };

int Example::MinValue = 0;

class ExampleInit
    {
    private:
        static int InitDone;
    public:
        ExampleInit()
            {
            printf("Enter minimum value: ");
            scanf("%i",&Example::MinValue);

            InitDone = 1;
            }
    };

int ExampleInit::InitDone = 0;
```

```
ExampleInit EI;

int main()
    {
    Example::Print();
    }
```

One object for the initialization class is instantiated; it initializes the value of the static variable for which it is defined. To prevent other *ExampleInit* objects from being created, and thus resetting the static member of *Example*, a static member of *ExampleInit* is set to a non-zero value once the initialization has occurred.

None of these techniques is perfect, but at least they do the job!

Customized Dynamic Memory Management

As mentioned in Chapter Two, the global *new* and *delete* operators can be redefined. This gives a C++ programmer the ability to build a customized memory allocation system that has the same interface as the default system.

The following is a C++ header file called *dynamic.hpp*:

```
extern "C"
    {
    #include "stddef.h"
    }

void * operator new (size_t size);

void operator delete (void * ptr);

extern "C" {
    void * _vec_new (
        void *      aptr,
        unsigned int num,
        size_t      size,
        void *      (*ctor)(void *));

    void _vec_delete (
        void *      aptr,
        unsigned int num,
```

```
    size_t      size,
    int         (*dtor)(int, void *),
    int         freeup);
}
```

dynamic.hpp declares operator functions for both *new* and *delete*. It also defines two other functions, *_vec_new* and *_vec_delete*, which are used to allocate arrays of objects. This is the file *dynamic.cpp*, which implements these functions:

```
#include "Dynamic.hpp"

extern "C"
    {
    #include "stdlib.h"
    }

void * operator new (unsigned int size)
    {
    void * temp = malloc(size);

    return temp;
    }

void operator delete (void * ptr)
    {
    free(ptr);
    }

void * _vec_new(
    void *        aptr,
    unsigned int  num,
    size_t        size,
    void *        (* ctor)(void *))
    {
    aptr = malloc(num * size);

    if ((ctor != NULL) && (aptr != NULL))
        {
        for (unsigned int n = 0; n < num; ++n)
            ctor((char *)aptr + n * size);
        }

    return aptr;
    }
```

```
void _vec_delete(
    void *       aptr,
    unsigned int num,
    size_t       size,
    int          (*dtor)(int, void *),
    int          freeup)
    {
    if (aptr == NULL)
        return;

    if (dtor != NULL)
        {
        for (unsigned int n = 0; n < num; ++n)
            dtor(2,(char *)aptr + n * size);
        }

    if (freeup)
        free(aptr);
    }
```

The implementation of *new* and *delete* is relatively straightforward. *new* always return a void pointer, and must always be defined as having one *size_t* parameter. Additional parameters for *new* can be specified if you wish. *delete* returns nothing, and always has a single void * parameter.

When an array of objects that lacks constructors is called, the *new* function is called to allocate sufficient array space. If specific constructor arguments are declared for each object in an array, *new* is called to allocate the array space and a separate constructor call is made for each object in the array. If a destructor is not defined for the class, an array of objects is deleted using *delete*. All of this is transparent to the programmer; you merely use the *new* and *delete* operators to create and destroy arrays.

Two cases are not covered by this approach. When an array of objects is created and the objects have a default constructor, *_vec_new* is called. *_vec_new* allocates space for the array, then calls the default constructor for each element of the array. Similarly, if an array of objects with destructors is deleted, *_vec_delete* is called. *_vec_delete* calls the destructor for each object in the array before deallocating the entire array.

_vec_new_ and _vec_delete_ are probably the most under-documented features of C++ memory allocation. I spent nearly two days just figuring out the proper return values and argument types for these functions. What really took time to figure out is that these are C-type functions, and they must be prototype use the _extern "C" { ... }_ syntax.

_vec_new_ must be defined with four parameters: a _void_ pointer to the array being allocated, an unsigned _int_ number of array elements, a _size_t_ length for each array element (stated in bytes), and a function pointer to the constructor to be called for each object. _vec_delete_ is defined with five parameters: a _void_ pointer to the array, the number of array elements, the size of each element, a pointer to the destructor, and an integer flag generally called _freeup_. If _freeup_ is not equal to zero, the memory for the array is freed; otherwise, the memory remains allocated.

Bear in mind that _vec_new_ and _vec_delete_ are only called when you allocate an array of objects from a class for which a default (no argument) constructor or a destructor is defined. They have no affect on other types of arrays.

The implementations of the _new, delete, _vec_new_, and _vec_delete_ functions in _dynamic.cpp_ duplicate the actions of the default versions they replace. You can think of _dynamic.cpp_ as a template from which to design your own memory allocation system. You might, for example, want to develop a set of memory allocation functions that trap bad pointers. _delete_ could be defined to call an exception handler when an invalid pointer is deallocated. The possibilities are endless.

One last caution: the _new_handler_ function pointer described in Chapter Two is specific to the default _new_ and _delete_ operators. The dynamic example given here doesn't implement a similar feature. If you want the same capability to trap memory-allocation errors in your own _new_ operator function, you'll need to define it yourself.

Class-Specific *new* and *delete*

There are times when you want the flexibility to define versions of *new* and *delete* to make them specific to a class. This is done by defining *new* and *delete* operators for a class, just as you would define any other sort of operator. Here is a class that defines its own versions of *new* and *delete*:

```
// a class defining new and delete

extern "C"
    {
    #include "stdio.h"
    }

class Number
    {
    private:
        double N;

    public:
        static unsigned int OnHeap;

        Number()
            {
            N = 0.0;
            }

        Number(double d)
            {
            N = d;
            }

        void * operator new (size_t Size);

        void operator delete (void * p);
    };

unsigned int Number::OnHeap = 0;

void * Number::operator new (size_t Size)
    {
    ++OnHeap;

    return ::new char [Size];
    }
```

```
void Number::operator delete (void * p)
    {
    --OnHeap;

    delete p;
    }
```

Basically, the *Number* class keeps track of how many instances of it-self have been allocated in dynamic memory. If you are defining class-specific *new* and *delete* operators, you must be careful. Since operator functions are inherited by derived classes, any class derived from *Number* will inherit *Number::new* and *Number::delete*. Unless the derived classes define their own versions of *new* and *delete* (either as overriding or virtual methods), the *new* and *delete* that have been defined for the base class must be flexible enough to handle the additional requirements of the derived classes.

In particular, a class-specific *new* should always allocate memory based on the value passed to it in the *Size* parameter, instead of using the *sizeof(classname)* operator. C++ compilers are intelligent enough to pass the actual size of a derived class to *new*; however, if the derived class differs in size from the base class, and the base class method allocates space based on the size of a base class object, problems will certainly occur.

I did encounter an unexpected problem while defining class-specific *new* and *delete* operators. The *_vec_new* and *_vec_delete* methods do not call class-specific memory allocation functions. Instead, they call the *global*; functions. This program prints 1 instead of 11:

```
#include "number.hpp"

extern "C" {
        #include "stdio.h"
        }

int main()
        {
        Number * n1 = new Number;
        Number * n2 = new Number [10];
```

```
        printf("%u",Number::OnHeap);
        }
```

The ten *Number*s allocated in the *n2* array are never counted by the *Number* class because *Number::new* is not called by *_vec_new*. So, if you're going to do class-specific memory allocation, be sure there are no dependencies on the class's *new* and *delete* operators for arrays of objects.

Objects and Files

Some object-oriented programming languages provide object persistence. A persistent object is one that retains its value between different executions of the same program. An object that can be shared between multiple programs is also persistent. In essence, a persistent object is an object that can be stored in a file or other form of mass storage for later retrieval.

Reading and writing C++ objects to files can be very tricky. On the surface, it might seem to be no more difficult to store a *class*-type object than it is to store a *struct*-type object in C. C++ is not C, however. In C++, a class may have "hidden" members that store things such as pointers to virtual methods. In addition, a C++ object may represent a complex data structure, such as a linked list. Writing the *Container* class to a file requires more than simply writing the basic *Container* object to disk.

If the objects of a class are to be used with files, it's best to define a pair of *ReadFile* and *WriteFile* methods for the purpose. This class does exactly that:

```
class TwoInts
        {
        private:
                int Value1, Value2;
        public:
                TwoInts(int v1, int v2)
                        {
                        Value1 = v1;
```

```
                        Value2 = v2;
                        }

            void WriteFile(FILE * f)
                        {
                        fprintf(f,"%i %i",Value1, Value2);
                        }

            void ReadFile(FILE * f)
                        {
                        fscanf(f,"%i %i",&Value1, &Value2);
                        }
    };
```

TwoInts objects can now be read and written to any text file simply by calling the *ReadFile* and *WriteFile* methods. The only drawback to this example is that it lacks the ability to tell you that you're in the right place in the file to read a *TwoInts* object. Of course, C's file I/O functions don't offer any guarantees either, so you should be used to this problem.

If a class contains static members, you'll need to make a decision. If you know the format of your file, you can store the static members in a "header" record. Otherwise, you'll have to assume that the values of the static members are good for any object read from a file.

Streams

C comes with an extensive library of functions to handle I/O. Every C programmer is familiar with *printf, puts, fopen, fwrite, fclose*, and related I/O functions defined in the header file *stdio.h*. These functions have served programmers well, but they are inadequate and clumsy when used in object-oriented programming. There is no way to add a new format specifier for *printf/scanf* functions for a programmer-created data type. In addition, the *stdio.h* functions are inconsistent in parameters ordering and semantics.

C++'s class mechanism allows it to create an extensible, consistent system for I/O. Known as the streams library, these classes form a powerful system that can be modified and expanded to incorporate user-defined type and programmer-designed modifications. In C++, a stream is a source and/or destination of a collection of characters. Output streams allow you to store (write) characters; characters can be fetched (read) from input streams. Some streams can be both input and output streams.

The streams library is a hierarchy of classes. The *streambuf* class is the basis of all streams; it defines the basic characteristics of buffers that hold characters for input or output. The *ios* class is derived from *streambuf.ios* defines the basic formatting and error control capabilities used on *streambuf*s. *ios* is a virtual base class for the classes *istream* (input stream) and *ostream* (output stream). The *iostream* (input/output stream) class is derived from both *istream* and *ostream*.

Stream Insertion

The traditional beginners C program is usually called "hello world," for obvious reasons:

```
#include "stdio.h"

int main(void)
    {
    puts("Hello, world!");
    }
```

puts is a standard function in the C library that sends characters to the standard output device (usually a terminal screen). "Hello world" also will work with C++, but the program could be rewritten to use C++ streams:

```
#include "iostream.hpp"

int main()
    {
    cout << "Hello, world!\n";
    }
```

iostream.hpp (or *iostream.h* in some cases) is the standard header file that defines the classes in the streams library. *cout* is a predefined output stream attached to the standard output device. C++ overloads the << left-shift operator to send characters to an output stream. When used for output, << is referred to as the insertion operator. Basically, the text string to the right of the insertion operator is "stored" in the stream on the left.

C programmers often use the *printf* function to format output. This is a typical C-language function that uses *printf*:

```
void show_it(char * name, int quantity)
    {
    printf("%s %i\n",name,quantity);
    }
```

show_it calls *printf* to display name and quantity. The first argument to *printf* is a format string that tells *printf* the type and output format of its other parameters. %*s* tells *printf* that it's first parameter is a char * string, and the %*i* says that the second parameter is an *int*. Of course, \n is an escape sequence representing the new-line character.

C++'s stream library and insertion operator can be used to accomplish the same task. A C++ version of *show_it* would look like this:

```
void show_it(char * name, int quantity)
    {
    cout << name << ' ' << quantity << '\n';
    }
```

As you can see, insertion operators can be "stringed" together in a single statement to perform several output operations. Each insertion operator returns a reference to the output stream for which it was called. Since the << operator associates from left to right, this return value is passed to each << operator in succession. First, *name* is output; the return value of that insertion is a reference to *cout*, which is used to output a single space character. The insertion of the space also returns a reference to *cout*, which in turn is passed on to the insertion operator associated with the output of *quantity*. This continues until the last insertion in the statement is performed.

Note that the order of operator precedence is not changed with <<'s new use. While you can write a statement like this

```
cout << x + y << '\n';
```

if you write a statement like this

```
cout << x & y << '\n';
```

your C++ compiler will complain that *y* is not a valid stream. The << operator is processed after + but before an operator like &. In any situation where other operators are embedded in a string of insertion operators, it's best to use parentheses to avoid ambiguities:

```
cout << (x & y) << '\n';
```

Stream Extraction

The opposite of insertion is extraction, which "fetches" data from an input stream. *cin* is the predefined input stream generally associated with the standard input device. The >> operator is overloaded to serve as the insertion operator. This code fragment will read an *int* from *cin*:

```
int i;

cin >> i;
```

There are built-in extraction operators for every intrinsic type. By default, the extractor for an intrinsic type skips leading white space by default, and then reads in the characters appropriate to the type in question.

The extractors for integral types skip white space and read input characters until a character is encountered that cannot be part of the requested integral type. White space is defined as those characters for which the boolean *isspace* function is true. For instance, if you entered <space><space>123X2 in response to the example above, *i* would contain the value *123*. The two spaces would be skipped, "123" would be read as the value of *i*, and the input pointer would be positioned at 'X'.

Floating-point extractors work in the same fashion as integral extractors; bypassing white space and then reading input characters until a non-floating-point character is found.

The *char* extractor may not work as you expect. It reads the next character in the input stream, after skipping white space. If you enter

<space>*X*, the *char* extractor will ignore the space and return 'X'. There is a way to get the next character, white space or not, which will be discussed a bit later when I discuss binary I/O.

To read in strings of data, the *char* * extractor is used. It skips white space, then reads all input characters until another space character is found. This isn't the way the *stdio* functions *fgets* and *gets* work — those functions read all characters, including white, space until a new line character is encountered.

This code fragment uses the *char* * extractor:

```
char buffer[20];

cin >> buffer;

cout << buffer;
```

If you enter "Jack Sprat," only the string "Jack" will be stored in the buffer. "Sprat" will remain in the input stream buffer until it is extracted.

Like insertion operators, extraction operators can be chained together so that multiple data items can be read in a single statement:

```
char name[20];
int age;

cin >> name >> age;
```

There's a problem here, however. What if you type in a value for *name* that is longer than 20 characters? In the example, the input text will overflow the memory area reserved for *name*, overwriting age and possible parts of the program's executable instructions. This obviously isn't a good situation; there needs to be a way to tell the stream exactly how long *name* is.

Formatting

In cases like the example above, you'll want to control how the computer formats input and output. This can be done with some special methods defined for stream objects. To set the maximum number of characters stored in a buffer, you can use the *width* method:

```
char buffer[20];

cin.width(20);
cin >> buffer;
```

The call to *width* tells *cin* to allow extractors to only read 20 characters at a time.

width also works for output streams:

```
int x = 1;

cout.width(5);
cout << x;
```

The value of x will be displayed right justified in a field five characters long. If the length of x is greater than the current *width*, the *width* setting is ignored and the entire value of x is displayed. The default value *width* for a stream is zero, which means that an insertion is made in its entirety, without any padding. After each insertion, *width* is reset to zero. The following program code

```
int x = 1, y = 2;

cout.width(5);
cout << x << ' ' << y;
```

will insert x in a five-character-wide field and display the space and *y* in as much space as they need.

width isn't the only method that can be used to change the characteristics of a stream:

```
float pi = 3.1415927;

int orig_prec = cout.precision(2);
cout << pi;
cout.precision(orig_prec);
```

If the value set using *width* is greater than the length of the inserted value, a *fill* character is used to "pad" the extra space. A space is the default *fill* character, although the *fill* method can change it to any other character. This code fragment

```
int x = 10;

cout.fill('0');
cout.width(5);
cout << x;
```

will display

```
00010
```

precision sets the number of digits to be displayed after the decimal point when a *float* or *double* is inserted. *precision* with or without an argument returns the current number of decimal places. The default precision is 6.

Streams recognize several flags that further control the format of input and output. These flags are:

skipws — If set, leading white space is ignored on extraction. If unset, white space is not ignored. By default, *skipws* is set.

left, right, internal — Only one of these may be set at any time. If *left* is set, inserted data will be left-justified in a field of characters *width* wide, with extra space filled by the *fill* character (specified by the *fill* method). If *right* is set (or the other two flags are not set), inserted data will be right-justified. If *internal* is set, the sign of a numeric value will be left-justified while the numeric value is right-justified, and the area between will contain the *pad* character.

dec, oct, hex — Only one of these can be set at any time. These control the base in which numbers are displayed. Setting the *oct* flag, for example, causes all integral insertions to be in octal format. Unlike the other format flags, these flags affect extractions, too. If *hex* is set, extracted integral values are interpreted and assumed to be in hexadecimal format. By default, *dec* is set.

showbase — If *showbase* is set, this flag prefaces integral insertions with the "base indicators" used with C++ constants. If *hex* is set, for instance, a "0x" will be inserted in front of any integral insertion. This flag is not set by default.

showpos — If this flag is set, a "+" sign will be inserted before any integral insertion. It remains unset by default.

uppercase — If set, all letters in numeric insertions (like the 'x' in *hex* notation) will be converted to upper case. The default is unset.

showpoint — When set, this flag forces the display of trailing zeros and decimal points in *float* and *double* insertions. This flag is unset by default.

scientific, fixed — When *scientific* is set, floating-point values are inserted using scientific notation. There will be one digit before the decimal point and precision digits after it, followed by an upper or lower case 'e' (depending on the setting of upper case), followed by the exponent value. When *fixed* is set, the value is inserted using decimal notation, with precision digits following the decimal point. If neither *scientific* or *fixed* is set (as defined by the default), scientific notation will be used when the exponent is less than -4 or greater than *precision*. Otherwise, fixed notation is used.

unitbuf — When *unitbuf* is set, the stream is "flushed" after every insertion. See the section below on "buffered" streams. This flag is unset by default.

stdio — This flag "flushes" the *stdout* and *stderr* devices defined in *stdio.h*. (See the section below on "Mixing *stdio* and Streams.") This is unset by default.

These flags are stored as bits in a long member of every stream. They can be set, unset, and read by these stream methods:

long flags() returns the current format flags.

long flags(long f) sets the format flags to *f*; returns the previous flag values.

long setf(long f) sets the flags that are set in f; returns the previous flag value.

long unsetf(long f) unsets the flags that are set in *f*; returns the previous flag value.

Basically, *flags* change all of the flags to a specific value, while *set* and *unset* change only those flags specified by their argument. This program shows how flags can be manipulated:

```
#include "iostream.hpp"

int main()
    {
    double pi = 3.1415927;
    int x = 1234;

    // save original flag values
    long orig_flags = cout.flags();

    // set some flags
    cout.setf(ios::hex | ios::showbase | ios::uppercase
                    | ios::scientific);
```

```
cout << "\nx = " << x << " pi = " << pi;

// reset to original flag values
cout.flags(orig_flags);

cout << "\nx = " << x << " pi = " << pi;

return 0;
}
```

The program's output will be:

```
x = 0X4D2 pi = 3.141593E+00
x = 1234 pi = 3.141593
```

The bit values for the flags are members of an unnamed enumerated type defined in the *ios* class. This is why the flag identifiers need to be prefaced with *ios::*. The flags can be or'd together to set/unset several flags in one statement.

There are some user-definable format flags, and a few additional methods to handle format flags. You'll need to check your C++ implementation for further details.

Manipulators

Format control methods like *width* are useful, but they can be clumsy to use. For instance:

```
int x = 1, y = 2;

cout.width(5);
cout << x;
cout.width(2);
cout << y;
```

C++ provides a better approach using a manipulator:

```
int x = 1, y = 2;

cout << setw(5) << x << setw(6) << y;
```

A manipulator like *setw* is a special stream function that changes the characteristics of how I/O is done. For example, in C, a programmer can use extended format specifiers to tell *printf* how to display numbers. The code fragment

```
int i = 160;
printf("%i %x %04i\n",i,i,i);
```

will display

```
160 A0 0160
```

on the standard output device. In C++, the same thing could be accomplished using this string of insertion operations:

```
cout << i
     << hex << i
     << dec << setfill('0') << setw(4) << i
     << setfill(' ') << newl;
```

hex, dec, setfill, setw, and *newl* are manipulators. Manipulators change the format flags and values for a stream. All manipulators, except *setw*, permanently set their flags or values. A field width set with *setw*, like *width*, is in effect only for the next data insertion. The *setfill* function is called once to set a new *fill* character, and again to set the *fill* character back to space.

The predefined manipulators are:

hex, dec, oct — These manipulators change the base of inserted or extracted integral values. The original default for a stream is *dec*.

ws — This is the only predefined manipulator for input streams. *ws* extracts white space characters and can be very handy when the *skipws* format flag is unset.

endl — This manipulator inserts a *newline* ('\n') character.

ends — This manipulator inserts a NUL (0) character and is usually used to terminate a string.

flush — This manipulator forces all insertions in the stream to be physically written to the appropriate device.

setfill(char f) — This changes the fill character to *f*. The default fill character is a space.

setw(int w) — This manipulator changes the field width to *w*, but only for the next insertion. The default field width is 0.

setprecision(int p) — This sets the precision for floating-point insertions to *p*. The default precision is 6.

setiosflags(long f) — This manipulator performs the same function as the *setf* method. The flags represented by the set bits in *f* are set.

resetiosflags(long) — This performs the same function as the *unsetf* method. The flags represented by the set bits in *f* are unset.

The *dec, hex, oct, ws, endl, ends,* and *flush* manipulators are defined in *iostream.hpp*. The other manipulators are defined in *iomanip.hpp*, which must be included into any program that employs them.

Other Input Stream Functions

tie is a method that attaches an output stream to an input stream. With this method, the output stream is flushed before any extractions are performed on the input stream. For example,

```
cin.tie(cout);
```

will cause *cout* to be flushed every time an extraction is performed on *cin*. In fact, the C++ streams library already performs this statement, since you always want the standard output device to be flushed before you accept any input to be sure any prompts are displayed before inputting anything. In addition, *cerr* and *clog* are tied to *cout* automatically.

Sometimes, you'll want a stream to skip a number of input characters, whether they are white space or not. The *ignore* method will do just that. In this example, *cin* is told to unconditionally ignore the next five input characters:

```
cin.ignore(5);
```

peek let's you look at the next character in an input stream without actually fetching that character from the stream:

```
char ch = cin.peek();
```

When parsing an input stream, it can be useful to be able to "put back" a character that has just been fetched. The *putback* method returns the last character read to the input buffer:

```
char ch;

cin >> ch;
cin.putback(ch);
```

You can only *putback* the last character read. Otherwise, a stream error will occur. An error may also occur if the stream cannot accept the *putback* character for some reason.

On an input stream, you can read a single character — white space or not — using the *get* method. A call to *get* looks like this:

```
char ch = cin.get();
```

get is heavily overloaded. Here are some of its common variants:

*get(char * str, int len, char delim = '\n')* fetches characters from the input stream into the character array pointed to by *str. fetch*ing stops when len characters have been fetched, or when the character specified by *delim* is encountered. The terminating character is not extracted.

get(char & ch) fetches the next character in the stream and stores it in *ch*.

*getline(char * str, int len, char delim = '\n')* works like the *get* function above, except that it extracts the terminator.

A single character can be written to an output stream without translation using the *put* method:

```
cout.put('a');
```

Several other stream methods, including *seekg, tellg, gcount*, and *read*, are used to do binary input from streams. Binary output on streams is performed using the *write* method. These methods will be discussed a bit later in the chapter in the section on "Binary Stream I/O."

Error Handling

C's handling of file errors, is, to say the least, weak. About all you can tell about a file in C is that something has gone wrong, which usually isn't much help. C++ streams, however, have an improved error-control system.

First, you can tell if something is wrong with a stream by applying the *!* operator:

```
if (!cin)
    {
    cout << "error in input!" << endl;
    }
```

An operator function is defined for *!*. If an error has occurred in the stream, the *!* function returns a non-zero value; if everything with the stream is okay, *!* returns a zero.

However, you cannot do the opposite:

```
if (cin)
    {
    cout << "input okay!" << endl;
    }
```

There's no way to define a function for "no operator".

Every stream has a "state" that indicates if an error has occurred and what that error is. The state is indicated by the setting of a set of bits, and these bits are defined by the *io_state* enumeration defined by the *ios* class. These bits are:

goodbit — actually indicates that no bits are set and everything is okay.

eofbit — set when an input stream is at its end to indicate that no more characters are available for extraction.

failbit — is set when the last insertion or extraction has failed.

badbit — is set when an attempted insertion or extraction is illegal.

hardfail — when this bit is set, a serious failure has occurred. Generally, an error that sets *hardfail* is unrecoverable.

Several stream methods check the current state of status bits for a stream:

int good() returns non-zero if the stream is okay, and returns 0 if an error has occurred.

int bad() returns non-zero if the *badbit* or *hardfail* bits are set, otherwise it returns 1. The *!* operator works in the same way.

int eof() returns non-zero is the *eofbit* is set. Otherwise it returns 0.

int fail() returns non-zero if the *failbit, badbit,* or *hardfail* bits are set. Otherwise it returns 0.

int rdstate() returns the current error state bits

There is one stream method that can set the value of the error state bits:

void clear(int ef = 0) sets the error flags equal to *ef*. By default, *ef* equals zero, which resets all the error bits.

Predefined Streams

There are four predefined streams that are initialized during program start-up. I've already discussed *cin* and *cout*, which are attached to standard input (keyboard) and output (screen) devices. *cerr* is attached to the standard error device and is usually the same as *cout*. *clog* is the same as *cerr*, except that *clog* is buffered whereas *cerr* is not.

Creating Your Own Streams

So far, I've only shown you how to work with the streams predefined by the *iostream.hpp* header. You can create your own streams using the classes defined in the header file *fstream.hpp*.

There are three file-oriented stream classes derived from the *istream*, *ostream*, and *iostream* classes: *ifstream*, *ofstream*, and *fstream* respectively. Each class has four constructors that can create file streams from different sources. The *ifstream* class, for instance, has these constructors:

?fstream() — This creates an unopened stream.

?fstream(char * name, int mode, int prot) — This constructor will create a stream that is attached to the specified file. The value of *mode* controls how the files is opened (input, output, etc.). *prot* defines the protection level of the stream. You can generally ignore *prot* since it is assigned a default parameter. Under MS-DOS, *prot* is basically ignored. Be sure to check the documentation for your implementation to see what the *prot* parameters mean for your programs.

?fstream(int fd) — Constructs a stream from an existing, open file handle or descriptor. This is useful for hooking a stream to files that have predefined descriptors. To create an output stream attached to the standard printer on an MS-DOS computer, you could use the statement:

ofstream cprn(4); // 4 is the handle of stdprn

?fstream(int fd, char * p, int l) — This allows you to construct a buffered stream that is attached to a file descriptor. *p* points to a buffer *l* bytes in length. If *p* is NULL or *l* is 0, the stream will not be buffered. To create a buffered stream that is attached to the standard printer device in MS-DOS, you could use these statements:

```
char * prnbuf = new char [1000];

ofstream cprn(4,prnbuf,1000);
```

The *?* in the constructor represents an *i*, *o*, or no character at all, depending on whether you're constructing an *ifstream*, *ofstream*, or a *fstream*, respectively.

The *mode* parameter for the second constructor can be set using a bit mask formed from enumerated constants defined in the class *ios*. The possible mode bits are:

app — all data written out will be appended to the stream.
ate — the file pointer will start at the end of the stream.
in — the stream is open for input.
out — the stream is open for output.
trunc — if a file exists, truncate it.
nocreate — if the file requested is missing, fail.
noreplace — if the file requested exists, fail,

To open an input/output stream named *input* that is attached to the file *data.dat* and truncating any existing file, you could use the statement:

```
fstream input("data.dat",ios::in|ios::out|ios::trunc);
```

The constructors for the *ifstream* and *ofstream* default the value of *mode* to *ios::in* and *ios::out*, respectively. If you specify a value for *mode*, and do not include either *ios::in* or *ios::out*, the stream will be constructed for input.

All three file stream classes support a set of four methods that can change the characteristics of a stream object. These methods are:

attach(int d) — This connects a stream to file descriptor *d*. If the stream is already attached, this method sets *failbit*.

close() — This method closes a file associated with a stream and clears the stream's error state.

open(char * name, int mode, int prot) — This opens the file name and associates it with the stream. *mode* and *prot* mean the same thing they did in the constructors.

setbuf(char * p, int l) — This allows you to change the buffer associated with a stream. *p* points to a buffer *l* bytes in length. If *p* is NULL or *l* is 0, the stream will not be buffered.

Binary I/O

All the stream I/O I've shown so far have been translated and interpreted. Specifically, these I/O methods shown pertain primarily to text streams. For many streams, you'll want to read and write values without modification. In other words, you'll want to do binary I/O. The streams library provides a set of methods that perform binary I/O.

The *put* and single-character *get* methods are used to output a single character without text-file translation. The *write* and *read* methods correspond to the *read* and *write* functions in ANSI C; they write and read a block of memory of a given length to a stream.

write(void * buffer, int len) — This method writes *len* binary characters to the stream from the buffer that is pointed to by *buffer*.

read(void * buffer, int len) — This reads *len* binary characters from an input stream into the memory area pointed to by *buffer*.

The *seekg* method is used to change the position from which data is fetched in a file associated with a stream. It has two forms:

seekg(long pos) — This sets the position pointer for a file associated with a stream to *pos* bytes from the beginning of the file. If *pos* is beyond the end of the file, the methods sets the *eofbit*.

seekg(long offset, seek_dir dir) — *offset* is the number of bytes from which the file position pointer is to be moved relative to the beginning of the file (if dir = *ios::beg*), end of the file (if dir = *ios::end*), or the current file position (if dir = *ios::cur*).

The *tellg* method returns the current value of the file position pointer:

```
long where = ifile.tellg();
```

Defining Insertion and Extraction Operators

printf requires format specifiers to identify the types and number of parameters it is to receive. The format specifiers available through *printf* are fixed; they cannot be changed, and new format specifiers cannot be added to *printf*. If you develop a new data type, there is no way to tell *printf* about that new type.

The stream insertion operator doesn't rely upon format specifiers. There's an insertion operator function defined for each intrinsic data type (*int*, *float*, etc.), and the actual function called by an insertion operation is determined by the type of the argument placed to the right of the operator. For example:

```
cout << 10;      // calls int insertion operator
cout << "hello"; // calls char * insertion operator
cout << 'a';     // calls char insertion operator
```

Unlike *printf*, the insertion operator can be overloaded to handle the output of user-defined types. The extraction operator can be overloaded, too, for your own types. Here's an example:

```
#include "iostream.hpp"
#include "iomanip.hpp"

extern "C"
    {
    #include "string.h"
    }

class Quantity
    {
    private:
        double Value;
        char * Type;
    public:
        Quantity()
            {
```

```
                    Value = 0.0;
                    Type  = NULL;
                    }

            friend istream & operator >> (istream & i,
                                          Quantity & q);
            friend ostream & operator << (ostream & o,
                                          Quantity & q);
        };

    istream & operator >> (istream & i, Quantity & q)
        {
        char buffer[40];

        i >> setw(40) >> buffer;
        i >> q.Value;

        q.Type = strdup(buffer);

        return i;
        }

    ostream & operator << (ostream & o, Quantity & q)
        {
        o << q.Value << ' ' << q.Type;

        return o;
        }

    int main()
        {
        Quantity q1;

        cout << "? ";
        cin >> q1;
        cout << '\n' << q1 << '\n';
        }
```

The insertion and extraction operators are defined as *friend* functions so they have access to the internal data elements of a *Quantity* object. As you can see, a *Quantity* object can be included in a string of insertion/extraction operators. In C++, this class effectively extends the capabilities of streams to support its own input and output capabilities, something that could not be done with the *printf* function in C.

User-Defined Manipulators

A programmer can define manipulators, too. The way in which a manipulator is implemented depends upon the number and type of parameters is it expecting. Both *iostream.hpp* and *iomanip.hpp* must be *#include*d in a source file that defines manipulators.

Most video display systems support ANSI-standard "escape sequences" that can move the cursor, change the display mode, and clear the screen. An escape sequence consists of a string of characters, beginning with an ESC (hex 1B) character, which are interpreted by the video system as a command. It would be useful to build a set of manipulators to embed ANSI escape sequence commands into stream output functions. Note that on some systems, particularly MS-DOS, a special device driver must be loaded to install support for ANSI escape sequences.

Let's start with the simplest case, a manipulator with no parameters. endl is an example of a predefined manipulator that lacks parameters. Here's a manipulator that uses an escape sequence to clear the screen:

```
//------------------------------------------------
// simple manipulator

ostream & ANSIclear(ostream & o)
    {
    return o << "\x1B[2J";
    }
```

The *ANSIclear* manipulator stores an escape sequence into the stream. It would be used like this:

```
cout << ANSIclear;
```

Note that, unlike regular calls to functions without parameters, calls to parameter-less manipulators do not require a set of empty parentheses after the manipulator name.

Things become more complicated when a manipulator requires parameters. If only one parameter of type *int* or *long* is needed, the definition must be made in two parts. A manipulator that uses an escape sequence to change the display mode would be defined as:

```
//------------------------------------------------
// manipulator with single int parameter

ostream & ANSIsetmode(ostream & o, int mode)
    {
    return o << "\x1B[" << mode << "h";
    }

OMANIP(int) ANSIsetmode(int mode)
    {
    return OMANIP(int) (ANSIsetmode, mode);
    }
```

ANSIsetmode can now be used as a manipulator:

```
cout << ANSIsetmode(1); // set to 40 column mode
```

OMANIP is one of several macros defined in *iomanip.hpp*. There are families of macros for different types of streams in *iomanip.hpp*. If you were making a manipulator for an input stream, you would use the *IMANIP* macro. Each implementation defines these macros differently, and to understand how they affect your C++ compiler, you will need to look at *iomanip.hpp*.

An integer that denotes the video mode to be set is passed as a parameter to *ANSIsetmode*. Mode 0 sets a 40-column-by-25-line black-and-white mode; mode 1 sets a 40-column-by-25-line mode with color; mode 2 sets an 80-column-by-25-line mode in black-and-white; mode 3 sets an 80-column-by-25-line mode with color.

Using explicit *int* value to represent the video mode is prone to errors. A better approach is to use an enumerated type to assign symbolic constants to the different mode values. However, the *iomanip.hpp* file only predefines the constructs needed for *int* and *long* parameters.

Therefore, to use a non-*int*, non-*long* type for a parameter, more work needs to be done:

```
//-------------------------------------------------
// manipulator with single non-int, non-long parameter

enum ANSImode {ANSI_40x25_BW, ANSI_40x25_Color,
               ANSI_80x25_BW, ANSI_80x25_Color};

IOMANIPdeclare(ANSImode);

ostream & ANSIsetmode(ostream & o, ANSImode mode)
    {
    return o << "\x1B[" << (int)mode << "h";
    }
```

The *ANSIsetmode* manipulator is used after a declaration is made:

```
int main()
    {
    OAPP(ANSImode) ANSIsetmode = ::ANSIsetmode;

    cout << ANSIsetmode(ANSI_40x25_Color);
    }
```

OAPP is a macro that preprocesses into a class name. The first *ANSIsetmode* is a variable; the second represents that address of the *ANSIsetmode* function. The scope operator is used so the variable is assigned the address of the global function.

A similar technique is used to create a manipulator with more than one parameter. The macros in *iomanip.hpp* are set up for only one parameter. Therefore, we need to use a structure as an intermediary. The structure should contain data elements representing the different parameters for the manipulator.

The ANSI escape sequence for cursor positioning, which requires both line and column parameters, could be implemented with this code:

```
//-------------------------------------------------------
// manipulator w/ two parameters!

struct ANSIcoord
    {
    int l, c;
    };

IOMANIPdeclare(ANSIcoord);

ostream & ANSIsetpos (ostream & o, ANSIcoord p)
    {
    return o << "\x1B[" << p.l << ';' << p.c << 'H';
    }

OMANIP(ANSIcoord) ANSIsetpos(int line, int col)
    {
    ANSIcoord p;

    p.l = line;
    p.c = col;

    return OMANIP(ANSIcoord)(ANSIsetpos,p);
    }
```

Overloading is used to create two *ANSIsetpos* functions. The second one is called first to construct a structure, and then call the first *ANSIsetpos* function to do the actual work. Now, statements of this type can be included in your programs:

```
cout << ANSIsetpos(10,10) << "Hello!";
```

Understanding how manipulators are created will require so practice and intuitive programming. To see how these macros work, I strongly urge you to read the *iomanip.hpp* header file that comes with your compiler.

Buffering

When a stream is buffered, each insertion or extraction does not have a corresponding I/O operation to physically write or read data to a device. Instead, insertions and extractions are stored in a buffer from which data is written or read in chunks.

It's possible to force data buffered in an output stream to be written. This is called "flushing," and ensures that everything stored in an output stream has been displayed. In general, flushing is done when interactive input is requested by the user, so that the program can be sure that the screen is completely up to date. *cout* can be flushed using this statement:

```
cout.flush();
```

A program can "tie" an input stream to an output stream. In this case, the output stream is flushed of any contents before characters are fetched from the input stream. For example, *cin* is automatically tied to *cout* to be sure that everything has been physically displayed before any input occurs. You can tie your own streams together using the *tie* method:

```
istream input;
ostream output;

input.tie(output);
```

This statement forces output to be flushed before every fetch from input.

Conclusion

The streams library is a powerful set of tools that can be used to handle I/O tasks. It also provides an excellent example of those things C++ does best by providing an extensible abstraction of file operations. Studying this library will help you better understand class hierarchies.

CHAPTER

8

Container Classes

The "correct" practices for object-oriented programming aren't always intuitive. In fact, when it comes to determining how to assemble the pieces to actually build an application, they can be downright obscure and confusing. The question I hear most often from newly initiated object-oriented programmers is, "How do I use this stuff? I know the syntax, and I've heard the explanations and definitions, but how do I actually use it?"

Since it has the ability to support both structured and object-oriented programming, C++ does not foster an absolute adherence to object-oriented programming techniques. This leads many C programmers to treat C++ as an extended version of C. Of course, some features of C++ can be treated this way, however, when it comes to object-oriented programming, C programmers often fail to learn concepts that are fundamental to the paradigm.

Container Classes

The term "container class" seems to be used a lot in object-oriented circles, but very few C++ programmers are really sure what it means. Actually, it's a very literal term. A container class defines objects that in turn contain other objects, such as linked lists and binary trees. The pure object-oriented programming language, Smalltalk, comes with a dizzying array of container classes, ranging from simple "bags" that hold an unordered collection of data to indexed "ordered collections."

Containers are the fundamental building blocks for computer programs. I've rarely written a complex program that doesn't have at least one linked list or tree structure. Since C++ lacks a set of standard container classes, it's useful to add them. What's more, building your own library of container classes will help demonstrate the practical uses of many of the concepts presented in previous chapters.

The goal of this chapter is to help you understand inheritance and polymorphism. I'm not going to offer a tutorial in data structures, nor will I explain the details of how lists, stacks, and queues work. As I pointed out in the first chapter, I'm assuming that you're an experienced C programmer who already knows the fundamentals of algorithms and data structures.

General Design Concepts

When you try to build generic data structures in C++, three problems present themselves. First, the intrinsic data types, such as *int* and *float*, are not classes. Second, C++ classes are not all derived from a single root class, as is the case with languages like Smalltalk, so there is no generic facility that encompasses all data types.

I want the container classes to be polymorphic, so that, for example, the code for a stack or a queue is interchangeable. This presents the third problem in building generic container classes: C++ requires virtual functions to have an identical type in every class for which it is defined. So, we need to find some method to reference objects of all types in a generic fashion.

The best solution is to use *void* pointers. A *void* pointer can point to anything, whether it is an intrinsic type or a class object. So, the container classes presented here store pointers to actual objects. This eliminates the need to allocate space to store duplicates of objects and data items, but it also forces us to be careful not to store any pointers in a container that will be deleted before the container itself is deleted. Unfortunately, no type-checking can be done on assignments made to and from *void* pointers.

The Container Class

All of the container classes will be derived from *Container*, which is the file that holds the container class definition:

```
#if !defined(__CONTAINR_HPP)
#define __CONTAINR_HPP 1

class Container
    {
    protected:
        // number of items in this list
        unsigned long Count;

        // pointer to exception handler
        void (* ErrorHandler)();

    public:
        // constructor
        Container();

        // copy constructor
        Container(const Container & c);

        // assignment operator
        void operator = (const Container & c);

        // store an item
        virtual int Store(void * item) = 0;

        // examine an item
        virtual void * Examine() = 0;

        // retrieve an item
        virtual void * Retrieve() = 0;

        // eliminate contents
        virtual void Empty() = 0;

        // return number of items in a container
        unsigned long GetCount()
            {
```

```
                return Count;
                }

        // set function for exception handler
        void AssignHandler(void (* userHandler)())
                {
                ErrorHandler = userHandler;
                }
    };

#endif
```

This is *Container*'s implementation file:

```
#include "Containr.hpp"

extern "C"
    {
    #include "stdio.h"
    }

// prototypes
static void DefaultHandler();

// default exception handler
static void DefaultHandler()
    {
    puts("\aContainer Error: memory allocation failure!");
    }

// constructor
Container::Container()
    {
    Count = 0;
    ErrorHandler = DefaultHandler;
    }

// copy constructor
Container::Container(const Container & c)
    {
    Count = c.Count;
    ErrorHandler = c.ErrorHandler;
    }

// assignment operator
void Container::operator = (const Container & c)
    {
    Count = c.Count;
    ErrorHandler = c.ErrorHandler;
    }
```

There are only two data members defined by *Container*: a count of the number of items stored in the *Container*, and a pointer to a function that is called when an error in a *Container* occurs, such as a memory allocation error. Remember the earlier discussion about exception handlers? In this case, *ErrorHandler* points to the exception handler for a *Container*.

The constructor for *Container* does not have any arguments; it merely assigns 0 to the data element *Count*. The assignment operator is defined to copy the values of *Count* and *ErrorHandler* from the source object to the destination object. No destructor is required by *Container* since it requires no cleanup.

It may seem a bit odd to define a constructor and assignment operators for a class as simple as *Container*. Their purpose is to provide an interface to the requirements common to all container classes. Every container object, for example, must assign zero to the *Count* data member inherited from *Container*. Rather than have each container class make the same assignment in their constructors, it is better to use the base class constructor. An additional benefit is that any changes to the basic requirements of a container can be reflected in all of the classes derived from *Container* simply by changing *Container*'s methods.

There are no implementations of the last four methods defined for *Container*, since they are all virtual methods. *Store* places its pointer parameter into the *Container*. *Examine* and *Retrieve* both return the current item pointer in a *Container* -- the difference is that *Retrieve* deletes all references to that item from the list. Finally, the *Empty* method removes all item pointers from a *Container*.

These four methods are virtual methods because they depend upon the type of *Container* to which they are being applied. *Store*, for example, works very differently for a *Stack* than it does for *Queue*. *Container* is an abstract class that defines the general capabilities of a group of classes. Since it doesn't need to implement these four methods, it defines them as pure virtual methods.

The last two methods defined for *Container* are utilitarian. *GetCount* returns the value of the *Count* instance variable, and *AssignHandler* is used to assign a pointer to a function that is to be used as an exception handler. If *AssignHandler* is not called, the default exception handler is used, as predefined in the *containr.cpp* implementation of the *Container* class.

Singly Linked Lists

A singly linked list is one of the fundamental building blocks of programs. This is a class-definition header file for a singly linked list class:

```
#if !defined(__SINGLIST_HPP)
#define __SINGLIST_HPP 1

#include "Containr.hpp"

class SinglyLinkedList : public Container
    {
    protected:
        // structure of a node in a list
        struct ListNode
            {
            ListNode  *  Next;
            void      *  DataPtr;
            };

        ListNode * Head;  // pointer to first node
        ListNode * Tail;  // pointer to the last node

        // duplication method
        void Copy(const SinglyLinkedList & sl);

    public:
        // constructor
        SinglyLinkedList();
```

```
      // copy constructor
      SinglyLinkedList(const SinglyLinkedList & sl);

      // assignment operator
      void operator = (const SinglyLinkedList & sl);

      // destructor
      ~SinglyLinkedList();

      // store an item
      virtual int Store(void * item) = 0;

      // examine an item
      virtual void * Examine() = 0;

      // retrieve an item
      virtual void * Retrieve() = 0;

      // remove all items from a list
      virtual void Empty();
   };

#endif
```

SinglyLinkedList is the base class for other singly linked list classes, and is derived from the abstract class *Container*. In fact, *SinglyLinkedList* is itself an abstract class in that it defines three pure virtual methods.

SinglyLinkedList's primary contribution to the container class hierarchy is the addition of the data structures used by singly linked lists. The *ListNode* structure defines the format of a node within a list. While *ListNode* is defined within the definition of *SinglyLinkedList*, it is actually a globally scoped structure. Any type definitions contained in the definitions of classes (or *structs* or *unions*) are actually public, regardless of the access mode under which they are defined.

The data members *Head* and *Tail* are pointers to the first and last members of the list.

Copy is the first private member function I've used in this book. *Copy* duplicates the linked list of pointers to *ListNodes* from one *SinglyLinkedList* to another. It's used by both the copy constructor and the assignment operator, and it simplifies the program code to make this process a method. Since we don't want the *Copy* method to be called directly outside of the class scope, it's protected by private access.

Here are the implementations of *SinglyLinkedList*'s methods:

```cpp
#include "SingList.hpp"

extern "C"
    {
    #include "stddef.h"
    }
// duplication method
void SinglyLinkedList::Copy(const SinglyLinkedList & sl)
    {
    Head = NULL;
    Tail = NULL;

    ListNode * temp = sl.Head;

    while (temp != NULL)
        {
        if (Tail == NULL)
            {
            Tail = new ListNode;

            if (Tail == NULL)
                ErrorHandler();

            Head = Tail;

            Tail->Next    = NULL;
            Tail->DataPtr = temp->DataPtr;
            }
        else
            {
            Tail->Next = new ListNode;

            if (Tail->Next == NULL)
                ErrorHandler();

            Tail->Next->Next    = NULL;
            Tail->Next->DataPtr = temp->DataPtr;

            Tail = Tail->Next;
            }
```

```
    temp = temp->Next;
    }
}

// constructor
SinglyLinkedList::SinglyLinkedList() : Container()
    {
    Head  = NULL;
    Tail  = NULL;
    }

// copy constructor
SinglyLinkedList::SinglyLinkedList(const SinglyLinkedList & sl) :
Container(sl)
    {
    Copy(sl);
    }

// assignment operator
void SinglyLinkedList::operator = (const SinglyLinkedList & sl)
    {
    this->Empty();

    Count = sl.Count;

    Copy(sl);
    }

// destructor
SinglyLinkedList::~SinglyLinkedList ()
    {
    this->Empty();
    }

// remove all items from a list
void SinglyLinkedList::Empty()
    {
    ListNode * temp, * hold;

    temp = Head;

    while (temp != NULL)
        {
        hold = temp->Next;
        delete temp;
        temp = hold;
        }
    }
```

Even though *SinglyLinkedList* does not implement the methods that
store and read items from a list, it does know enough about singly
linked list structures to be able to implement the constructors, destructor, and *Empty* methods. *SinglyLinkedList* may be an abstract base
class, but it provides the implementations of the utility methods that
are used by the classes derived from it.

Stacks and Queues

Stacks and queues are similar forms of singly linked lists. In a stack,
items are stored in such a way that the last item stored is the first
item retrieved. A queue works in the opposite direction, so the first
item stored is the first item retrieved. The primary difference between stacks and queues is in how items are stored. In a stack stores,
new items are stored at the head of the list, while a queue stores new
items at the tail of the list.

The definition of the *Stack* class is based on the *SinglyLinkedList*
class:

```
#if !defined(__STACK_HPP)
#define __STACK_HPP 1

#include "SingList.hpp"

class Stack : public SinglyLinkedList
    {
    public:
        // constructor
        Stack();

        // copy constructor
        Stack(const Stack & st);

        // assignment operator
        void operator = (const Stack & st);

        // store an item in a stack
        virtual int Store(void * item);

        // examine the top item in the stack
        virtual void * Examine();
```

```
        // retrieve the top item in a stack (and remove it)
        virtual void * Retrieve();
    };

#endif
```

Stack doesn't define any data members; everything it needs is inherited from *SinglyLinkedList*, which in turn inherits from *Container*. *Stack*'s constructors are simple, too — they merely pass arguments on to the constructors for *SinglyLinkedList*. The assignment operator for *Stack* shows how to call an inherited operator method. This is one instance where the *this* pointer to the implicit object comes in handy.

As shown below, there's nothing remarkable about *Stack*'s methods:

```
#include "Stack.hpp"

extern "C"
    {
    #include "stddef.h"
    }
// constructor
Stack::Stack() : SinglyLinkedList()
    {}
// copy constructor
Stack::Stack(const Stack & st) : SinglyLinkedList(st)
    {}
// assignment operator
void Stack::operator = (const Stack & st)
    {
    this->SinglyLinkedList::operator = (st);
    }
// add new item
int Stack::Store(void * item)
    {
    ListNode * new_node;

    new_node = new ListNode;

    if (NULL == new_node)
        return 1;
```

```
    new_node->Next    = Head;
    new_node->DataPtr = item;

    Head = new_node;

    if (Tail == NULL)
        Tail = new_node;

    ++Count;

    return 0;
    }

// examine the top item on the stack
void * Stack::Examine()
    {
    if (Count == 0)
        return NULL;

    return Head->DataPtr;
    }

// read and remove the top item on the stack
void * Stack::Retrieve()
    {
    ListNode * temp;
    void *     value;

    if (Count == 0)
        return NULL;

    value = Head->DataPtr;
    temp  = Head->Next;

    delete Head;

    Head = temp;

    --Count;

    return value;
    }
```

Store places the new item at the beginning of the list, while *Retrieve* and *Examine* return the item pointer stored at the head of the list.

Since the only difference between a stack and a queue is the way in which they store items, *Queue* is derived from *Stack*:

```
#if !defined(__QUEUE_HPP)
#define __QUEUE_HPP 1

#include "Stack.hpp"

class Queue : public Stack
    {
    public:
        // constructor
        Queue();

        // copy constructor
        Queue(const Queue & q);

        // assignment constructor
        void operator = (const Queue & q);

        // store an item in a queue
        virtual int Store(void * item);
    };

#endif
```

Queue defines only the bare necessities: the constructors, the assignment operator, and its own version of *Store* to place new items at the end of the list.

As discussed earlier, constructors and assignment operator defined in a base class are not inherited by a derived class. Therefore, *Queue* must define its own versions of these methods since they are not inherited from *Stack*. The implementation of *Queue*'s methods is very short:

```
#include "Queue.hpp"

extern "C"
    {
    #include "stddef.h"
    }

// constructor
Queue::Queue() : Stack()
    {}
```

```
// copy constructor
Queue::Queue(const Queue & q) : Stack(q)
    {}

// assignment constructor
void Queue::operator = (const Queue & q)
    {
    this->Stack::operator = (q);
    }

// add new item
int Queue::Store(void * item)
    {
    ListNode * new_node;

    new_node = new ListNode;

    if (NULL == new_node)
        return 1;

    new_node->Next    = NULL;
    new_node->DataPtr = item;

    if (Count > 0)
        {
        Tail->Next = new_node;
        Tail       = new_node;
        }
    else
        {
        Head = new_node;
        Tail = new_node;
        }

    ++Count;

    return 0;
    }
```

The program *condemo.cpp* demonstrates how the *Stack* and *Queue* classes work:

```
extern "C"
    {
    #include "stdio.h"
    }

#include "Stack.hpp"
#include "Queue.hpp"
```

```
Stack s, s2;
Queue q, q2;

int i, a[10], * ip;

int main();

int main()
    {
    for (i = 0; i < 10; ++i)
        {
        a[i] = i;
        s.Store(&(a[i]));
        q.Store(&(a[i]));
        }

    s2 = s;
    q2 = q;

    printf("\nstack2 = ");

    while (NULL != (ip = (int *)(s2.Retrieve())))
        printf("%3d",*ip);

    printf("\nqueue2 = ");

    while (NULL != (ip = (int *)(q2.Retrieve())))
        printf("%3d",*ip);

    printf("\nstack  = ");

    while (NULL != (ip = (int *)(s.Retrieve())))
        printf("%3d",*ip);

    printf("\nqueue  = ");

    while (NULL != (ip = (int *)(q.Retrieve())))
        printf("%3d",*ip);

    printf("\n");
    }
```

condemo.cpp creates a single array of integer values ranging from 1 to 10, and then assigns the addresses of the array elements to *Stack* and *Queue* objects *s* and *q*. The assignment operator is then used to make copies of these two containers. The items stored in the *Stack*s and *Queue*s are then displayed. The simple program above should give you some idea of how these classes work.

Doubly Linked Lists

In a singly linked list, each element in the list maintains a pointer to the item that follows it. In a doubly linked list, each element stored maintains an additional pointer to the item preceding it. A singly linked list is processed faster than a doubly linked list, but a doubly linked list can be used for more complicated tasks than a singly linked list.

Here's the definition of a doubly linked list class:

```
#if !defined(__DBLLIST_HPP)
#define __DBLLIST_HPP 1

#include "Containr.hpp"

class DoublyLinkedList : public Container
    {
    protected:
        // structure of a node in a list
        struct DListNode
            {
            DListNode * Prev;
            DListNode * Next;
            void       * DataPtr;
            };

        // pointers to first and last nodes in list
        DListNode * Head;
        DListNode * Tail;

        // duplication method
        void Copy(const DoublyLinkedList & sl);

    public:
        // constructor
        DoublyLinkedList();

        // copy constructor
        DoublyLinkedList(const DoublyLinkedList & sl);

        // assignment operator
        void operator = (const DoublyLinkedList & sl);

        // destructor
        ~DoublyLinkedList();
```

```
        // store an item
        virtual int Store(void * item) = 0;

        // examine an item
        virtual void * Examine() = 0;

        // retrieve an item
        virtual void * Retrieve() = 0;

        // remove all items from a list
        virtual void Empty();
    };

#endif
```

The types of methods and data elements defined by *DoublyLinkedList* correspond to those defined in *SinglyLinkedList*. Like the *SinglyLinkedList* class, *DoublyLinkedList* is an abstract class that is meant to provide a basis for other doubly linked list classes. Its implementation is:

```
#include "DblList.hpp"

extern "C"
    {
    #include "stddef.h"
    }

// duplication method
void DoublyLinkedList::Copy(const DoublyLinkedList & dl)
    {
    Head = NULL;
    Tail = NULL;

    DListNode * temp = dl.Head;

    while (temp != NULL)
        {
        if (Tail == NULL)
            {
            Tail = new DListNode;

            if (Tail == NULL)
                ErrorHandler();

            Head = Tail;
```

```
            Tail->Next    = NULL;
            Tail->Prev    = NULL;
            Tail->DataPtr = temp->DataPtr;
            }
        else
            {
            Tail->Next = new DListNode;

            if (Tail->Next == NULL)
                ErrorHandler();

            Tail->Next->Next    = NULL;
            Tail->Next->Prev    = Tail;
            Tail->Next->DataPtr = temp->DataPtr;

            Tail = Tail->Next;
            }

        temp = temp->Next;
        }
    }

// constructor
DoublyLinkedList::DoublyLinkedList() : Container()
    {
    Head  = NULL;
    Tail  = NULL;
    }

// copy constructor
DoublyLinkedList::DoublyLinkedList(const DoublyLinkedList & dl)
    {
    Copy(dl);
    }

// assignment operator
void DoublyLinkedList::operator = (const DoublyLinkedList & dl)
    {
    this->Empty();

    Count = dl.Count;

    Copy(dl);
    }

// destructor
DoublyLinkedList::~DoublyLinkedList()
    {
    this->Empty();
    }
```

```
// remove all items from a list
void DoublyLinkedList::Empty()
    {
    DListNode * temp, * hold;

    temp = Head;

    while (temp != NULL)
        {
        hold = temp->Next;
        delete temp;
        temp = hold;
        }
    }
```

The WorkList Class

The only class discussed in this book that is derived from *DoublyLinkedList* is a class I call *WorkList*. *WorkList* is a very flexible type of list, and it is used in several of the programming projects later in this book. The *WorkList* class definition looks like this:

```
#if !defined(__WORKLIST_HPP)
#define __WORKLIST_HPP 1

#include "DblList.hpp"

class WorkList : public DoublyLinkedList
    {
    protected:
        DListNode * Current; // selected node in the list

    public:
        // constructor
        WorkList();

        // copy constructor
        WorkList(const WorkList & wl);

        // assignment operator
        void operator = (const WorkList & wl);

        // store an item
        virtual int Store(void * item);

        // examine an item
        virtual void * Examine();
```

```
        // read and remove an item
        virtual void * Retrieve();

        // delete an item from the list
        virtual int Delete(void * item);

        // go to head of list
        virtual void GoToHead();

        // go to end of list
        virtual void GoToTail();

        // go to next item in list
        virtual void GoNext();

        // go to previous item in list
        virtual void GoPrev();
    };

#endif
```

Perhaps the best thing that the *WorkList* class demonstrates is the extent to which a derived class can modify a base class. *WorkList* adds a data element and five methods to those it inherits from *DoublyLinkedList*. The new data element is a pointer to the currently selected item in a *WorkList*. Unlike the other list types presented so far, any item pointer stored in a *WorkList* can be selected for examination.

Here's how the methods for *WorkList* are implemented:

```
#include "WorkList.hpp"

extern "C"
    {
    #include "stddef.h"
    }

// constructor
WorkList::WorkList() : DoublyLinkedList()
    {
    Current = NULL;
    }
```

```
// copy constructor
WorkList::WorkList(const WorkList & wl) : DoublyLinkedList(wl)
    {}

// assignment operator
void WorkList::operator = (const WorkList & wl)
    {
    DoublyLinkedList::operator = (wl);

    Current = Head;
    }

// store an item
int WorkList::Store(void * item)
    {
    DListNode * new_item;

    new_item = new DListNode;

    if (item == NULL)
        return 1;

    new_item->Prev    = NULL;
    new_item->Next    = NULL;
    new_item->DataPtr = item;

    if (Head == NULL)
        {
        Head    = new_item;
        Tail    = new_item;
        Current = new_item;
        }
    else
        {
        Head->Prev = new_item;
        new_item->Next = Head;
        Head = new_item;
        }

    ++Count;

    return 0;
    }

// examine an item
void * WorkList::Examine()
    {
    if (Current == NULL)
        return NULL;
```

```
        else
            return Current->DataPtr;
        }

// read and remove an item
void * WorkList::Retrieve()
        {
        void * value = Examine();

        Delete(value);

        return value;
        }

// delete an item from the list
int WorkList::Delete(void * item)
        {
        DListNode * temp;

        temp = Head;

        while (temp != NULL)
            {
            if (temp->DataPtr == item)
                {
                if (temp == Current)
                    Current = temp->Next;

                if (temp->Prev == NULL)
                    {
                    Head = temp->Next;

                    if (Head != NULL)
                        Head->Prev = NULL;

                    if (temp->Next == NULL)
                        Tail = NULL;
                    }
                else
                    {
                    temp->Prev->Next = temp->Next;

                    if (temp->Next == NULL)
                        Tail = temp->Prev;
                    else
                        temp->Next->Prev = temp->Prev;
                    }

                delete temp;
```

```
            --Count;

            return 0;
            }

        temp = temp->Next;
        }

    return 1;
    }
// go to head of list
void WorkList::GoToHead()
    {
    Current = Head;
    }

// go to end of list
void WorkList::GoToTail()
    {
    Current = Tail;
    }

// go to next item in list
void WorkList::GoNext()
    {
    if (Current != NULL)
        Current = Current->Next;
    }

// go to next item in list
void WorkList::GoPrev()
    {
    if (Current != NULL)
        Current = Current->Prev;
    }
```

Pointers to items are stored at the end of the list by the *Store* method. The *Delete* method searches the stored item pointers for one that matches the item pointer given as an argument. If a match is found, the item pointer and its node are removed from the list.

The item pointers stored in a *WorkList* can be thought of as a ladder. Think of the node pointed to by *Head* as the base of the ladder, while the node pointed to by *Tail* is the top of the ladder. The *Current* pointer indicates which step of the ladder (or node) is selected. The *Examine* and *Retrieve* methods return the value of the item pointer stored in the node indicated by *Current*. *Retrieve* will also delete all references to the currently selected item from the *WorkList*. *GoToHead* sets *Current* to point to the bottom of the ladder (*Head*), while *GoToTail* selects the top of the ladder (*Tail*). *GoNext* moves *Current* to the next item up the ladder toward *Tail*, and *GoPrev* moves *Current* down the ladder toward *Head*.

Programs throughout the remainder of this book demonstrate the uses of *WorkList*. *WorkList* is used most extensively in the Window class and the simulation program, both of which are developed in later chapters.

Other Container Classes

Obviously, this class hierarchy doesn't cover all of the possible container types. Some containers, such as binary trees, would allow item pointers to be stored and retrieved based on a key value. Developing a tree of keyed container classes would be an excellent exercise for those of you who want to become more comfortable with C++, inheritance, and polymorphism.

9

Sets

Programmers tend to be somewhat elitist about their programming language. If Joe's programming language can jettison its flotsam and Sally's language can't, Joe will say that his language is better. It doesn't matter that jettisoning flotsam may be only marginally useful, or that Sally's language can whack a dingbat. Some of the most colorful arguments in which I've been involved have revolved around proving that one language is better than another.

Having made that statement, I would like to now sing the praises of C++'s classes. Classes can be used to add new features to the language. If you like using sets in Pascal or Modula-2, there's no reason you can't develop classes in C++ that provide a set type. In fact, because you can custom-design a class, the sets you create for C++ can be more flexible than their "hard-wired" counterparts in Pascal and Modula-2.

What's a Set?

If you haven't worked with Pascal or Modula-2, you may not recall what a set is. Sets are a mathematical concept usually taught in elementary school. In simple terms, a set is a collection of objects of the same type. The objects are called elements of the set. If two sets contain exactly the same elements, they are equal. If the elements of set A are all elements of set B, a is called a subset of B. The intersection of two sets is a set made up of the elements common to both original sets. Finally, a union of sets A and B is a set that contains all of the items that are in either A or B.

That's the mathematical definition. Programming languages approach sets from a slightly different angle. In programming, a set contains a series of bits that represent a series of binary (on-off) switches stored in sequence from 0 through the maximum number of items in the set. Each switch represents the presence of an element in the set, so if the switch is on, the set contains the element corresponding to that switch.

The easiest data type to use with a set is an integer. The bits directly correspond to the value of the integer stored in the set. For example, this 8-bit (one-byte) set contains the integers 0, 1, 4, and 7:

```
bit          0 1 2 3 4 5 6 7
--------------------
set: 1 1 0 0 1 0 0 1
```

To find out if an integer value is "stored" in the set, you merely need to check the value of the bit in the correct position. This means that anything represented by an integer value can be stored in a set.

Defining the BitSet Class

In general, the type of set I just described is called a bit set. They're very useful, as you'll see. Let's begin by designing the *BitSet* class.

First, each *BitSet* must contain an array of bits. Different types of sets will have different numbers of elements, so the size of the array should be flexible. The number of required bits should be specified when a set is instantiated. The bit array will then by dynamically allocated. Since most computers allocate space in 8-bit bytes, we'll need to allocate space in units of 8 bits, even if this results in a few wasted bits.

All of the standard set operations should be available for a *BitSet*. Naturally, there will have to be methods to include and exclude values from a set. The class will also need to provide a method to determine if a value is stored in the set. Union and intersection sets should be calculable from other sets. Set comparison methods will also be useful. Of course, the class will need the standard copy constructor, destructor (to deallocate the array of bits), and assignment operator methods. Finally, we'll want to the *BitSet* class to provide a basis for other set classes.

There's one more goal to reach in the design of *BitSet* — the class must be reasonably efficient. Common operations on *BitSet*s should be as quick as possible to make the class practical.

Defining BitSet

With a design in hand, you can now proceed to build a *BitSet* class. The definition of the *BitSet* class is contained in the file bitset.*hpp*:

```
#if !defined(_BitSet_HPP)
#define _BitSet_HPP 1

extern "C"
    {
    #include "stddef.h"
    #include "string.h"
    }

class BitSet
    {
    protected:
        unsigned long   Length;
        unsigned char * Data;

        BitSet()
            {
            Length = 0L;
            Data   = NULL;
            }

    public:
        // constructors
        BitSet(unsigned long size);
```

```
    BitSet(BitSet & bs);

// destructor
~BitSet(void);

// assignment operator
void operator = (BitSet & bs);

// Get number of bits in set
unsigned long Size()
    {
    return Length;
    }

// operation methods
void Include(unsigned long bit)
    {
    if (bit < Length)
        Data[bit / 8] |= (unsigned char)(1 << (bit & 7));
    }

void Exclude(unsigned long bit)
    {
    if (bit < Length)
        Data[bit / 8] &= ~(unsigned char)(1 << (bit & 7));
    }

// turn all bits in set on
void AllOn()
    {
    memset(Data,'\xFF',(Length + 7) / 8);
    }

// turn all bits in set off
void AllOff()
    {
    memset(Data,'\x00',(Length + 7) / 8);
    }

// union operators
BitSet operator & (BitSet & bs);
BitSet operator &= (BitSet & bs);

// synonyms for union operators
BitSet operator +  (BitSet & bs);
BitSet operator += (BitSet & bs);

// intersection operators
BitSet operator |  (BitSet & bs);
BitSet operator |= (BitSet & bs);
```

```
    // difference operators
    BitSet operator -  (BitSet & bs);
    BitSet operator -= (BitSet & bs);

    // complement operator
    BitSet operator ~ ();

    // comparison operator
    int operator == (BitSet & bs);
    int operator != (BitSet & bs);

    // value retrieval method
    int operator [] (unsigned long bit)
        {
        if (bit < Length)
            return (Data[bit/8] & (1 << (bit&7)));
        else
            return 0;
        }
};

#endif
```

The *BitSet* class defines two private data members. *Length* holds the numbers of bits stored in the set, and *Data* is a pointer to the bits themselves. Bits are allocated in groups of eight, which is the number of bits in one *char*. There may be some unused bits. For example, a *BitSet* with a *Length* of 11 will have two *char*s allocated to it for a total of 16 bits. This is because memory can only be allocated in units of eight bits (one *char*). The few wasted bits should not seriously affect the size of your programs, since no more than seven bits can be wasted in any *BitSet*.

BitSet defines its default constructor as an inline private member. This might seem strange, since a private constructor cannot be used to create objects outside of the scope of the class. The design of *BitSet* requires that the numbers of bits in the set be provided when a *BitSet* object is created. The default constructor is only needed (and used) by a few class methods, and as such it is made private.

There are two public constructors for *BitSet*. One constructor accepts an unsigned *long* parameter that defines the number of bits in the newly created set. The other constructor is a copy constructor. Since *BitSet*s allocate dynamic memory, a destructor is required for clean-up when an object is destroyed.

```
// constructors
BitSet::BitSet(unsigned long size)
    {
    unsigned long alloc;

    Length = size;
    alloc  = (size + 7) / 8;
    Data   = new unsigned char[(unsigned int)alloc];

    memset(Data,'\x00',(unsigned int)alloc);
    }

BitSet::BitSet(BitSet & bs)
    {
    unsigned long alloc;

    Length = bs.Length;
    alloc  = (bs.Length + 7) / 8;
    Data   = new unsigned char[(unsigned int)alloc];

    memcpy(Data,bs.Data,(unsigned int)alloc);
    }
```
BitSets allocate memory, so a destructor is required:
```
// destructor
BitSet::~BitSet(void)
    {
    if (Data != NULL)
        delete Data;
    }
```

One BitSet can be made equal to another by using the assignment operator:

```
// assignment operator
void BitSet::operator = (BitSet & bs)
    {
    unsigned long alloc;

    if (Length != bs.Length)
        {
        Length = bs.Length;

        alloc = (bs.Length + 7) / 8;
```

```
        if (Data != NULL)
            delete Data;

        Data = new unsigned char[(unsigned int)alloc];

        memcpy(Data,bs.Data,(unsigned int)alloc);
        }
    else
        memcpy(Data, bs.Data,
                    (unsigned int)((Length + 7) / 8));
    }
```

Size is an inline method that returns the value of *Length* for a *BitSet*. *Length* could have been made a public member of *BitSet*, which would eliminate the need for a separate function. However, that would have allowed the modification of a *BitSet*'s *Length* from outside of the class scope — definitely an undesirable situation. By defining the *Size* method as an inline function, it is just as efficient at run-time as accessing *Length* directly.

Include and *Exclude* are also inline methods that respectively set and reset single bits in the *BitSet*. When a bit is set (given a value of 1), the unsigned *long* value corresponding to that location is said to be included in the set. Turning a bit off (setting it to 0) removes an unsigned *long* value from the set.

AllOn and *AllOff* merely set all of the bits in a *BitSet* to 1 or 0, respectively. They are implemented inline because of their simplicity.

The operator *&* is defined to calculate the union of two *BitSet*s. Both the binary and assignment forms of the operator are defined. The + operator is a synonym for *&*, and performs exactly the same function.

```
// union operators
BitSet BitSet::operator & (BitSet & bs)
    {
    BitSet result;

    unsigned long bit;

    if (Length < bs.Length)
        {
        result = bs;

        for (bit = 0; bit < Length; ++bit)
            if ((*this)[bit])
                result.Include(bit);
        }
    else
        {
        result = *this;

        for (bit = 0; bit < bs.Length; ++bit)
            if (bs[bit])
                result.Include(bit);
        }

    return result;
    }

BitSet BitSet::operator &= (BitSet & bs)
    {
    *this = *this & bs;

    return *this;
    }

// synonyms for union operators
BitSet BitSet::operator + (BitSet & bs)
    {
    BitSet result = *this & bs;

    return result;
    }

BitSet BitSet::operator += (BitSet & bs)
    {
    BitSet result = *this &= bs;

    return result;
    }
```

The intersection of two sets is calculated by the | operators:

```
// intersection operators
BitSet BitSet::operator | (BitSet & bs)
    {
    BitSet result;

    unsigned long max;

    if (Length > bs.Length)
        {
        result = BitSet(Length);
        max    = bs.Length;
        }
    else
        {
        result = BitSet(bs.Length);
        max    = Length;
        }

    for (unsigned long bit = 0; bit < max; ++bit)
        if ((*this)[bit] & bs[bit])
            result.Include(bit);

    return result;
    }

BitSet BitSet::operator |= (BitSet & bs)
    {
    *this = *this | bs;

    return *this;
    }
```

The difference between two sets is calculated by removing the members of one set from another set. The *BitSet* uses the - operator for this purpose:

```
// difference operators
BitSet BitSet::operator - (BitSet & bs)
    {
    BitSet result = *this;

    unsigned long stop = (Length < bs.Length) ? Length : bs.Length;

    for (unsigned long bit = 0; bit < stop; ++bit)
        if (bs[bit])
            result.Exclude(bit);
```

```
    return result;
    }

BitSet BitSet::operator -= (BitSet & bs)
    {
    *this = *this - bs;

    return *this;
    }
```

The unary ~ operator reverses the settings of the bits in a set:

```
// complement operator
BitSet BitSet::operator ~ ()
    {
    BitSet result(Length);

    for (unsigned long bit = 0; bit < Length; ++bit)
        if ((*this)[bit])
            result.Exclude(bit);
        else
            result.Include(bit);

    return result;
    }
```

Comparisons between two sets are handled by defining the == and != operators. The concept of one set being greater than another does not exist, so the relative comparison operators are not needed.

```
// comparison operators
int BitSet::operator == (BitSet & bs)
    {
    if (Length != bs.Length)
        return 0;

    for (unsigned long bit = 0; bit < Length; ++bit)
        if ((*this)[bit] != bs[bit])
            return 0;

    return 1;
    }

int BitSet::operator != (BitSet & bs)
    {
    if (Length != bs.Length)
        return 1;
```

```
unsigned long bit = 0;

while (bit < Length)
    if ((*this)[bit] == bs[bit])
        ++bit;
    else
        return 1;

return 0;
}
```

BitSet uses the *[]* operator to determine if a value is a member of a set. This inline method uses bit manipulation operators and is defined inline to make it as fast as possible. Note that some C++ translators and compilers will not inline a function that contains a conditional statement, but this limitation will disappear as C++ compilers become more sophisticated.

BitSet demonstrates a useful C++ technique. The assignment forms of the *BitSet* operators are defined as calls to their binary siblings. The + operators are defined as direct calls to the & operators. This style puts all of the actual code for a given operation in one location, even though there may be some slight loss in efficiency.

The operators are the only methods that use the default constructor. They need to define a *BitSet* object without having any space allocated for it. These operators set the value of the local *BitSet* to that of one of their *BitSet* parameters before calculations begin.

Here's a program to demonstrate how *BitSet* works:

```
#include "BitSet.hpp"

extern "C"
    {
    #include "stdio.h"
    #include "string.h"
    }

void ShowBitSet(BitSet & bs);

void ShowBitSet(BitSet & bs)
    {
    for (int i = 0; i < bs.Size(); ++i)
        if (bs[i])
            putchar('1');
        else
            putchar('0');

    putchar('\n');
    }

int main()
    {
    unsigned int i;

    BitSet bs1(76);
    BitSet bs2(13);
    BitSet bs3(8);

    for (i = 0; i < bs1.Size(); ++i)
        {
        if (i % 2)
            bs1.Include(i);
        else
            bs1.Exclude(i);
        }

    ShowBitSet(bs1);

    bs3 = bs1;

    ShowBitSet(bs3);

    for (i = 0; i < bs2.Size(); ++i)
        {
        if (i % 2)
            bs2.Exclude(i);
        else
```

```
        bs2.Include(i);
    }

for (i = 4; i < bs3.Size(); ++ i)
    {
    bs2.Exclude(i);
    }

ShowBitSet(bs2);

bs3 = bs2 + bs1;
ShowBitSet(bs3);

bs3 = ~bs2;
ShowBitSet(bs3);

bs2 = bs1 | bs3;
ShowBitSet(bs2);

bs2 -= bs3;
ShowBitSet(bs2);

bs2 = bs1 - bs3;
ShowBitSet(bs2);

bs3 += bs1;
ShowBitSet(bs3);

bs3.AllOn();
ShowBitSet(bs3);

bs3.AllOff();
ShowBitSet(bs3);

bs3 = bs2;

if (bs3 == bs1)
    puts("bs3 == bs1");

if (bs3 == bs2)
    puts("bs3 == bs2");

if (bs3 != bs1)
    puts("bs3 != bs1");

if (bs3 != bs2)
    puts("bs3 != bs2");
}
```

The CharSet Class

Now that we have a working *BitSet* class, we can build classes from it. One of the more useful class types defined by Pascal is the *SET OF CHAR*, which is a set of all the character codes for a given system. A set of characters can be useful when you need to check one-key responses against a set of valid responses.

Basically, a *CharSet* is a special form of a *BitSet* that uses *char* values as indexes to individual set bits. Since there are 256 characters in the ASCII character set (the most common character set), a *CharSet* can be defined as a fixed-length, 256-bit *BitSet*. Since it can inherit almost all of *BitSet*'s methods, *CharSet* turns out to be very simple to implement. Its definition is:

```
#if !defined(__CHARSET_HPP)
#define __CHARSET_HPP 1

#include "BitSet.hpp"

class CharSet : public BitSet
    {
    public:
        // constructors
        CharSet() : BitSet(256)
            {}

        CharSet(CharSet & cs) : BitSet(cs)
            {}

        CharSet(char * Values);

        // assignment operator
        void operator = (CharSet & cs)
            {
            BitSet::operator = (cs);
            }
    };

#endif
```

The implementation of *CharSet* is equally simple — it contains only the implementation of the constructor that converts a C-type, null-terminated string of characters into a *CharSet*:

```
#include "CharSet.hpp"

CharSet::CharSet(char * Values) : BitSet(256)
    {
    while (*Values != '\x00')
        {
        Include(*Values);
        ++Values;
        }
    }
```

CharSet defines its own default and copy constructors, which simply call the equivalent methods for *BitSet*. The length of a *CharSet* is not specified, since it has a fixed length of 256 bits. The assignment operator is equally simple.

The program *csdemo.cpp* shows how to use the *CharSet* class:

```
#include "CharSet.hpp"

extern "C"
    {
    #include "stdio.h"
    }

char ics[] = "CharSetTestProgram*&!*&^@01293845";

CharSet cs1;
CharSet cs2;
CharSet cs3;

int main()
    {
    unsigned int i;

    cs1  = "ABCDEFGHIJKLMNOPQRSTUVWXYZ";
    cs2  = ics;
    cs3  = cs1;
    cs2 -= cs1;
    cs3 -= CharSet("DEFGHI");
    cs3 += cs2;
```

```
    printf("set 1 = [");
    for (i = 0; i < 255; ++i)
        if (cs1[i])
            printf("%c",i);

    printf("]\nset 2 = [");
    for (i = 0; i < 255; ++i)
        if (cs2[i])
            printf("%c",i);

    printf("]\nset 3 = [");
    for (i = 0; i < 255; ++i)
        if (cs3[i])
            printf("%c",i);

    printf("]\n");

    return 0;
    }
```

The BitGrid Class

This example shows the other class I've derived from *BitSet*:

```
#if !defined(__BITGRID_HPP)
#define __BITGRID_HPP 1

#include "BitSet.hpp"

class BitGrid : public BitSet
    {
    private:
        unsigned long Width;

    public:
        // constructor
        BitGrid(unsigned long x_dim,
                        unsigned long y_dim)
            : BitSet(x_dim * y_dim)
            {
            Width = x_dim;
            }

        // include a bit
        void Include(unsigned long x_pos,
                            unsigned long y_pos)
            {
            BitSet::Include(y_pos * Width + x_pos);
            }
```

```
        // exclude a bit
        void Exclude(unsigned long x_pos,
                                unsigned long y_pos)
            {
            BitSet::Exclude(y_pos * Width + x_pos);
            }

        //
        int IsSet(unsigned long x_pos,
                        unsigned long y_pos)
            {
            return BitSet::operator []
                                        (y_pos * Width +
x_pos);
            }
    };

#endif
```

A *BitGrid* is a two-dimensional form of *BitSet*. It's defined entirely inline in its header file, since none of its methods have more than one executable program line in them. I've found a two-dimensional grid of bits to be very useful, particularly in graphics applications where I need to keep track of the status of individual pixels. The *BitGrid* class is used in Chapter 14 [[check chapter reference]] in the simulated ecosystem program.

10

A Dynamic String Class

The first project many budding C++ programmers undertake is to develop a character string class. One of C's primary shortcomings is that it lacks the sophisticated string handling available in languages such as Pascal and Basic. Strings are quite useful, and nearly every program manipulates text data of one type or another. Developing a string class was one of my first C++ projects, and during the two years since I created it the class has undergone substantial changes.

As my understanding of C++ has grown, so has my ability to build a better class. After two years, the *String* class has undergone four major versions. I'm quite happy with the incarnation presented here, which works well in applications ranging from databases to text editors. Appendix A contains the complete implementations of the *String* class in files *str.hpp* and *str.cpp*.

My goal was to create a dynamically allocated string class that provides all the functionality of standard, NUL-terminated C character arrays (which I call C-strings). However, I wanted to avoid the pitfalls of C-strings. For instance, errors often occur when working with C-strings because they fail to do any sort of range or validity checking. In addition, the *start* library functions defined in *string.h* are missing important features. In order for strings to be useful in a wide variety of applications, they need manipulation routines not normally found in C function libraries, such as those for inserting and deleting data.

The Class Definition

The definition of the *String* class begins with the definition of three enumerated types: *StrCompVal, StrCompMode*, and *StrError*. *StrCompVal* is the return value of the *Compare* method. *StrCompMode* is used to indicate whether *String* comparisons are case-sensitive or not. *StrError* is used by the exception handler. I use enumerations for these types to control the validity of values passed to and returned from methods. The types must be public so that the enumeration constants are available to the class user.

The class definition for the *String* class looks like this:

```
enum StrCompVal  {SC_LESS, SC_EQUAL,
                  SC_GREATER, SC_ERROR};
enum StrCompMode {SM_SENSITIVE, SM_IGNORE};
enum StrError    {SE_ALLOC, SE_TOO_LONG};

class String
    {
    private:
        // instance variables
        unsigned int Siz;    // allocated size
        unsigned int Len;    // current length
        char * Txt;          // pointer to text

        // class constant
        static unsigned int AllocIncr;

        // pointer to exception handler
        static void (*ErrorHandler)(StrError err);

        // shrinks string to minimum allocation
        void Shrink();

    public:
        // constructor
        String();
        String(const String & str);
        String(const char * cstr);
        String(char fillCh, unsigned int count);
```

```
// destructor
~String();

// value return methods
unsigned int Length();
unsigned int Size();

// Assign an exception handler
static void SetErrorHandler(
        (void (* userHandler)(StrError)));

// create a c-string from String method
operator const char * ();

// assignment method
void operator = (const String & str);

// concatenation methods
friend String operator + (const String & str1,
                                const String & str2);

void operator += (const String & str);

// comparison methods
int operator <  (const String & str);
int operator >  (const String & str);
int operator <= (const String & str);
int operator >= (const String & str);
int operator == (const String & str);
int operator != (const String & str);

StrCompVal Compare(const String & str,
            StrCompMode caseChk = SM_IGNORE);

// substring search methods
int Find(const String & str,
        unsigned int & pos,
        StrCompMode caseChk = SM_IGNORE);

// substring deletion method
void Delete(unsigned int pos,
                unsigned int count);

// substring insertion methods
void Insert(unsigned int pos, char ch);
void Insert(unsigned int pos,
                        const String & str);

// substring retrieval method
String SubStr(unsigned int start,
                        unsigned int count);
```

```
      // character retrieval method
      char operator [] (unsigned int pos):

      // case-modification methods
      String ToUpper();
      String ToLower();
  };
```

A *String* is defined as having three private instance variables: *Siz*, *Len*, and *Txt*. *Siz* contains the currently allocated length of the *Txt* pointer. *Len* holds the actual number of characters stored in the *String*. The *char* pointer *Txt* points to the location on the heap of the buffer containing the *String*'s text data.

AllocIncr is a private static class member. As discussed in Chapter Four[[ck ref]], any class data item defined as static has only one occurrence shared by the entire class. In this case, there is only one copy of *AllocIncr*, which is common to all *String* objects. The purpose of private static class members is to eliminate global variables. Private static class members should be used whenever there is a data item that is accessed only from within a class scope. There's no need for anything external to the *String* class to "see" *AllocIncr*, so it is safely locked away from outside manipulation.

An Exception Handler

ErrorHandler is an exception handler shared by all *String* objects. *ErrorHandler* accepts a single parameter of type *StrError*. *StrError* is an enumerated type that identifies the type of error for which *ErrorHandler* is being called. Currently, two errors can occur for a *String*: either the program has run out of memory (*SE_ALLOC*), or a method has tried to create a string longer than 65,535 characters (*SE_TOO_LONG*).

A default exception handler can be defined for *ErrorHandler* by defining a function whose address is assigned to *ErrorHandler* during static member initialization. In an implementation file, I define the default exception handler like this:

```
// prototype for default error handler
static void DefaultHandler(StrError err);

void (*(String::ErrorHandler))(StrError) =
        DefaultHandler;

// default exception handler
static void DefaultHandler(StrError err)
    {
    printf("\aERROR in String object: ");

    switch (err)
        {
        case SE_ALLOC :
            printf("memory allocation failure");
            break;
        case SE_TOO_LONG :
            printf("exceeded %d character limit"
                            ,UINT_MAX);
        }

    printf("\n");

    exit(1);
    }
```

When a program that uses the *String* class starts up, it will do all initializations associated with *String*'s static members. *ErrorHandler* can be set to point to a programmer-defined function with the *SetErrorHandler* method:

```
// Assign a function to the exception handler
void String::SetErrorHandler(
    void (* userHandler)(StrError))
    {
    ErrorHandler = userHandler;
    }
```

Methods

In general, class methods are made public to facilitate their use by user-defined objects. In the case of the *String* class, however, the method *Shrink* is used only internally by the class. *Shrink* adjusts the allocated buffer space for a string to eliminate wasted space. This is its implementation:

```
// shrinks allocated size of a string
void String::Shrink()
    {
    char * temp;

    if ((Siz - Len) > AllocIncr)
        {
        Siz = ((Len+AllocIncr)/AllocIncr)*AllocIncr;

        temp = new char [Siz];

        if (temp != NULL)
            {
            strcpy(temp,Txt);
            delete Txt;
            Txt  = temp;
            }
        else
            ErrorHandler(SE_ALLOC);
        }
    }
```

Shrink is not meant to be called from outside of the class scope, so it is declared in the private section of the *String* class definition.

The default constructor *String()* creates an empty, uninitialized string:

```
// constructor
String::String()
    {
    Len = 0;
    Siz = AllocIncr;

    Txt = new char[Siz];

    if (Txt == NULL)
        ErrorHandler(SE_ALLOC);
```

```
Txt[0] = '\x00';
}
```

The class also defines a copy constructor to create a new *String* from an existing one:

```
String::String(const String & str)
    {
    Len = str.Len;
    Siz = str.Siz;

    Txt = new char[Siz];

    if (Txt == NULL)
        ErrorHandler(SE_ALLOC);

    strcpy(Txt,str.Txt);
    }
```

*String(char * Cstr)* allows a newly-created *String* to be initialized with the value of a C-string.

```
String::String(const char * cstr)
    {
    if ((cstr == NULL) || (cstr[0] == '\x00'))
        {
        Len = 0;
        Siz = AllocIncr;
        }
    else
        {
        Len = strlen(cstr);
        Siz = ((Len + AllocIncr) / AllocIncr) * AllocIncr;
        }

    Txt = new char [Siz];

    if (Txt == NULL)
        ErrorHandler(SE_ALLOC);

    if (Len > 0)
        strcpy(Txt,cstr);
    else
        Txt[0] = '\x00';
    }
```

The last constructor, *String(char FillCh, unsigned int Count)*, creates a new string which contains *Count FillCh* characters:

```
String::String(char fillCh, unsigned int count)
    {
    Siz = ((count + AllocIncr) / AllocIncr) * AllocIncr;
    Len = Siz;

    Txt = new char[Siz];

    if (Txt == NULL)
        ErrorHandler(SE_ALLOC);

    memset(Txt,fillCh,count);

    Txt[count] = '\x00';
    }
```

The *String* class requires a destructor to delete the memory allocated to the *Txt* instance variable.

```
// destructor
String::~String()
    {
    delete Txt;
    }
```

The *Length* and *Size* methods simply return the current length and allocation size of a string, respectively. *Length* corresponds to the *string.h* function *strlen*. *Size* was originally created to help test the class. Since it is so simple, I just left it in for future use. Both can be defined as inline methods in the class header file:

```
// value return methods
inline unsigned int String::Length()
    {
    return Len;
    }

inline unsigned int String::Size()
    {
    return Siz;
    }
```

A programmer will often want to use a *String* in place of a standard *char* array. This conversion can be accomplished by defining a conversion operator for *String*:

```
// create a c-string from String method
String::operator const char * ()
    {
    return Txt;
    }
```

The function above allows a *String* to be cast to a const char *. The conversion would be used like this:

```
String Str = "Hello!";
const char * s = (const char *)Str;
```

The *const* specifier is used to prevent modification of the *char* array pointed to by *Txt*. In other words, *s* can be used to examine the value of *Str*, but it cannot change it.

The definition of the assignment operator comes next:

```
// assignment method
void String::operator = (const String & str)
    {
    Len = str.Len;
    Siz = str.Siz;

    delete Txt;

    Txt = new char[Siz];

    if (Txt == NULL)
        ErrorHandler(SE_ALLOC);

    strcpy(Txt,str.Txt);
    }
```

The + and += operators are used to concatenate two strings, performing the same function as the standard *strcat* function. The two methods look similar:

```
// concatenation methods
String operator + (const String & str1,
                                const String & str2)
    {
    unsigned long totalLen;
    unsigned int newLen, newSiz;
    String tempStr;
    char * temp;

    totalLen = str1.Len + str2.Len;

    if (totalLen > UINT_MAX)
        String::ErrorHandler(SE_TOO_LONG);

    newLen  = (unsigned int)totalLen;
    newSiz  = str1.Siz + str2.Siz;
    temp    = new char[newSiz];

    if (temp == NULL)
        String::ErrorHandler(SE_ALLOC);

    strcpy(temp,str1.Txt);
    strcpy(&temp[str1.Len],str2.Txt);

    tempStr = temp;
    return tempStr;
    }

// another concatenation method
void String::operator += (const String & str)
    {
    unsigned long totalLen;
    unsigned int newLen, newSiz;
    char * temp;

    totalLen = str.Len + Len;

    if (totalLen > UINT_MAX)
        ErrorHandler(SE_TOO_LONG);

    newLen  = (unsigned int)totalLen;
    newSiz  = Siz + str.Siz;

    temp = new char[newSiz];
```

```
if (temp == NULL)
    ErrorHandler(SE_ALLOC);

strcpy(temp,Txt);

delete Txt;

Txt = temp;

strcpy(&Txt[Len],str.Txt);

Len = newLen;
Siz = newSiz;

Shrink();
}
```

If a C-string is passed to either of these methods, the conversion constructor will convert it to a temporary *String* object before calling the function.

Several comparison operators are defined for *String*s. The symbolic comparison operators are most efficiently implemented inline, and they all call the *Compare* method:

```
// comparison methods
inline int String::operator <  (const String & str)
    {
    return (Compare(str) == SC_LESS);
    }

inline int String::operator >  (const String & str)
    {
    return (Compare(str) == SC_GREATER);
    }

inline int String::operator <= (const String & str)
    {
    return (Compare(str) != SC_GREATER);
    }

inline int String::operator >= (const String & str)
    {
    return (Compare(str) != SC_LESS);
    }
```

```
inline int String::operator == (const String & str)
    {
    return (Compare(str) == SC_EQUAL);
    }

inline int String::operator != (const String & str)
    {
    return (Compare(str) != SC_EQUAL);
    }
```

Basically, these methods use symbolic comparison operators as a shell over the *Compare* method. Thus, no efficiency is lost, and a program using these operators will look more natural when read.

Compare literally compares two *String*s and returns an enumeration value of type *StrCompVal*, which indicates the relationship between the two values. This works very much like the standard function *strcmp*, with the exception that the *Case* parameter determines whether the comparison is case-sensitive. It's implementation is:

```
StrCompVal String::Compare(const String & str,
                                    StrCompMode caseChk)
    {
    char * tempStr1, * tempStr2;
    StrCompVal compVal;

    tempStr1 = strdup(Txt);

    if (tempStr1 == NULL)
        ErrorHandler(SE_ALLOC);

    tempStr2 = strdup(str.Txt);

    if (tempStr2 == NULL)
        ErrorHandler(SE_ALLOC);

    if (caseChk == SM_IGNORE)
        {
        strupr(tempStr1);
        strupr(tempStr2);
        }

    switch (strcmp(tempStr1,tempStr2))
        {
        case -1:
            compVal = SC_LESS;
```

```
        break;
    case 0:
        compVal = SC_EQUAL;
        break;
    case 1:
        compVal = SC_GREATER;
        break;
    default:
        compVal = SC_ERROR;
    }

delete tempStr1;
delete tempStr2;

return compVal;
}
```

The method *Find* duplicates the purpose of the standard library function *strstr*, by locating a given *String* within another *String*. It returns an index that indicates where the substring begins. Like *Compare*, the *Case* parameter defaults to *SF_IGNORE* to indicate a case-insensitive comparison. The search can be made case-sensitive by specifying the *Case* parameter as *SF_SENSITIVE*.

This is the implementation of *Find*:

```
// substring search methods
int String::Find(const String & str, unsigned int & pos, StrCompMode
caseChk)
    {
    char * tempStr1, * tempStr2;
    unsigned int lastPos, searchLen, tempPos;
    int found;

    tempStr1 = strdup(Txt);

    if (tempStr1 == NULL)
        ErrorHandler(SE_ALLOC);

    tempStr2 = strdup(str.Txt);

    if (tempStr2 == NULL)
        ErrorHandler(SE_ALLOC);

    if (caseChk == SM_IGNORE)
        {
        strupr(tempStr1);
```

```
        strupr(tempStr2);
        }

pos     = 0;
tempPos = 0;
found   = 0;

searchLen = str.Len;
lastPos   = Len - searchLen;

while ((tempPos <= lastPos) && !found)
    {
    if (0 == strncmp(&tempStr1[tempPos],
                                tempStr2, searchLen))
        {
        pos   = tempPos;
        found = 1;
        }
    else
        ++tempPos;
    }

delete tempStr1;
delete tempStr2;

return found;
}
```

The *Delete* method removes a specified number of characters from a string:

```
// substring deletion method
void String::Delete(unsigned int pos,
                            unsigned int count)
    {
    unsigned int copyPos;

    if (pos > Len)
        return;

    copyPos = pos + count;

    if (copyPos >= Len)
        Txt[pos] = 0;
    else
        while (copyPos <= Len + 1)
            {
            Txt[pos] = Txt[copyPos];
            ++pos;
```

```
        ++copyPos;
        }

    Len -= count;

    Shrink();
    }
```

The parameter *Pos* provides the index of the first character to be
deleted, and the *Count* parameter indicates how many characters
should be deleted.

Characters and strings can be inserted into a *String* at any position
with the Insert methods. The first *Insert* method listed inserts a single character:

```
// substring insertion methods
void String::Insert(unsigned int pos, char ch)
    {
    char * temp;

    if (pos > Len)
        return;

    if (Len + 1 == Siz)
        {
        Siz  += AllocIncr;
        temp  = new char[Siz];

        if (temp == NULL)
            ErrorHandler(SE_ALLOC);

        strcpy(temp,Txt);

        delete Txt;

        Txt = temp;
        }

    for (unsigned int col = Len + 1; col > pos; --col)
        Txt[col] = Txt[col-1];

    Txt[pos] = ch;

    ++Len;
```

```
Txt[Len + 1] = '\x00';
}
```

The second inserts an entire *String*:

```
void String::Insert(unsigned int pos,
                               const String & str)
    {
    unsigned long totalLen = str.Len + Len;

    if (totalLen > UINT_MAX)
        ErrorHandler(SE_TOO_LONG);

    unsigned int SLen = str.Len;

    if (SLen > 0)
        for (unsigned int i = 0; i < SLen; ++i)
            {
            Insert(pos,str.Txt[i]);
            ++pos;
            }
    }
```

Once again, the conversion constructor permits the use of a C-string in place of the *String* parameter in both *Insert* methods.

Occasionally, it is necessary to extract a section of a *String*. The *SubStr* method accomplishes this by copying *Count* characters beginning at *Pos* into another *String*:

```
// substring retrieval method
String String::SubStr(unsigned int start,
                                 unsigned int count)
    {
    String tempStr;
    char * temp;

    if ((start < Len) && (count > 0))
        {
        temp = new char [count + 1];

        memcpy(temp,&Txt[start],count);

        temp[count] = '\x00';
        }
    else
```

```
        temp = "";

    tempStr = temp;

    delete temp;

    return tempStr;
    }
```

The indexing operator *[]* is defined for *String*. This makes it possible to extract single characters at specific positions within a *String* in the same fashion as if you were working with a C-string. If the position given is beyond the last character of the *String*, a NUL character is returned. This is a simple method, and I implement it inline:

```
// character retrieval method
inline char String::operator [] (unsigned int pos)
    {
    if (pos >= Len)
        return '\x00';
    else
        return Txt[pos];
    }
```

The last two methods for *String* are *ToUpper* and *ToLower*, which convert all of the characters in a *String* to upper or lower case, respectively:

```
// case-modification methods
String String::ToUpper()
    {
    String tempStr = *this;

    strupr(tempStr.Txt);

    return tempStr;
    }

String String::ToLower()
    {
    String tempStr = *this;

    strlwr(tempStr.Txt);

    return tempStr;
    }
```

These methods perform the same actions performed by the *strupr* and *strlwr* functions in the standard C library.

Implementation Notes

If you examine the methods that return a *String*, you will see what appears to be a violation of proper programming practice. For example, *SubStr* copies the substring into a local *String* object, *TempStr*. *SubStr* then returns *TempStr*, which seems to be dangerous. After all, isn't the destructor for *TempStr* called when the method is exited, which means that the recipient of the method's return value will get garbage?

Again, C++ is trickier than it looks. When an object is returned from a function, the copy constructor is called first to copy the return value into its destination, and then the destructor is called. This makes it much easier to write methods that return objects.

The *String* class does not contain many inline methods. I tend to be very cautious about making methods inline. Remember that, under the C++ definition, inline methods can be treated as regular method functions by the compiler. I know of no C++ compiler that will actually inline a method that contains complex control statements like loops and switches. These methods are made into function methods regardless of their declaration as inline.

A String Example

The following program shows how the *String* objects can be used. If you make changes to the *String* class, you might want to use test your changes with a variant of this program:

```
#include "Str.hpp"

extern "C"
    {
    #include "stdio.h"
    }
```

```
void print_string(String & S);

String s1;
String s2("This is the second string!");

int main()
    {
    String ls;
    String ls2("Another local string");
    StrCompVal v;

    unsigned int pos, i;
    char ch;

    s1 = s2;

    if (s1 == s2)
        printf("s1 equals s2!\n");
    else
        printf("\as1 is not equal to s2!\n");

    ls = "This is the local string";
    print_string(s1);
    print_string(s2);
    print_string(ls);
    print_string(ls2);
    printf("\n");

    s1 = s2 + ls;
    print_string(s1);

    v = s1.Compare(s2);

    switch (v)
        {
        case SC_LESS :
            printf("s1 < s2\n");
            break;
        case SC_EQUAL :
            printf("s1 = s2\n");
            break;
        case SC_GREATER :
            printf("s1 > s2\n");
        }

    s1 = "String one has a value";
    print_string(s1);

    s2 += ls;
    print_string(s2);
```

```
    printf("\n");

    if (s2.Find("Burfulgunk",pos))
        printf("first search = %d\n",pos);

    if (s2.Find(ls,pos))
        printf("second search = %d\n",pos);

    ls2 = "&&";

    s1.Insert(10,'*');
    s1.Insert(15,ls2);
    print_string(s1);

    s1.Insert(s1.Length(),'%');
    print_string(s1);

    for (i = 0; 0 != (ch = s1[i]); ++i)
        putchar(ch);

    putchar('\n');

    s1.Insert(2,"<><><><><>");
    print_string(s1);

    s1.Delete(2,10);
    print_string(s1);

    s2 = s1.ToUpper();
    print_string(s2);

    s2 = s1.ToLower();
    print_string(s2);

    s1 = s2.SubStr(2,10);
    print_string(s1);

    return 0;
    }

void print_string(String & S)
    {
    const char * buffer;

    buffer = (const char *)S;

    if (buffer != NULL)
        printf("%s ",buffer);

    printf("Len = %u Siz = %u\n",S.Length(),S.Size());
    }
```

CHAPTER

11

Object-Oriented Windows

Every program displays information on the screen, and "windows" have become the most common display metaphor. A window is a section of the screen delimited by a border that is treated as a small screen in its own right. One or more windows can be on-screen simultaneously, and the user can select between various windows to access their contents. In many ways, windows increase the amount of information that can be displayed by a program. All of today's sophisticated program are expected to have a windowed interface through to present its output.

Windows come in all types and sizes, which is one reason they are used so often as examples of object-oriented programs. Once you've built a general window class, you can derive further classes for menus, dialog boxes, and other window-like displays. Unfortunately, most object-oriented windowing examples are limited in their capability. They're used to illustrate the concept of class hierarchies, but they also tend to be incomplete and impractical.

This chapter presents a complete implementation of a window class, and provides an excellent basis for other classes. You should be able to assemble your own specialized window classes by building on the information presented in this chapter.

Defining A Window

The requirements for a window class are somewhat complicated. First, you must choose between two types of windows: tiled and stacked.

Every window in a tiled window system is completely visible at all times, and the windows adjust their sizes to make room for new windows. In essence, tiled windows are like tiled floors: they fit together like a jigsaw to cover the entire screen without covering each other. As more windows are added to the display, less space is available for each individual window. Generally, tiled windows are considered archaic and very few programs use them.

In a stacked window system, any window can be made any size up to the full size of the screen. Stacked windows are like stacked pieces of paper. To better understand this analogy, you can take several pieces of paper and cut them into different rectangular shapes, each representing a window. Then, mark off a rectangular area on a table top to represent the entire video display. Place the rectangles of paper (the windows) inside of the rectangular area (the display).

As you'll see, some pieces of paper are covered by other pieces, so one or more "windows" may be completely visible. Likewise, the display windows on the top of the "stack" may cover portions of the windows lower down. One or more windows may be completely visible, if they're small enough to fit on the display without overlapping.

Stacked windows are more flexible than their tiled counterparts. Therefore, the class described in this chapter implements stacked windows.

A stacked window class must provide access to all windows on the screen, even those screens that are completely or partially covered by other windows. Windows display information, and methods to implement that display must be developed. Windows can be of any dimension up to the full screen size, they must be movable and rearrangeable, and they should be able to become invisible when they're not needed. Windows must also be quick, since slow programs are unusable. Finally, the programmer should have complete control over window colors and cursor positioning.

However, before we dive into creating our window environment, we need to think about what is NOT needed as well. In this case, we don't want to define methods to accept data into our basic class. Some windows are used only for display purposes so they don't need data entry methods.

Portability is also important. Programs that use the window class should be relatively easy to port to new display environments. To provide portability, I've broken the windowing system into two classes: *Screen* and *Window*. *Screen* defines the fundamental operations that can take place on a video display, and *Window* goes through *Screen* to access the display. As discussed in Chapter Five[[ck ref]], this encapsulates the implementation-dependent parts of the windowing system to a single class. When the *Screen* class is modified for a new environment, the *Window* class automatically inherits the ability to work in the new environment.

PC Video Displays

The *Screen* class in this book is implemented for the MS-DOS operating system on a computer with a standard IBM PC-compatible display. So, before discussing the implementation of the *Screen* class, it would be helpful to explore the nature of PC-compatible displays.

There are three basic ways to display information on the PC screen: through MS-DOS services, by calling the computer's Basic I/O System (BIOS), and by placing data directly into video memory. Each of these methods has advantages and disadvantages, and you must determine which method is most appropriate to the window class.

Using MS-DOS services is the most portable way of displaying data. These services exist on all computers that run or emulate MS-DOS, and programs that use MS-DOS video services can run on any MS-DOS compatible system. By using the ANSI escape sequences (provided by the ANSI.SYS device driver), the programmer has complete control of cursor positioning and text attributes. The significant drawback to using MS-DOS is that it is slow. Even on a fast 80386fbased PC, the MS-DOS display services are too slow for practical programs.

The second alternative uses BIOS, which is stored in Read-Only Memory (ROM) and contains routines to display data. These routines are more flexible than those provided by MS-DOS, and are generally considerably faster. All IBM-PC compatibles support a standard set of BIOS video routines, so BIOS calls are portable. However, BIOS calls are still not fast enough for most of today's applications, especially on whey they are run older and slower PCs.

The final method to display information involves writing the data directly to the video display memory. Video memory is arranged as a simple array; a standard 80-column by 25-line screen requires 2,000 memory locations (80 times 25) to store its text. Each character on the screen actually consists of two bytes. The first byte holds the character graphic information (such as the character 'A'), and the second byte holds data relating to the character's color attributes. So a standard 25-by-80 screen actually represents an array in memory of 2,000 words or 4,000 bytes.

In order to store information directly into the PC's video memory, it is necessary to understand how memory is addressed. The microprocessor in all MS-DOS PCs can access up to one megabyte of memory. It uses two values to locate a given location in memory: a segment, which is the base address of a section of memory; and an offset, which is the number of the byte being accessed within that segment. Both the segment and offset are stored as a word, or 16-bit, quantity. To get the actual memory location of a given byte of memory, the processor multiplies the segment by 16, then adds the offset to get an absolute location within its megabyte of memory. For all intents and purposes, though, segments and offsets can be treated as 16-bit numbers without any concern for exactly how the microprocessor calculates physical memory addresses.

Video memory is located at different memory addresses on different types of graphics cards. When you use a Hercules or Monochrome Display Adapter (MDA), the video memory is located at segment 0xB000. The CGA, EGA, and VGA color video adapters locate their video memory at segment 0xB800. The type of adapter installed can be determined by calling the BIOS video service 15, which returns the current video mode. The only mode used by MDA and Hercules cards is mode 7, so when mode 7 is returned by service 15 you know you are working with a monochrome card with video memory located at segment 0xB000. Otherwise, you have a color graphic card and video memory is located at segment 0xB800.

In order to provide high-speed performance, the window class displays information by "poking" characters and their attributes directly into video memory. The only drawback to this approach is that some older CGA-type video cards display an interference pattern called "snow" when data is written to video memory. Snow can be eliminated, but that is best done with an assembly language routine. Luckily, most people are moving to EGA and VGA systems. With this in mind, the windowing module avoids the extra complexity of assembly language routines by ignoring the elimination of snow.

The Screen Class

Before the *Window* class can be created, the underlying *Screen* class must be developed. The definition of *Screen* is contained in the file *screen.hpp,* shown here:

```
#if !defined(__SCREEN_HPP)
#define __SCREEN_HPP 1

#include "Str.hpp"

extern "C"
    {
    #include "peekpoke.h"
    #include "stddef.h"
    }

enum BoxType {BT_NONE, BT_SINGLE, BT_DOUBLE, BT_SOLID};

class Screen
    {
    protected:
        static unsigned int  Width;
        static unsigned int  Length;
        static unsigned int  BaseAdr;
        static unsigned int  CursorShape;
        static int           CursorHidden;
        static unsigned int  HowMany;

    public:
        // constructor
        Screen();

        // destructor
        ~Screen();

        // retrieve screen size method
        static void Dimensions(unsigned int & wid,
                               unsigned int & len);

        // cursor methods
        static void CursorHide();
        static void CursorUnhide();

        static void CursorSetPos(unsigned int line,
                                 unsigned int col);
```

```
            static void CursorGetPos(unsigned int & line,
                                     unsigned int & col);

            // data display methods
            static void PutChar(unsigned int line,
                                unsigned int col,
                                unsigned char attr,
                                char ch);

            static void PutStr(unsigned int line,
                               unsigned int col,
                               unsigned char attr,
                               String & str);

            // data retrieval methods
            static void GetChar(unsigned int line,
                                unsigned int col,
                                unsigned char & attr,
                                char & ch);

            // box display method
            static void DrawBox(unsigned int topLine,
                                unsigned int leftCol,
                                unsigned int btmLine,
                                unsigned int rightCol,
                                unsigned char attr,
                                BoxType typeBox);

            // screen clearing methods
            static void Clear();
            static void ClearLine(unsigned int line,
                                  unsigned int col = 0);
    };

// character display method
inline void Screen::PutChar(unsigned int line,
                            unsigned int col,
                            unsigned char attr,
                            char ch)
    {
    unsigned int v = ((unsigned int)attr << 8) |
                     (unsigned char)ch;

    Poke(BaseAdr, (line * Width * 2) + (2 * col), v);
    }


// data retrieval methods
inline void Screen::GetChar(unsigned int line,
                            unsigned int col,
                            unsigned char & attr,
                            char & ch)
```

```
    {
    unsigned int v = Peek(BaseAdr, (line * Width * 2) +
                                   (2 * col));

    attr = v >> 8;
    ch   = v & 0xFF;
    }
```

```
extern Screen Display;
```

```
#endif
```

Screen is an example of a one-instance class (see Chapter 6). All of *Screen*'s members are static (with the exception of constructors and destructors, which cannot be static), meaning that all *Screen* objects will share the same set of static members, so in effect, every *Screen* object is identical. With very few exceptions, a computer will have only one video display.

The *Screen* class defines six static data members. The number of columns and rows on the display are stored in *Width* and *Length*. While most PC video displays have 80 columns and 25 rows of characters, some displays can handle other sizes. Full-page displays may have 66 rows, and the EGA and VGA adapters were designed with 43- and 50-line modes in mind. The implementation of *Screen*'s constructor determines the current dimensions of the display and stores those values in *Width* and *Length*.

BaseAdr holds the display memory segment — 0xB000 for a monochrome display card and 0xB800 is for color displays. The *CursorHidden* flag is used to remember whether the cursor has been turned on or off. *CursorShape* holds the original shape of the cursor when it is hidden.

HowMany counts the number of times *Screen* has been instantiated and is used by the constructor and destructor methods. The constructor for *Screen* is used to set the class's static data members, depending on the type of video display installed, and should only be called once in any program. Whenever a *Screen* object is created, the constructor is automatically called, despite the fact that all *Screen* objects are the same object. So, the constructor increments the *HowMany* flag every time a *Screen* object is instantiated. If the *HowMany* flag is greater than 1, the constructor simply exits without doing anything.

Screen's destructor also uses *HowMany*. The destructor should only do its work when the last *Screen* object is destroyed. So, the destructor checks the value of *HowMany* before it does any of its work. If *HowMany* is greater than 1, the destructor knows that it is being called for a *Screen* object other than the first one. In that case, the destructor merely decrements *HowMany*, and returns. If *HowMany* is 1, then the destructor can go ahead and clear the screen and home the cursor.

One *Screen* object, *Display*, is instantiated in the definition and implementation of the *Screen* class. The purpose of *Display* is to execute the constructor and destructor calls that set up the *Screen* class. When the *Screen* class is used by a program, its constructor is called for the *Display* object when the program starts. When the program ends, *Display* is destroyed and the destructor is called. While it's possible to instantiate new Screen objects, there's absolutely no need to do so.

Screen is implemented in a file called *screen.cpp*. The complete version of that file is in Appendix A, but here we'll look at individual portions of *screen.cpp*.

Screen's static members and the *Display* object are initialized like this:

```
// assign values to static class members
unsigned int  Screen::Width        = 0;
unsigned int  Screen::Length       = 0;
unsigned int  Screen::BaseAdr      = 0;
unsigned int  Screen::CursorShape  = 0;
int           Screen::CursorHidden = 0;

Screen Display;
```

The constructor determines the type of video display (color or monochrome), and the number of lines and columns of text available. It also clears the screen:

```
// constructor
Screen::Screen()
    {
    ++HowMany;

    if (HowMany > 1)
        return;

    union REGS regs;

    regs.h.ah = 0x0f;

    int86(0x10,&regs,&regs);

    if (regs.h.al == 0x07)
        BaseAdr = 0xB000;
    else
        BaseAdr = 0xB800;

    Width = (int) regs.h.ah;

    regs.x.ax = 0x1130;
    regs.h.bh = 0;
    regs.x.dx = 0;

    int86(0x10,&regs,&regs);

    Length = regs.x.dx + 1;

    if (Length == 1)
        Length = 25;

    Clear();

    CursorHidden = 0;
    }
```

The destructor decrements *HowMany*. If *HowMany* becomes zero, the destructor knows that it is being called for the first *Screen* created (which will be the automatically created *Display*), and clears the screen.

```
// destructor
Screen::~Screen()
    {
    --HowMany;

    if (HowMany > 0)
        return;

    Clear();

    CursorSetPos(0,0);
    }
```

The *Dimensions* method is used to retrieve the *Width* and *Length* values for the current screen. An intelligent program will examine these values so that it can adjust the actual screen size.

```
// access methods
void Screen::Dimensions(unsigned int & wid,
                        unsigned int & len)
    {
    wid = Width;
    len = Length;
    }
```

All of the cursor-handling methods use calls to the BIOS cursor functions. *CursorHide* makes the cursor invisible, and *CursorUnhide* restores the cursor if it is hidden.

```
// cursor methods
void Screen::CursorHide()
    {
    if (CursorHidden)
        return;

    union REGS regs;

    regs.h.ah = 3;
    regs.h.bh = 0;

    int86(0x10,&regs,&regs);

    CursorShape = regs.x.cx;

    regs.h.ah = 1;
    regs.x.cx = 0x2000;
```

```
    int86(0x10,&regs,&regs);

    CursorHidden = 1;
    }

void Screen::CursorUnhide()
    {
    if (!CursorHidden)
        return;

    union REGS regs;

    regs.h.ah = 1;
    regs.x.cx = CursorShape;

    int86(0x10,&regs,&regs);

    CursorHidden = 0;
    }
```

CursorSetPos will move the cursor to any specific location on the
screen, and *CursorGetPos* will obtain the current cursor location.

```
void Screen::CursorSetPos(unsigned int line,
                          unsigned int col)
    {
    union REGS regs;

    regs.h.ah = 2;
    regs.h.bh = 0;
    regs.h.dh = line;
    regs.h.dl = col;

    int86(0x10,&regs,&regs);
    }

void Screen::CursorGetPos(unsigned int & line,
                          unsigned int & col)
    {
    union REGS regs;

    regs.h.ah = 3;
    regs.h.bh = 0;

    int86(0x10,&regs,&regs);

    line = regs.h.dh;
    col  = regs.h.dl;
    }
```

PutChar and *GetChar* are used to display and retrieve a character from display memory, respectively. They have parameters for a line and column number to indicate the character in question, and a pair of char values that contain the graphic and attribute to be stored or read.

PutChar and *GetChar* are implemented as inline methods. *PutChar* uses a function called *Poke* to store the calculated character/attribute value at a given location within video memory. *GetChar* uses a complimentary function called *Peek* that retrieves a 16-bit word value from a specific memory location.

Some compilers provide *Peek*- and *Poke*-like functions in their standard library, and others don't. To make the system more portable between C++ implementations, I wrote my own *Peek* and *Poke* functions in 8086 macro assembler. The source files for these functions are *peekpoke.h* and *peekpoke.asm*:

```
/* peekpoke.h */

void Poke(unsigned int segm, unsigned int offs, unsigned int value);

unsigned int Peek(unsigned int segm, unsigned int offs);
```

```
; peekpoke.asm
.8086

.CODE

PUBLIC Peek
PUBLIC Poke

Peek        PROC      segm:WORD, offs:WORD
            push      es
            push      si
            mov       ax,segm
            mov       es,ax
            mov       si,offs
            mov       ax, es:[si]
            pop       si
            pop       es
            ret
Peek        ENDP
```

```
Poke        PROC    segm:WORD, offs:WORD, value:WORD
            push    es
            push    di
            mov     ax,segm
            mov     es,ax
            mov     di,offs
            mov     cx,value
            mov     es:[di], cx
            pop     di
            pop     es
            ret
Poke        ENDP

END
```

The *Peek* and *Poke* functions are defined as C-type functions, and the extern "C" {...} syntax is used to bracket the inclusion of the *peekpoke.h* header file. This way, the *Peek* and *Poke* functions can be written using the simpler C interface, which does not involve C++'s name-mangling.

PutChar and *GetChar* don't do any range-checking. If you put a character at line 200, column 99, *PutChar* will merrily calculate the address of that theoretical screen location and place your character and its attribute in never-never land. This can be dangerous, to say the least, since the location to which you are poking may contain information vital to the BIOS or MS-DOS.

Why, then, forego range-checking? Simply because range-checking adds overhead and complexity. The overhead of checking the line and column parameters of *PutChar* and *GetChar* against *Length* and *Width* slows those functions by 20 to 40 percent. The additional complexity may force these inline functions to become regular functions, which further degrades performance. To improve execution speed, it's sometimes necessary to leave out the seat belts.

PutStr uses *PutChar* to display a *String* value (see Chapter Ten [[ck ref]]for the *String* class).

```
// display a text string method
void Screen::PutStr(unsigned int line,
                    unsigned int col,
                    unsigned char attr,
                    String & str)
    {
    for (unsigned int i = 0; str[i] != '\000'; ++i)
        PutChar(line, col + i, attr, str[i]);
    }
```

DrawBox displays a rectangle using one of four border styles. The enumerated type *BoxType* is defines the various border types.

```
// box display methods
void Screen::DrawBox(unsigned int topLine,
                     unsigned int leftCol,
                     unsigned int btmLine,
                     unsigned int rightCol,
                     unsigned char attr,
                     BoxType typeBox)
    {
    if ((typeBox == BT_NONE) ||
            (leftCol >= rightCol) ||
            (topLine >= btmLine))
            {
        return;
            }

    char v, h;

    switch (typeBox)
        {
        case BT_SINGLE:
            v = '\xB3';
            h = '\xC4';
            PutChar(topLine, leftCol,  attr, '\xDA');
            PutChar(topLine, rightCol, attr, '\xBF');
            PutChar(btmLine, leftCol,  attr, '\xC0');
            PutChar(btmLine, rightCol, attr, '\xD9');
            break;
        case BT_DOUBLE:
            v = '\xBA';
            h = '\xCD';
            PutChar(topLine, leftCol,  attr, '\xC9');
            PutChar(topLine, rightCol, attr, '\xBB');
            PutChar(btmLine, leftCol,  attr, '\xC8');
            PutChar(btmLine, rightCol, attr, '\xBC');
            break;
        case BT_SOLID:
```

```
        v = '\xDB';
        h = '\xDB';
        PutChar(topLine, leftCol,  attr, '\xDB');
        PutChar(topLine, rightCol, attr, '\xDB');
        PutChar(btmLine, leftCol,  attr, '\xDB');
        PutChar(btmLine, rightCol, attr, '\xDB');
        }

    for (int c = leftCol + 1; c < rightCol; ++c)
        {
        PutChar(topLine, c, attr, h);
        PutChar(btmLine, c, attr, h);
        }

    for (int l = topLine + 1; l < btmLine; ++l)
        {
        PutChar(l, leftCol,  attr, v);
        PutChar(l, rightCol, attr, v);
        }
    }
```

Finally, the *Clear* method fills the entire screen with blanks, and the *ClearLine* method clears a single line from the column indicated by the *c* parameter to the end of the line.

```
// screen clearing methods
void Screen::Clear()
    {
    for (int l = 0; l < Length; ++l)
        {
        for (int c = 0; c < Width; ++c)
            PutChar(l,c,7,' ');
        }
    }

void Screen::ClearLine(unsigned int line,
                       unsigned int col)
    {
    for (int c = col; c < Width; ++c)
        PutChar(line,c,7,' ');
    }
```

This class is very useful for programs where a full-blown window class is not needed. It's performance rivals that of assembly-language video display libraries, thus proving that the advantages of object-oriented programming do not automatically incur a performance penalty as some experts claim.

The *Window* Class

A complication arises when you wish to have multiple windows active at the same time. How does the window class know which screen location is to be used by a given window? It's possible for several windows to simultaneous "occupy" the same screen location, yet only the "highest" level window can actually display anything at that location.

The solution is to create an array of window objects with the same dimensions as the screen. Since an object is actually a pointer to an object, this array contains object references. When a window displays information, it checks to be sure that it "owns" the location to which it is displayed by comparing its object identifier with the one stored in the screen ownership array. If the window owns that screen location, it displays a character; otherwise, it does nothing.

Window is the most complicated class yet presented in this book. It contains several member objects, dynamically allocated arrays of object pointers, and several private member functions. The class is defined in the file *window.hpp*. Implementation of the member functions are broken into several source files. *wdw_main.cpp* implements most of the private member functions; *wdw_ctdt.cpp* contains the constructors and destructors; *wdw_copy.cpp* implements the copy constructor and assignment operator; *wdw_disp* defines the methods used to store data in a *Window* and display a *Window*; *wdw_misc.cpp* contains the methods that change the position and attributes of a window; and *wdw_err.cpp* implements the error handling methods and initialization code. The complete form of these listings can be found in Appendix A.

As a reference, here's the definition of the *Window* class:

```
#if !defined(__WINDOW_HPP)
#define __WINDOW_HPP 1

#include "Screen.hpp"
#include "Str.hpp"
#include "WorkList.hpp"

extern "C"
    {
    #include "stddef.h"
    }

class Window
    {
    protected:
        static WorkList   WdwList;
        static Window ** ScrnOwner;
        static int        Initialized;
        static Window *  TopWindow;

        static unsigned int MaxLength;
        static unsigned int MaxWidth;

        unsigned int HomeLine;
        unsigned int HomeCol;
        unsigned int Length;
        unsigned int Width;
        unsigned int CrsLine;
        unsigned int CrsCol;

        unsigned char InsideColor;
        unsigned char BorderColor;

        BoxType Border;

        // header text
        String Header;

        // flags
        int Wrapped;
        int Concealed;

        // buffer for this window
        struct WindowWord
            {
            unsigned char Attribute;
            char Symbol;
            };
```

```
        WindowWord * BufferSW;

        // private methods
        static void FirstTime();

        void Display(int line, int col,
                    unsigned char attr, char ch);

        static void Restack();

        void PlotOwnership();

        static void (* ErrorHandler)();
public:
    // constructor
    Window(unsigned int  line, unsigned int  col,
           unsigned int  len, unsigned int  wid,
           unsigned char iattr, unsigned char battr,
           BoxType bord,
           String & heading, int wrapMode = 0);

    // copy constructor
    Window(const Window & w);

    // assignment operator
    void operator = (const Window & w);

    // destructor
    ~Window();

    // assign an exception handler
    static void SetErrorHandler (void (* userHandler)());

    // paint a window
    void Paint();

    // paint a line
    void PaintLine(unsigned int line);

    // change position
    void Move(unsigned int line, unsigned int col);

    // make this the top window
    void Hoist();

    // conceal this window
    void Conceal();
```

```
                   // reveal this window
                   void Reveal();

                   // turn wrap on
                   void WrapOn();

                   // turn wrap off
                   void WrapOff();

                   // change headings
                   void SetHead(String & heading);

                   // set the cursor position
                   void SetCursor(unsigned int line,
                             unsigned int col);

                   // get the cursor position
                   void GetCursor(unsigned int & line,
                             unsigned int & col);

                   // store a character
                   void PutChar(unsigned int  line,
                             unsigned int col,
                             unsigned char attr, char c);

                   // store a string
                   void PutStr(unsigned int line,
                             unsigned int col,
                             unsigned char attr, String & s);

                   // clear entire window
                   void ClearAll();

                   // clear one line of window
                   void ClearLine(unsigned int line,
                             unsigned int col = 0);
          };

#endif
```

Six static members of *Window* define the shared data elements for all *Window* objects. *WdwList* is a *WorkList* object that maintains the order of the window stack on the screen. While the windows are organized into a "stack," it isn't quite the same kind of stack implemented by the *Stack* class (see Chapter 8 for an explanation of the *Stack* and *WorkList* container classes). A standard stack allows only the item most recently stored to be deleted or examined. The more flexible *WorkList* class allows for object pointers to be deleted, no matter where they are in the stack.

ScrnOwner is a dynamically allocated, two-dimensional array of *Window* pointers, and it has the same dimensions as the rest of the screen. When a *Window* owns a screen location, its address is assigned to the corresponding *Window* pointer in *ScrnOwner*. Then, when a window tries to display a character at a given location, it can check to see if it owns that screen location by comparing its pointer (*this*) to the pointer stored in *ScrnOwner* for the screen location.

Initialized is simply a flag that tells a *Window* that the *Window* class has been globally initialized. *Window*'s constructor calls the private member function *FirstTime* if *Initialized* is set to 0. It then sets *Initialized* to 1 so that subsequent creations of *Window* objects avoid calling *FirstTime*.

TopWindow is a pointer to the *Window* on the top of the stack. Some operations can only be performed on the uppermost *Window*. For example, the cursor is only displayed in the *TopWindow*.

MaxLength and *MaxWidth* are set to the number of lines and columns available in the current screen. They are set by a call to *Screen::Dimensions*, which is made in the method *FirstTime*.

The next twelve private members of *Window* define the private instance variables of *Window* objects. Most of these maintain the information provided in the constructor call used to create a *Window*. *HomeLine* and *HomeCol* store the position of the upper-left-hand corner of the window, while *Length* and *Width* contain the length and width of the window. *CrsLine* and *CrsCol* keep track of the current cursor position within the window. *InsideColor* is the default attribute for characters displayed inside of the *Window*, and *BorderColor* is the attribute of the *Window*'s border. Border stores the style of the *Window*'s border, and *Header* is a *String* that contains the text of the *Window*'s title.

The *Wrapped* and *Concealed* flags set the nature of how a window works. If *Wrapped* is true (non-zero), long lines displayed within the *Window* are wrapped to a new line if they extend beyond the edge of the *Window*. When *Concealed* is true, the *Window* is hidden and not displayed.

The *WindowWord* structure holds a character symbol and its attribute. *BufferSW* is a dynamically allocated array of *WindowWords*, which holds the current information displayed inside of a window. Since a *Window* may not always be completely displayed on the screen, a buffer is needed to keep track of the data it contains. When a window is "painted" on the screen, the data to be displayed is taken from the *BufferSW* array.

One (and only one) of initialization file must contain the initializations of the *Window* class's static members. In my design, I put these initializations into *wdw_main.cpp*:

```
// initialize static class members!
WorkList        Window::WdwList;
Window **       Window::ScrnOwner   = NULL;
int             Window::Initialized = 0;
Window *        Window::TopWindow   = NULL;
unsigned int    Window::MaxLength   = 0;
unsigned int    Window::MaxWidth    = 0;
```

The standard constructor is implemented in *wdw_ctdt.cpp*. Its parameters define the new *Window*'s location, size, default attributes, and border. With the exception of some minor changes, these values are copied directly into the instance variables for the *Window* object. A newly-created *Window* is always the *TopWindow*. Once it has been added to the *WdwList*, the area of the screen owned by the new window is plotted with *PlotOwnership*, the window is filled with blanks, and it is then painted on the screen:

```
// constructor
Window::Window(unsigned int line, unsigned int col,
               unsigned int len,  unsigned int wid,
               unsigned char iattr,
               unsigned char battr,
```

```
            BoxType bord, String & heading,
            int wrapMode)
: Header(heading)
{
if (!Initialized)
    FirstTime();

// make sure window is created on the scree
if ((line > MaxLength) || (col > MaxWidth))
    {
    line = 0;
    col  = 0;
    }

// set instance variables
HomeLine = line;
HomeCol  = col;
Length   = len;
Width    = wid;
CrsLine  = 0;
CrsCol   = 0;

InsideColor = iattr;
BorderColor = battr;

Border = bord;

Wrapped   = wrapMode;
Concealed = 0;

// no border, no heading
if (Border == BT_NONE)
    Header = "";

// add the window to the list
WdwList.Store(this);

// allocate buffer to store window contents
BufferSW = new WindowWord [Length * Width];

if (BufferSW == NULL)
    ErrorHandler();

// make the new window the top window
TopWindow = this;

PlotOwnership();

// clear the window
ClearAll();
```

```
// and display it
Paint();
}
```

Window's destructor, which is also defined in *wdw_ctdt.cpp*, deletes
the *Window* object being destroyed from *WdwList* and *Restack*s the
remaining windows. It also deallocates the memory used by the object's *BufferSW* array.

```
// destructor
Window::~Window()
    {
    // remove window from list
    WdwList.Delete(this);

    // get a new top window
    WdwList.GoToHead();

    TopWindow = (Window *)WdwList.Examine();

    // free buffer space
    delete BufferSW;

    // restack all windows
    Restack();
    return;
    }
```

The copy constructor and assignment operator are, as always, very
similar. They duplicate the contents and characteristics of a window.
Their implementations are stored in *wdw_copy.cpp*;

```
// copy constructor
Window::Window(const Window & w) : Header(w.Header)
    {
    // duplicate instance variables
    HomeLine = w.HomeLine;
    HomeCol  = w.HomeCol;
    Length   = w.Length;
    Width    = w.Width;
    CrsLine  = w.CrsLine;
    CrsCol   = w.CrsCol;

    InsideColor = w.InsideColor;
    BorderColor = w.BorderColor;
```

```
    Border = w.Border;

    Wrapped   = w.Wrapped;
    Concealed = w.Concealed;

    // allocate a buffer

    BufferSW = new WindowWord [Length * Width];

    if (BufferSW == NULL)
        ErrorHandler();

    // copy existing buffer into new buffer
    for (unsigned int l = 0; l < Length; ++l)
        {
        for (unsigned int c = 0; c < Width; ++c)
            BufferSW[l * Width + c] = w.BufferSW[l * Width + c];
        }

    // add window to list
    WdwList.Store(this);

    // make this the top window
    TopWindow = this;

    // plot what it owns
    PlotOwnership();

    // display it
    Paint();
    }

// assignment operator
void Window::operator = (const Window & w)
    {
    // free old buffer
    delete BufferSW;

    // copy instance variables
    HomeLine = w.HomeLine;
    HomeCol  = w.HomeCol;
    Length   = w.Length;
    Width    = w.Width;
    CrsLine  = w.CrsLine;
    CrsCol   = w.CrsCol;

    InsideColor = w.InsideColor;
    BorderColor = w.BorderColor;

    Border = w.Border;
```

```
    Wrapped   = w.Wrapped;
    Concealed = w.Concealed;

    Header = w.Header;

    // allocate new buffer
    BufferSW = new WindowWord [Length * Width];

    if (BufferSW == NULL)
        ErrorHandler();

    // copy buffer from existing window
    for (unsigned int l = 0; l < Length; ++l)
        {
        for (unsigned int c = 0; c < Width; ++c)
            BufferSW[l * Width + c] = w.BufferSW[l * Width + c];
        }

    // plot what this window owns
    PlotOwnership();

    // paint all windows
    Restack();
    }
// first time initialization function
void Window::FirstTime()
    {
    Initialized = 1;

    // obtain screen dimensions
    Screen::Dimensions(MaxWidth, MaxLength);

    unsigned int area = MaxLength * MaxWidth;

    // using malloc due to bug in cfront
    ScrnOwner = (Window **)malloc (area * sizeof(Window *));

    if (ScrnOwner == NULL)
        ErrorHandler();

    // clear the ownership array
    for (unsigned int l = 0; l < MaxLength; ++l)
        {
        for (unsigned int c = 0; c < MaxWidth; ++c)
            ScrnOwner[l * MaxWidth + c] = NULL;
        }
    }
```

Display (defined in *wdw_main.cpp*) is the function that actually displays characters via the *Screen* class method *PutChar*:

```
// actually display a character
void Window::Display(int line, int col,
                     unsigned char attr, char ch)
    {
    unsigned int rl = line + HomeLine;
    unsigned int rc = col  + HomeCol;

    if ((rl >= MaxLength) || (rc >= MaxWidth))
        return;

    if (this == ScrnOwner[rl * MaxWidth + rc])
        Screen::PutChar(rl,rc,attr,ch);
    }
```

A character stored in a *Window* is placed at a line and column location relative to the upper-left-hand corner of the *Window*. Naturally, the position of a *Window* on the physical display changes the physical screen location of the upper-left-hand corner of the *Window*. When a character is placed in line 5, column 2 of a *Window* whose origin is at line 10, column 20 of the physical screen, the character needs to be displayed at line 15, column 22 on the physical screen. The *Display* method handles this conversion, as well as determining that the screen position to which the character is displayed is owned by the *Window* in question.

Occasionally, it's necessary to redisplay the entire stack of windows, such as when a *Window* is deleted or moved. The *Restack* method begins by clearing the physical screen and the *ScrnOwner* array. It then goes through the list of Windows from bottom to top, recalculating the ownership of the various screen positions while it paints the *Window*s.

```
// restack all windows
void Window::Restack()
    {
    Screen::Clear();

    // clear screen ownership grid
    for (unsigned int l = 0; l < MaxLength; ++l)
```

```
        {
        for (unsigned int c = 0; c < MaxWidth; ++c)
            ScrnOwner[l * MaxWidth + c] = NULL;
        }


    // start with the "lowest" window in the list
    WdwList.GoToTail();

    Window * curWdw = (Window *)WdwList.Examine();

    while (curWdw != NULL)
        {
        // plot what a Window owns
        curWdw->PlotOwnership();

        // the paint it
        curWdw->Paint();

        // get the next window
        WdwList.GoPrev();

        curWdw = (Window *)WdwList.Examine();
        }
    }
```

PlotOwnership is called for a *Window* when it needs to mark the screen locations it owns. Hidden (non-visible) *Window*s do not own any part of the screen. This method is called by *Restack* and the constructor, and should only be called by the *TopWindow*. In the case of *Restack*, it begins at the "lowest" *Window* in the stack, and calls *PlotOwnership* for each Window in the stack as it moves toward the top. The screen locations owned by a lower-level window will be claimed by calls to *PlotOwnership* for windows that overlap it.

```
// plot which screen locations belong to this window
void Window::PlotOwnership()
    {
    unsigned int l, c;

    if (Concealed)
        return;

    // mark locations own by display area of window
    if ((Length == MaxLength) && (Width == MaxWidth))
        {
        for (l = 0; l < Length; ++l)
```

```
        for (c = 0; c < Width; ++c)
            ScrnOwner[l * MaxWidth + c] = this;
    }
else
    {
    for (l = HomeLine; l < HomeLine + Length; ++l)
        for (c = HomeCol;c < HomeCol + Width; ++c)
            if ((l < MaxLength) && (c < MaxWidth))
                ScrnOwner[l * MaxWidth + c] = this;
    }

// mark border locations
if (Border != BT_NONE)
    {
    if (HomeCol > 0)
        {
        if (HomeLine > 0)
            ScrnOwner[(HomeLine - 1) * MaxWidth +
                                    (HomeCol - 1)] = this;

        if (Length < MaxLength)
            ScrnOwner[(Length+HomeLine)*MaxWidth+
                                    (HomeCol-1)] = this;
        }

    if (Width < MaxWidth)
        {
        if (HomeLine > 0)
            ScrnOwner[(HomeLine - 1) * MaxWidth +
                                    (Width + HomeCol)] = this;

        if (Length < MaxLength)
            ScrnOwner[(Length+HomeLine)*MaxWidth+
                                    (Width + HomeCol)] = this;
        }

    if ((HomeLine + Length) < MaxLength)
        {
        for (c = HomeCol;c <= HomeCol + Width; ++c)
            ScrnOwner[(Length+HomeLine)*MaxWidth+c]
                        = this;
        }

    if (HomeLine > 0)
        {
        for (c = HomeCol;c <= HomeCol + Width; ++c)
            ScrnOwner[(HomeLine-1)*MaxWidth+c]
                        = this;
        }
```

```
        if ((HomeCol + Width) < MaxWidth)
            {
            for (l=HomeLine;l <= HomeLine + Length;++l)
                ScrnOwner[l*MaxWidth+Width+HomeCol]
                            = this;
            }

        if (HomeCol > 0)
            {
            for (l=HomeLine;l <= HomeLine+Length; ++l)
                ScrnOwner[l * MaxWidth + HomeCol - 1]
                            = this;
            }
        }
    }
```

ErrorHandler, a pointer to an exception handler function, is called whenever a memory allocation error occurs while processing *Window*s. It is initially set by the *FirstTime* function (called when the first *Window* is constructed) to point to a default error handling function, but it can be changed to point to a user-defined function by using the static method *SetErrorHandler*. *SetErrorHandler* and the default error handling function are contained in the file *wdw_err.cpp*.

```
// internal prototype
wstatic void DefaultHandler();

void (* Window::ErrorHandler)() = DefaultHandler;

// default exception handler
static void DefaultHandler()
    {
    puts("\aWindow Error: allocation failure\n");
    }

// assign an exception handler
void Window::SetErrorHandler(void (* userHandler)())
    {
    ErrorHandler = userHandler;
    }
```

The methods that change and display the contents of a *Window* are implemented in *wdw_disp.cpp*. Two steps are required to display information on the screen through a *Window*. First, the information must be stored in the *Window* buffer *BufferSW*. Second, the buffer must be "painted" on the screen. Any number of changes can be made to the contents of a Window without those changes appearing on the screen. The current contents of the *Window* will appear when the window is painted.

The *Paint* method displays the complete contents of a *Window* on the screen. Of course, if the *Window* is overlapped by a another *Window*, all of its contents may not be displayed. *Paint* also redisplays the *Window*'s border and title, if one exists.

```
// paint entire window
void Window::Paint()
    {
    if (Concealed)
        return;

    unsigned int l, c, hpos;

    // draw border
    switch (Border)
        {
        case BT_SINGLE :
            Display(-1,-1,BorderColor,'\xDA');
            Display(Length,-1,BorderColor,'\xC0');
            Display(Length,Width,BorderColor,'\xD9');
            Display(-1,Width,BorderColor,'\xBF');

            if (Header.Length() == 0)
                for (c = 0; c < Width; ++c)
                    {
                    Display(-1,c,BorderColor,'\xC4');
                        Display(Length,c,BorderColor,
                                        '\xC4');
                    }
            else
                {
                hpos = 0;

                for (c = 0; c < Width; ++c)
                    {
                    if (hpos < Header.Length())
                        {
                        Display(f1,c,BorderColor,Header[hpos]);
                        ++hpos;
                        }
                    else
                            {
```

```
                    Display(f1,c,BorderColor,'\xC4');
                         }

               Display(Length,c,BorderColor,'\xC4');
               }
          }

    for (l = 0; l < Length; ++l)
         {
         Display(l,-1,BorderColor,'\xB3');
         Display(l,Width,BorderColor,'\xB3');
         }

    break;

case BT_DOUBLE :
    Display(-1,-1,BorderColor,'\xC9');
    Display(Length,-1,BorderColor,'\xC8');
    Display(Length,Width,BorderColor,'\xBC');
    Display(-1,Width,BorderColor,'\xBB');

    if (Header.Length() == 0)
        for (c = 0; c < Width; ++c)
             {
             Display(-1,c,BorderColor,'\xCD');
             Display(Length,c,BorderColor,'\xCD');
             }
    else
         {
         hpos = 0;

         for (c = 0; c < Width; ++c)
             {
             if (hpos < Header.Length())
                 {
                 Display(-1,c,BorderColor,Header[hpos]);
                 ++hpos;
                 }
             else
                         {
                 Display(-1,c,BorderColor,'\xCD');
                         }

             Display(Length,c,BorderColor,'\xCD');
             }
         }
```

```
        for (1 = 0; 1 < Length; ++1)
            {
            Display(1,-1,BorderColor,'\xBA');
            Display(1,Width,BorderColor,'\xBA');
            }
    }

unsigned int pos;

// display each character in buffer
for (1 = 0; 1 < Length; ++1)
    for (c = 0; c < Width; ++c)
        {
        pos = 1 * Width + c;
        Display(1, c, BufferSW[pos].Attribute,
                        BufferSW[pos].Symbol);
        }

// set the cursor position
SetCursor(CrsLine, CrsCol);
}
```

PaintLine is a simpler version of *Paint*. It merely displays a single line of the window on the screen. This method speeds operation when a change occurs in only one line of a *Window*.

```
// paint one line
void Window::PaintLine(unsigned int line)
    {
    if ((Concealed) || (line > Length))
        return;

    unsigned int pos;

    // draw just one line of contents
    for (unsigned int c = 0; c < Width; ++c)
        {
        pos = line * Width + c;
        Display(line, c, BufferSW[pos].Attribute,
                    BufferSW[pos].Symbol);
        }
    }
```

PutChar and *PutStr* are the methods that store characters into *BufferSW*. *PutChar* stores a single character at a specific location, while *PutStr* displays an entire String value. Remember that the

311

characters stored into a *Window* using these methods will not appear
on the physical screen until a *Paint* method is called.

```
// store a character in the window
void Window::PutChar(unsigned int line,
                     unsigned int col,
                     unsigned char attr, char ch)
    {
    if ((line >= Length) || (col >= Width))
        return;

    unsigned int pos = line * Width + col;

    // store the character...
    BufferSW[pos].Symbol = ch;

    // ... and its attribute
    if (attr != 0)
        BufferSW[pos].Attribute = attr;
    else
        BufferSW[pos].Attribute = InsideColor;
    }

// store a string in the window
void Window::PutStr(unsigned int line,
                    unsigned int col,
                    unsigned char attr,
                    String & s)
    {
    if ((line >= Length) || (col >= Width))
        return;

    if (attr == 0)
        attr = InsideColor;

    unsigned char l = line;
    unsigned char c = col;

    unsigned int spos = 0;
    unsigned int wpos;

    // display text
    while (s[spos] != '\x00')
        {
        wpos = l * Width + c;
```

```
        BufferSW[wpos].Symbol    = s[spos];
        BufferSW[wpos].Attribute = attr;

        if (c == (Width - 1))
            {
            if (!Wrapped)
                return;

            if (l < Length)
                {
                c = 0;
                ++l;
                }
            else
                return;
            }
        else
            ++c;

        ++spos;
        }
    }
```

There are several methods that will change the position and characteristics of a *Window*. These are all implemented in the *wdw_misc.cpp* file.

The position of a *Window* on the screen can be changed with the *Move* method, but moving a window does not changes its level in the stack. For example, if the second window from the top of a stack is moved, it remains the second window down.

```
// change position
void Window::Move(unsigned int line, unsigned int col)
    {
    if ((line > MaxLength) || (col > MaxWidth))
        return;

    // set new window position
    HomeLine = line;
    HomeCol  = col;

    // redisplay all windows
    Restack();
    }
```

Hoist changes the position of a Window in the stack by making it the top window. It's somewhat like removing a plate from the middle of a pile of dishes and placing on the top of the pile.

```
// make this the top window
void Window::Hoist()
    {
    // delete window from list
    WdwList.Delete(this);

    // add it to the list (making it the top window)!
    WdwList.Store(this);

    TopWindow = this;

    // redisplay all windows
    Restack();
    }
```

A *Window* does not have to be visible. The *Conceal* method makes any *Window* invisible. A *Conceal*ed *Window* does not own any screen locations, nor does it cover any windows beneath it. An invisible *Window* can have characters stored in its buffer. It can also be moved or destroyed. The *Reveal* method makes a *Conceal*ed *Window* visible again.

```
// conceal this window
void Window::Conceal()
    {
    Concealed = 0;

    Restack();
    }

// reveal this window
void Window::Reveal()
    {
    Concealed = 0;

    Restack();
    }
```

When a *Window* has its *Wrapped* flag on, any string of characters stored in its buffer by the *PutStr* method that would extend off the right side of the *Window* will wrap to a new line. If the *Wrapped* flag is off, long strings are chopped off at the right window border. The *WrapOn* and *WrapOff* methods change the setting of the *Wrapped* bit.

```
// turn wrap on
void Window::WrapOn()
    {
    Wrapped = 1;
    }

// turn wrap off
void Window::WrapOff()
    {
    Wrapped = 0;
    }
```

SetHead changes a *Window*'s heading value. A heading is a *String* displayed near the left side of the top border of a *Window*. An initial heading is provided when a *Window* is constructed.

```
// set the heading
void Window::SetHead(String & heading)
    {
    if (Border == BT_NONE)
        return;

    unsigned int c, hpos;
    char bordchar;

    // pick border character
    if (Border == BT_SINGLE)
        bordchar = 0xC4;
    else
        bordchar = 0xCD;

    Header = heading;

    // no header, fill in border
    if (Header.Length() == 0)
        {
        for (c = 0; c < Width; ++c)
            Display(-1,c,BorderColor,bordchar);

        return;
        }
```

```
        hpos = 0;

        // display header and border fragment
        for (c = 0; c < Width; ++c)
            if (hpos < Header.Length())
                {
                Display(-1,c,BorderColor,Header[hpos]);
                ++hpos;
                }
            else
                Display(-1,c,BorderColor,bordchar);
        }
```

SetCursor sets the position of the cursor within a *Window,* and *GetCursor* retrieves the current position of the cursor. *ClearAll* blanks the entire *Window,* and *ClearLine* erases only one line.

```
// set the cursor position
void Window::SetCursor(unsigned int line, unsigned int col)
    {
    // cursor can only be positioned within top window
    if ((line > Length)
    || (col > Width)
    || (this != TopWindow))
        return;

    unsigned char newl = line + HomeLine;
    unsigned char newc = col  + HomeCol;

    if ((newl > MaxLength) || (newc > MaxWidth))
        return;

    CrsLine = line;
    CrsCol  = col;

    // physically set cursor position
    Screen::CursorSetPos(newl, newc);
    }

// get the cursor position
void Window::GetCursor(unsigned int & line,
                                    unsigned int & col)
    {
    line = CrsLine;
    col  = CrsCol;
    }
```

```
// clear the entire window
void Window::ClearAll()
    {
    unsigned int pos = 0;

    for (unsigned char l = 0; l < Length; ++l)
        {
        for (unsigned char c = 0; c < Width; ++c)
            {
            BufferSW[pos].Symbol    = ' ';
            BufferSW[pos].Attribute = InsideColor;

            ++pos;
            }
        }
    }

// clear one line of the window
void Window::ClearLine(unsigned int line,
                       unsigned int col)
    {
    unsigned int pos;

    for (unsigned char c = col; c < Width; ++c)
        {
        pos = line * Width + c;

        BufferSW[pos].Symbol    = ' ';
        BufferSW[pos].Attribute = InsideColor;
        }
    }
```

The *Window* class is large, and possibly confusing to the novice C++ programmer. So, I've provided an example program, *wdw_demo.cpp*, which shows how the class can be used:

```
#include "Window.hpp"

extern "C"
    {
    #include "conio.h"
    #include "string.h"
    }

void f1();
void f2(Window * Parent);
void WaitForKey();

static Window * Wmain;
```

```
int main()
    {
    unsigned int l, c;

    // allocate main window
    Wmain = new Window(1,1,23,78,7,7,BT_DOUBLE,"",0);

    // fill the main window with stars
    for (l = 0; l < 25; ++l)
        for (c = 0; c < 80; ++c)
            Wmain->PutChar(l,c,0,'*');

    // paint the main window
    Wmain->Paint();

    WaitForKey();

    // work with other windows
    f1();
    WaitForKey();

    delete Wmain;
    }

void f1()
    {
    unsigned int l, c;
    char buf[128];

    Window W1(2,10,15,40,7,7,BT_DOUBLE,"Test Window 1",1);

    W1.PutStr(0,0,0,"This is a long sentence to"
                    "examine how wrapping works!");
    W1.PutChar(14,10,0,'*');
    W1.PutChar(5,29,0,'*');
    W1.Paint();

    WaitForKey();

    Wmain->SetHead("MAIN WINDOW!");

    WaitForKey();

    f2(&W1);

    WaitForKey();

    Wmain->PutStr(5,5,0,"This is also a very long"
                    "sentence, which should be clipped!");

    Wmain->Paint();
```

```
    WaitForKey();

    strcpy(buf,"Scott Ladd");

    W1.PutStr(11,0,0,buf);
    W1.Paint();

    WaitForKey();
    }

void f2(Window * Parent)
    {
    Window W2(10,25,8,20,7,7,BT_SINGLE,
                        "Test Window 2",0);

    W2.PutStr(3,4,15,"This should be truncated because"
                                "it is too long!");
    W2.Paint();

    WaitForKey();

    Parent->Hoist();

    WaitForKey();

    W2.Move(10,50);

    WaitForKey();
    }

void WaitForKey()
    {
    while (!kbhit()) ;

    if (!getch()) getch();
    }
```

Working with the *Screen* and *Window* classes, you should be able to define specific window classes with features like scroll bars, mouse input, and menus. You can think of classes as building blocks, with each block providing a foundation for other blocks. *Window* and *Screen* are the kind of building blocks every C++ programmer needs.

12

Simulation in C++

This is it — the last chapter. By now, you should have a feel for using C++ to build reusable, extensible classes that become the building blocks for programs. With all of that work behind us, it's time to have a little fun. I'm going to show you how I used C++ to simulate a simple ecological system. That's right — I'm talking about simulating life in a computer using object-oriented programming.

Actually, the program presented here is far too simple to be called a true simulation of life. Rather, it can be thought of as a computer-based laboratory in which you can perform experiments in the new science of artificial life.

Artificial Life: What Is It?

When the term "artificial life" is used, many people immediately think of some guy named Frankenstein who built a monster to terrorize eastern Europeans. Ever since humans first began building things, we've been trying to duplicate life. Even simple structures like statues are an attempt at imitate real life. Our ability to generate lifelike forms has improved at the same pace as improvements in our technology.

In the scientific world, the study of Artificial Life (AL) is quickly becoming an important adjunct to traditional biological research.

Biologists have always been hampered by the fact that we have only one form of biology to study — the carbon-chain-based life found here on Earth. There's no reason other types of life couldn't exist, and AL brings alternate life forms into the laboratory for study. In effect, we create an artificial environment using a computer simulation to better understand ourselves and the world of life around us.

Artificial Intelligence (AI) is related to Artificial Life, although the two sciences take opposite approaches to the same problem. AI researchers use a top-down approach. They begin by defining intelligence and, once they have a definition in hand, they write programs based on their definition. Neural networks are an example of this type of design. AL, on the other hand, uses a bottom-up approach. A central theory behind AL is that behavior is the result of an unbelievable number of underlying — and simple — actions. In reality, life is the behavior exhibited by a massively parallel system.

What is a human being? In a strictly biological sense, we are a colony of trillions of cells. These cells interact using simple rules. For example, light reaches part of our eye, which chemically reacts and sends electrical impulses to the brain, which in turn interprets the information. None of these electro-chemical reactions is particularly complex, but the sum of these reactions taken together is amazing.

In AL, it is how the system behaves that is important. If you look at a beehive, it can be seen as a single entity or as a colony of individual bees, just as the human being is a colony of cells. Each bee has a specific, simple task in the hive, such as gathering nectar to produce honey, and interacts with its fellow bees. An AL approach to simulating a bee hive would be to create parallel processes that imitate the behavior of individual bees. Each "bee-omata" would know exactly what its job was, and how it should interact with other bees. One bee-omata by itself is uninteresting, but put them together and they will act exactly like a real bee hive.

Computers and Life

For years, computers have been used to simulate the real world. One of the most popular "simulations" is Life, an elementary computerized imitation of a colony of cells. The system was developed by John Conway of the University of Cambridge (England) in the late 1960s. Cells live, die, and are born according to a simple set of rules. If exactly three "live" cells are adjacent to an empty cell, the empty cell comes to life. When a cell has four or more live neighbors, it dies from overcrowding. Any cell with two or three live neighbors survives.

From these three rules came a fascinating pastime for many people. The computer is given a pattern of live cells to begin with, then processes that pattern using the rules above. Fluctuating and oscillating patterns emerge, and have been given names such as "gliders" and "guns." It's even more fun when you add to the rules or change them. People have become quite creative in enhancing Life, adding different universes, modified rules, and creating "mutant" cells. It's fascinating to watch the patterns as they change. Even people who hate computers (are there such cretins?) will spend hours watching Life run its course.

Even in its extended forms, however, Life is not truly lifelike. It's a system to modify a pattern according to a set of extremely simple rules. Real life is a much more complicated interaction between an organism and its environment. Living creatures evolve as their environment changes. Is it possible to simulate evolving artificial creatures in a computer?

A simple AL program was written by a California high school teacher named Michael Palmiter. Palmiter's program simulates "bugs" living in a "dish" containing "bacteria," which are the bugs' primary food. The bugs begin by randomly moving about in the dish, eating any bacteria they encounter. The bacteria provide energy so the bugs can continue to move, and when the bugs are old enough and have sufficient energy, they reproduce by breaking into two new bugs. All of this is shown on a computer screen using graphics.

What makes Palmiter's program interesting is that he built a minimal amount of "genetic" information into each bug. Each bug has a set of genes to control its movement. Movement is determined by lottery so a random direction is picked for every turn. However, as the bugs reproduce, "mutations" are introduced that increase the probability that a given direction will be chosen. Where the first bugs tend to "jitter" about randomly, later bugs take on a more directed pattern of movement.

Those bugs that can find food will live long enough to reproduce, passing on their characteristics to a new generation of bugs. Jitter-bugs have a problem when food in their local area becomes scarce because they tend not to travel far from their origin point. Cruiser-bugs, which travel primarily in one or two directions, have the advantage of being able to seek out food in new locations. And zig-zag-cruisers have a greater advantage since they move in an erratic pattern that leads them in one direction but covers a greater area.

Palmiter's program is simple, yet elegant. As time goes on, the bugs seem to develop behavior patterns — even if the patterns are a bit random in nature. But is it 'real life on a computer screen?" No. Real life, even for single-cell organisms, is far more complicated than that represented by Palmiter's simulated bugs. Nevertheless, he has taken a major step forward in creating artificial life.

The program presented here represents an extension of the ideas Palmiter used for his program. Where his bugs randomly search for food, mine can gain the ability to "sense" food at a given distance. In addition, some creatures die of old age and others die of starvation. The program is built using object-oriented techniques, so you can develop your own specialized creatures to inhabit your computer universe.

Each creature appears as a square 9-by-9 grid of pixels on the screen. Food is shown as single-pixel spots on the screen. A creature can move in any of eight direction, moving one "square" in one direction during each click of the program's clock. Each movement expends a creature's energy supply. If any food particles are found in the new position, they are consumed to add to the creature's energy supply. If a creature runs out of energy, or if it reaches its maximum age, it dies and is removed from the ecosystem.

When a creature is old enough, it will split off a new creature. The new creature will be identical to its parent, with the possible exception of a single mutation to its genes. These genes determine the likelihood of the creature moving in a given direction, as well as its ability to sense food. Both positive and negative mutations should be supported.

Preliminaries

This program uses graphics, but since this book is about C++ and not about graphics, I won't spend a lot of time detailing how to make pixels appear on the screen.

I did build a short, simple graphics module called *GraphVGA* in C, which is used by this chapter's program. *GraphVGA* is designed to be used with an IBM PC-compatible VGA video adapter and display in 640-by-480 pixel mode (16 colors). It should be adaptable to other types of video displays, including the IBM EGA display. Appendix B provides the listings for *GraphVGA*, along with a short explanation of how it works. For the purposes of this chapter, I'll simply describe those functions of *GraphVGA* that are used here.

C++ Techniques and Applications

The *GraphInit* function sets the VGA adapter to 640-by-480-by-116 color mode. *GraphDone* is a complimentary function that restores the video to the mode selected before *GraphInit* was called. *PlotPixel* turns on a pixel at a given X-Y coordinate with a specific color value. The other functions in *GraphVGA* are not used in this chapter.

Now let's define our ecosystem.

Creatures

This program is designed to be flexible. While the example in this chapter uses only one type of creature, it should be possible to design several types of creatures, each with different characteristics. This sounds suspiciously like a class hierarchy, so I'll begin by building a universal base class for all creatures. The class is defined in the file *creature.hpp*, and it is implemented in the file *creature.cpp*. Both files are given, in their entirety, in Appendix A.

For reference purposes, here's the class definition:

```
#if !defined(__CREATURE_HPP)
#define __CREATURE_HPP 1

#include "WorkList.hpp"

class Creature
    {
    protected:
        unsigned char Color;
        int Energy;
        int Age;
        int AgeRep;
        int PosX, PosY;

    public:
        // public list of all creatures
        static WorkList CList;

        // constructor
        Creature(unsigned char c, int e, int x, int y);

        // ask creature to perform an action
        virtual int Move() = 0;
```

```
        // tell creature to draw itself
        virtual void Draw() = 0;

        // tell creature to erase itself
        virtual void Erase() = 0;
    };

#endif
```

And this is how I implemented the class:

```
// Program:    Creature
extern "C"
    {
    #include "stdio.h"
    #include "stdlib.h"
    }

#include "Creature.hpp"

// initialize static members
WorkList Creature::CList;

// constructor
Creature::Creature(unsigned char c, int e,
                            int x, int y)
    {
    // set values of members
    Color  = c;
    Energy = e;
    Age    = 0;
    AgeRep = 0;
    PosX   = x;
    PosY   = y;

    // add creature to creature list
    if (CList.Store(this))
        {
        printf("Creature cannot be added to list\n");
        exit(0);
        }
    }
```

*Creature*s have five characteristics defined by data members. *Color* is (obviously) the color used to display the creature. *Energy* represents the current level of energy a creature possesses. The number of "ticks" the creature has are its *Age*. *AgeRep* stores the number of ticks that have occurred since the creature last reproduced. Finally, *PosX* and *PosY* are the X and Y coordinates of the creature's current location on the screen.

Remember the *WorkList* class discussed in Chapter Eight[[ck ref]]? A static WorkList object is a public static member of *Creature*. Every *Creature* created is stored in *CList*. The main ecosystem program then sequentially executes a *Move* method for each of the *Creatures* stored in *Clist* for every "tick" of the program's clock.

The only constructor for *Creature* requires four arguments. When a *Creature* is instantiated, color, current energy level, and the initial position in the ecosystem must be indicated. These values correspond to the C, e, x, and y parameters in the constructor definition.

The *Move* method for a creature tells it to do whatever it wants to do for the current clock tick. Calling *Move* for a *Creature* is like telling it to take its turn in a game of checkers.

The *Draw* method tells a creature to draw itself on the screen, and the *Erase* method tells a creature to remove its picture from the screen. Like the *Move* method, *Draw* and *Erase* are virtual methods so that they can be polymorphically redefined by classes derived from *Creature*.

Grazers

The only class derived from *Creature* in this book is *Grazer*. A *Grazer* corresponds to one of Palmiter's "bugs." Basically, *Grazers* wander around the ecosystem searching for food particles. They are simple creatures, similar to single-celled plant and animal life forms. The class definition is located in the file *grazer.hpp*, while the implementation is in *grazer.cpp* (see Appendix A).

This is the *Grazer* class definition:

```
#if !defined(__GRAZER_HPP)
#define __GRAZER_HPP 1

#include "Creature.hpp"
#include "BitGrid.hpp"

class Grazer : public Creature
    {
    protected:
        unsigned char Movement[8];
        unsigned char MoveCount;

        unsigned char Sense;

        static int Count;

        static int MaxEnergy;
        static int MaxAge;
        static int MaxSense;
        static int ReproAge;
        static int RepEnergy;
        static int FoodValue;

        static int NoMoveGenes;

        static int MoveTable[8][2];

        static BitGrid *FoodSupply;

        static int MaxX;
        static int MaxY;

    public:
        // basic constructor
        Grazer(int x, int y);

        // copy constructor
        Grazer(const Grazer & G);

        // destructor
        ~Grazer();

        // retrieve number of living grazers
        static int Population()
            {
            return Count;
            }
```

```
        // set food supply and area dimensions
        static void SetRegion(BitGrid * food,
                                            int xmax, int ymax);

        // ask grazer to do something
        virtual int Move();

        // tell grazer to draw itself
        virtual void Draw();

        // tell grazer to erase itself
        virtual void Erase();
    };

#endif
```

The definition of the *Grazer* class declares a number of static data members. The array *Movement* holds integer values that represent the likelihood that a creature will move in a given direction. The higher the value of a *Movement* "gene," the higher the probability that the *Grazer* will move in that direction. *MoveCount* contains the total "genes" stored in *Movement*.

Sense is the only non-static data member added by *Grazer* to the data members inherited from *Creature*. The value of *Sense* indicates how many moves a *Grazer* can "look ahead" for food. Originally, *Grazers* cannot sense food and must randomly search for it. Eventually, the *Sense* value will mutate to a positive number in a newly created *Grazer*, and that *Grazer* will begin to look for food.

A census of *Grazers* is kept in *Count* and returned by the static *Population* method.

The next batch of static members defines limits and parameters for *Grazers*. *MaxEnergy* is the maximum value which that *Energy* can achieve. *MaxAge* is the number of ticks a *Grazer* can live before it dies of old age. The maximum value of *Sense* is stored in *MaxSense*. *ReproAge* is the number of ticks that must pass after a *Grazer* is created or born before it can reproduce. *GrazerEnergy* contains the minimum energy needed to reproduce. The amount of energy gained by consuming a food particle is stored in *FoodValue*.

MoveTable contains the offsets used to calculate movement. *FoodSupply* is a pointer to the *BitGrid* to indicate which pixel locations hold food particles. *MaxX* and *MaxY* control the boundaries of the area in which grazers can live. The last three instance variable describe the environment in which a *Grazer* exists, and are set by the global method *SetRegion*. The ecosystem must create and maintain a *BitGrid* in which bits are set to indicate the locations of food particles. The dimensions of the ecosystem and the address of its ecosystem must be given to *Grazer*s via the *SetRegion* method before any *Grazer*s are created.

The implementation of *Grazer* is contained in the file *grazer.cpp* (see Appendix A). In *grazer.cpp*, a macro is defined that returns random numbers within a given range. This simplifies working with random chance:

```
// this macro returns a random number between 1 and n
#define RandVal(n) ((rand() % n) + 1)
```

The static members of *Grazer* are initialized with *grazer.cpp* to these values:

```
// initialize the static members of Grazer class
int Grazer::Count        =    0;
int Grazer::MaxEnergy    = 3000;
int Grazer::MaxAge       =  300;
int Grazer::MaxSense     =    3;
int Grazer::ReproAge     =  100;
int Grazer::RepEnergy    = 2000;
int Grazer::FoodValue    =  150;
int Grazer::NoMoveGenes  =    8;

int Grazer::MoveTable[8][2] =
    { {-3, -3}, { 0, -3}, { 3, -3},
      {-3,  0},           { 3,  0},
      {-3,  3}, { 0,  3}, { 3,  3} };

// globals defining area which grazers live in
BitGrid * Grazer::FoodSupply = NULL;
```

```
int Grazer::MaxX = 0;
int Grazer::MaxY = 0;
```

As mentioned above, the *SetRegion* must be called before any *Grazer*s can be constructed:

```
// set food supply and area dimensions
void Grazer::SetRegion(BitGrid * food,
                                      int xmax, int ymax)
    {
    FoodSupply = food;

    MaxX = xmax;
    MaxY = ymax;
    }
```

There are two constructors for *Grazer*. One constructor is used to create "spontaneous" *Grazer*s at specific locations in the ecosystem. Spontaneous generation of *Grazer*s only occurs when the ecosystem generates its initial population. Once the ecosystem begins to operate, *Grazer*s are only created when they are "born" from another *Grazer*. New *Grazer*s are born via the copy constructor, which generates a duplicate of an existing *Grazer*, possibly with mutations. The copy constructor also modifies the original *Grazer* by reducing its *Energy* and setting *AgeRep* back to zero.

```
// basic constructor for a new creature
Grazer::Grazer(int x, int y)
    : Creature(15,1500,x,y)
    {
    for (int i = 0; i < NoMoveGenes; ++ i)
        Movement[i] = 1;

    MoveCount = NoMoveGenes;

    Sense = 0;

    ++Count;

    Draw();
    }

// copy constructor
Grazer::Grazer(const Grazer & G)
```

```
: Creature(15,G.Energy,G.PosX,G.PosY)
{
for (int i = 0; i < NoMoveGenes; ++i)
    Movement[i] = G.Movement[i];

MoveCount = G.MoveCount;

Sense = G.Sense;

int choice = RandVal(10);

switch (choice)
    {
    case 1: // modify movement genes
    case 2:
    case 3:
        int move = RandVal(NoMoveGenes) - 1;

        if (1 == RandVal(2))
            {
            if (Movement[move] == 1)
                {
                ++Movement[move];
                ++MoveCount;
                }
            }
        else
            {
            if (Movement[move] == 2)
                {
                --Movement[move];
                --MoveCount;
                }
            }
        break;

    case 4: // modify sense value
        if (1 == RandVal(2))
            {
            if (Sense < MaxSense)
                ++Sense;
            }
        else
            {
            if (Sense > 0)
                --Sense;
            }
    }

++Count;
```

```
      Draw();
      }
```

The destructor for a *Grazer* erases it from the screen, deletes it from
Clist, and decrements *Count.*

```
// destructor
Grazer::~Grazer()
    {
    if (CList.Delete(this))
        {
        printf("Creature can't be deleted from list");
        exit(0);
        }

    Erase();

    --Count;
    }
```

The *Move* method for *Grazer* is not as complex as it might look:

```
// ask grazer to do something
int Grazer::Move()
    {
    ++Age;
    ++AgeRep;

    if ((AgeRep >= ReproAge) && (Energy >= RepEnergy))
        {
        AgeRep = 0;

        Energy /= 2;

        Grazer * newG = new Grazer(*this);

        if (newG == NULL)
            {
            printf("Error! Grazer Repro\n");
            exit(1);
            }
        }

    int i, x, y, newx, newy, m, weight, move;

    if (Sense > 0)
        {
        int move_value, j, ix, iy;
```

```
        int hi_value = -1;

    move = 0;

    for (i = 0; i < NoMoveGenes; ++i)
        {
        move_value = 0;

        x = PosX;
        y = PosY;

        for (j = 0; j < Sense; ++j)
            {
            x += MoveTable[i][0];
            y += MoveTable[i][1];

            if (x < 1) x = MaxX;
            if (x > MaxX) x = 1;
            if (y < 1) y = MaxY;
            if (y > MaxY) y = 1;

            for (ix = x - 1; ix <= x + 1; ++ix)
                for (iy = y - 1; iy <= y + 1; ++iy)
                    if (FoodSupply->IsSet(ix,iy))
                        ++move_value;
            }

        if (move_value > hi_value)
            {
            hi_value = move_value;
            move = i;
            }
        else
            if ((move_value == hi_value)
                    && (Movement[i] >= Movement[move]))
                if ((Movement[i] > Movement[move])
                        || (RandVal(2) == 1))
                        {
                        move = i;
                        }
        }
    }
else
    {
    weight = Movement[0];
    m      = RandVal(MoveCount);

    move =  0;
```

```
    while (m > weight)
        {
        ++move;
        weight += Movement[move];
        }
    }

if ((move == 0) || (move == 2)
|| (move == 5) || (move == 7))
    Energy -= 5;
else
    Energy -= 3;

// did it die?
if ((Age == MaxAge) || (Energy <= 0))
    return 1;

newx = PosX + MoveTable[move][0];
newy = PosY + MoveTable[move][1];

Erase();

PosX = newx;
PosY = newy;

if (PosX < 1) PosX = MaxX;
if (PosX > MaxX) PosX = 1;
if (PosY < 1) PosY = MaxY;
if (PosY > MaxY) PosY = 1;

for (x = PosX - 1; x <= PosX + 1; ++x)
    for (y = PosY - 1; y <= PosY + 1; ++y)
        if (FoodSupply->IsSet(x,y))
            {
            Energy += FoodValue;
            FoodSupply->Exclude(x,y);
            }

Draw();

return 0;
}
```

Move begins by increasing the creature's age by 1. If it is old enough
and has sufficient *Energy*, the creature reproduces via the copy constructor. It then determines physical movement. If its sense value is
greater than zero, it searches the adjacent moves for food particles.
The direction in which the most food is found is the direction in

which the *Grazer* will move. If two or more directions have equivalent amounts of food, the *Grazer* chooses between them based on its *Movement* genes and/or a random selection.

If a *Grazer* does not have the ability to sense food (Sense = 0), it then randomly selects a direction based on the value of its *Movement* genes.

Once a direction has been selected, the energy required to move is subtracted from the *Grazer*'s *Energy* value. If the *Grazer*'s *Energy* reaches 0, or its age is equal to the maximum, the creature dies. Otherwise, it *Erases* itself and *Draws* itself at the new location. Any food particles located in the new position are consumed, which adds to the *Grazer*'s energy. Here's how *Grazer* implements the *Erase* and *Draw* methods:

```
// tell grazer to draw itself
void Grazer::Draw()
    {
    for (int x = PosX - 1; x <= PosX + 1; ++x)
        for (int y = PosY - 1; y <= PosY + 1; ++y)
            PlotPixel(x,y,Color);
    }

// tell grazer to erase itself
void Grazer::Erase()
    {
    for (int x = PosX - 1; x <= PosX + 1; ++x)
        for (int y = PosY - 1; y <= PosY + 1; ++y)
            PlotPixel(x,y,0);
    }
```

The EcoSystem

The ecosystem itself is a very simple program named *ecosys.cpp*, reproduced here and in Appendix A:

```
// include standard C libraries
extern "C"
    {
    #include "conio.h"
    #include "time.h"
    #include "stdio.h"
```

```
    #include "stdlib.h"
    #include "graphvga.h"
    }

// this macro returns a random number between 1 and n
#define RandVal(n) ((rand() % n) + 1)

// include C++ classes
#include "Creature.hpp"
#include "Grazer.hpp"
#include "BitGrid.hpp"

// These definitions change how food is distributed
// #define GARDEN 1
#define NORMAL_FOOD 1
#define NEW_FOOD 2

// constants which define the size of the grid array
const int MaxX = 630;
const int MaxY = 450;

// global data items
BitGrid * GrazerFood;

// function prototypes
int  Initialize();
void LifeCycle();
void cdecl Finish();
int  main();

int Initialize()
    {
    GraphInit();

    // set function to be called at exit
    if (atexit(Finish))
        return 1;

    srand(unsigned(time(NULL)));

    GrazerFood = new BitGrid (630, 450);

    Grazer::SetRegion(GrazerFood, MaxX, MaxY);

    Grazer * G;
    int i, x, y;

    for (i = 0; i < 40; ++i)
        {
        x = RandVal(MaxX);
        y = RandVal(MaxY);
```

```
        G = new Grazer(x,y);

        if (G == NULL)
            {
            printf("Error: Init Grazers\n");
            return 2;
            }
        }

    for (i = 0; i < 4000; ++i)
        {
        do  {
            x = RandVal(MaxX);
            y = RandVal(MaxY);
            }
        while (GrazerFood->IsSet(x,y));

        GrazerFood->Include(x,y);

        PlotPixel(x,y,14);
        }

    return 0;
    }

void LifeCycle()
    {
    Creature * C;
    unsigned long move;
    char stat_line[20];
    int x, y, i;

    move = 0L;

    while ((Grazer::Population() > 0) && !kbhit())
        {
        Creature::CList.GoToHead();

        while (1)
            {
            C = Creature::CList.Examine();

            if (NULL == C)
                break;

            Creature::CList.GoNext();

            if (C->Move())
                delete (Grazer *)C;
            }
```

```
            for (i = 0; i < NEW_FOOD; ++i)
                {
            #if defined(GARDEN)
                do  {
                        x = RandVal(100) + 270;
                        y = RandVal(100) + 175;
                        }
                    while (GrazerFood->IsSet(x,y));

                    GrazerFood->Include(x,y);

                    PlotPixel(x,y,14);
            #endif

            #if defined(NORMAL_FOOD)
                do  {
                        x = RandVal(MaxX);
                        y = RandVal(MaxY);
                        }
                    while (GrazerFood->IsSet(x,y));

                    GrazerFood->Include(x,y);

                    PlotPixel(x,y,14);
            #endif
                }

        ++move;

        sprintf(stat_line,"M: %6ld, C: %3d", move,
                                Grazer::Population());

        PutGraphString(465,10,stat_line,15,0);
            }
        }

void cdecl Finish()
    {
    while (!kbhit()) ;

    if (!getch()) getch();

    GraphDone();
    }

int main()
    {
    if (Initialize())
        return 1;
```

```
    LifeCycle();

    return 0;
}
```

The program creates 40 *Grazers* and 4,000 food particles in a 630-by-450-pixel area on the VGA screen. Once everything is set up, the ecosystem runs through cycles until all of the *Grazers* have died, or a key is pressed.

The *Initialize* function generates the ecosystem. It turns on the graphics, initializes the random number generator, and uses the *SetRegion* method to give the *Grazer* class the address of the *GrazerFood BitGrid* and the dimensions of the ecosystem. It then generates 40 spontaneous *Grazers* at random locations, and then places 4,000 bits of food on the screen and in *GrazerFood*.

The actual work is done by the *LifeCycle* function, which continues as long as there is a population of *Grazers* and a key is not pressed to interrupt the program. Inside the loop, the *CList* of *Creatures* is processed sequentially, and a *Move* method is invoked for each *Creature* found. Note that, because the classes based on *Creature* are polymorphic, other creature types could be added to the program without affecting this main loop. To add new creatures, just define a new class derived from the *Creature* class, and add objects of the type to *CList* when they are created. They'll be processed along with the *Grazers*.

Each cycle of the loop also generates more food particles. The value of the *NEW_FOOD* macro determines how many pieces of new food appear with each turn. If the *GARDEN* macro is defined, a square area in the center of the screen receives an extra ration of food particles.

At the end of every cycle, the current population of *Grazers* and the current cycle number are displayed at the bottom of the screen.

Farewell!

This is both a fun and educational program to work with. An earlier version written in C and published in *Micro Cornucopia Magazine* (issue #49) has been one of the most popular programs I've every written for publication.

Feel free to experiment. Try changing the parameters that affect the food supply or reproduction rate of the *Grazers*. I've written one version of the program to implement a *Hunter* class. *Hunters* chase down and eat *Grazers*. *Grazers*, of course, can use their sense to detect *Hunters*. Like life itself, the possibilities offered by this program are endless.

With this piece of scientific archania, I bid you adieu. I hope you've enjoyed this book. I know that I've enjoyed writing it.

Listings

This appendix should contain the following source files in this order. The copy editor should merge the listings in from the APPEND_A directory on the distribution disk. I'd suggest using a font which allows up to 80 characters per line, since that's how the listings are formatted.

Thanks!

Chapter 6

complex.hpp

```
// Header:     Complex
// Version:    2.20
//
// Language:   C++ 2.0
// Environ:    Any
//
// Purpose:    Provides the class "Complex" for C++ programs. The majority
//             of the class is implemented inline for efficiency. Only
//             the division, power, and i/o methods are actual functions.
//
// Written by: Scott Robert Ladd

#if !defined(__COMPLEX_HPP)
#define __COMPLEX_HPP 1

class Complex
    {
    private:
        double Real; // Real part
```

```
        double Imag; // Imaginary part

        static void (* ErrorHandler)();

    public:
        // constructors
        Complex (void);
        Complex (const Complex & c);
        Complex (const double & r, const double & i);
        Complex (const double & r);

        // method to set error handler function
        static void SetErrorHandler(void (* userHandler)());

        // value extraction methods
        friend double real(const Complex & c);
        friend double imag(const Complex & c);

        // assignment methods
        void operator = (const Complex & c);

        // utility methods
        friend double abs(const Complex & c);
        friend double norm(const Complex & c);
        friend double arg(const Complex & c);

        // unary minus method
        Complex operator - ();

        // calculation methods
        friend Complex operator + (const Complex & c1, const Complex & c2);
        friend Complex operator - (const Complex & c1, const Complex & c2);
        friend Complex operator * (const Complex & c1, const Complex & c2);
        friend Complex operator / (const Complex & c1, const Complex & c2);

        Complex operator += (const Complex & c);
        Complex operator -= (const Complex & c);
        Complex operator *= (const Complex & c);
        Complex operator /= (const Complex & c);

        // comparison methods
        friend int operator == (const Complex & c1, const Complex & c2);
        friend int operator != (const Complex & c1, const Complex & c2);

        friend int operator <  (const Complex & c1, const Complex & c2);
        friend int operator <= (const Complex & c1, const Complex & c2);

        friend int operator >  (const Complex & c1, const Complex & c2);
        friend int operator >= (const Complex & c1, const Complex & c2);
```

```
        // polar coordinate methods
        friend Complex polar(const double radius, const double theta = 0.0);
        friend Complex conj(const Complex & c);

        // trigonometric methods
        friend Complex cos(const Complex & c);
        friend Complex sin(const Complex & c);
        friend Complex tan(const Complex & c);

        friend Complex cosh(const Complex & c);
        friend Complex sinh(const Complex & c);
        friend Complex tanh(const Complex & c);

        // logarithmic methods
        friend Complex exp(const Complex & c);
        friend Complex log(const Complex & c);

        // "power" methods
        friend Complex pow(const Complex & c, const Complex & power);
        friend Complex sqrt(const Complex & c);

        // output method
        int Print() const;
    };

#endif
```

cp_util.cpp

```
// Module:     Cp_Util
// Version:    2.20
//
// Language:   C++ 2.0
// Environ:    Any
//
// Purpose:    Utility methods for Complex class
//
// Written by: Scott Robert Ladd

#include "Complex.hpp"

extern "C"
    {
    #include "math.h"
    #include "stdio.h"
    #include "stdlib.h"
    }
```

```
// prototype for default error handler
static void DefaultHandler();

// assignment of default handler address to error function pointer
void (* Complex::ErrorHandler)() = DefaultHandler;

// default error handler
static void DefaultHandler()
    {
    puts("\aERROR in complex object: DIVIDE BY ZERO\n");
    exit(1);
    }

// constructors
Complex::Complex (void)
    {
    Real = 0.0;
    Imag = 0.0;
    }

Complex::Complex (const Complex & c)
    {
    Real = c.Real;
    Imag = c.Imag;
    }

Complex::Complex (const double & r, const double & i)
    {
    Real = r;
    Imag = i;
    }

Complex::Complex (const double & r)
    {
    Real = r;
    Imag = 0.0;
    }

// method to set error handler function
void Complex::SetErrorHandler(void (* userHandler)())
    {
    ErrorHandler = userHandler;
    }

// value extraction methods
double real (const Complex & c)
    {
    return c.Real;
    }
```

```
double imag (const Complex & c)
    {
    return c.Imag;
    }

// assignment method
void Complex::operator = (const Complex & c)
    {
    Real = c.Real;
    Imag = c.Imag;
    }

// utility methods
double abs(const Complex & c)
    {
    double result = sqrt(c.Real * c.Real + c.Imag * c.Imag);

    return result;
    }

double norm(const Complex & c)
    {
    double result = (c.Real * c.Real) + (c.Imag * c.Imag);

    return result;
    }

double arg(const Complex & c)
    {
    double result = atan2(c.Imag, c.Real);

    return result;
    }
```

cp_ops.cpp

```
//  Module:      Cp_ops
//  Version:     2.20
//
//  Language:    C++ 2.0
//  Environ:     Any
//
//  Purpose:     Basic operators for Complex objects
//
//  Written by: Scott Robert Ladd

#include "Complex.hpp"

extern "C"
    {
```

```
    #include "math.h"
    }

// unary minus method
Complex Complex::operator - ()
    {
    Complex result;

    result.Real = -Real;
    result.Imag = -Imag;

    return result;
    }

// calculation methods
Complex operator + (const Complex & c1, const Complex & c2)
    {
    Complex result;

    result.Real = c1.Real + c2.Real;
    result.Imag = c1.Imag + c2.Imag;

    return result;
    }

Complex operator - (const Complex & c1, const Complex & c2)
    {
    Complex result;

    result.Real = c1.Real - c2.Real;
    result.Imag = c1.Imag - c2.Imag;

    return result;
    }

Complex operator * (const Complex & c1, const Complex & c2)
    {
    Complex result;

    result.Real = (c1.Real * c2.Real) - (c1.Imag * c2.Imag);
    result.Imag = (c1.Real * c2.Imag) + (c1.Imag * c2.Real);

    return result;
    }

Complex operator / (const Complex & c1, const Complex & c2)
    {
    Complex result;
    double den;

    den = norm(c2);
```

```
    if (den != 0.0)
        {
        result.Real = (c1.Real * c2.Real + c1.Imag * c2.Imag) / den;
        result.Imag = (c1.Imag * c2.Real - c1.Real * c2.Imag) / den;
        }
    else
        Complex::ErrorHandler();

    return result;
    }
```

cp_asop.cpp

```
// Module:      Cp_asop
// Version:     2.20
//
// Language:    C++ 2.0
// Environ:     Any
//
// Purpose:     Assignment operators for Complex objects
//
// Written by: Scott Robert Ladd

#include "Complex.hpp"

Complex Complex::operator += (const Complex & c)
    {
    Real += c.Real;
    Imag += c.Imag;

    return *this;
    }

Complex Complex::operator -= (const Complex & c)
    {
    Real -= c.Real;
    Imag -= c.Imag;

    return *this;
    }

Complex Complex::operator *= (const Complex & c)
    {
    double OldReal = Real; // save old Real value

    Real = (Real * c.Real) - (Imag * c.Imag);
    Imag = (OldReal * c.Imag) + (Imag * c.Real);
```

```
    return *this;
    }

Complex Complex::operator /= (const Complex & c)
    {
    double den = norm(c);

    if (den != 0.0)
        {
        double OldReal = Real;

        Real = (Real * c.Real + Imag * c.Imag) / den;
        Imag = (Imag * c.Real - OldReal * c.Imag) / den;
        }
    else
        Complex::ErrorHandler();

    return *this;
    }
```

cp_comp.cpp

```
// Module:     Cp_comp
// Version:    2.20
//
// Language:   C++ 2.0
// Environ:    Any
//
// Purpose:    Comparison operations for Complex class
//
// Written by: Scott Robert Ladd

#include "Complex.hpp"

extern "C"
    {
    #include "math.h"
    #include "stdlib.h"
    }

// comparison methods
int operator == (const Complex & c1, const Complex & c2)
    {
    return (c1.Real == c2.Real) && (c1.Imag == c2.Imag);
    }

int operator != (const Complex & c1, const Complex & c2)
```

```
        {
        return (c1.Real != c2.Real) || (c1.Imag != c2.Imag);
        }


int operator <  (const Complex & c1, const Complex & c2)
        {
        return abs(c1) < abs(c2);
        }

int operator <= (const Complex & c1, const Complex & c2)
        {
        return abs(c1) <= abs(c2);
        }


int operator >  (const Complex & c1, const Complex & c2)
        {
        return abs(c1) > abs(c2);
        }

int operator >= (const Complex & c1, const Complex & c2)
        {
        return abs(c1) >= abs(c2);
        }
```

cp_trig.cpp

```
//   Module:      Cp_trig
//   Version:     2.20
//
//   Language:    C++ 2.0
//   Environ:     Any
//
//   Purpose:     Trignometric functions for Complex class
//
//   Written by: Scott Robert Ladd

#include "Complex.hpp"

extern "C"
    {
    #include "math.h"
    #include "stdlib.h"
    }

// trigonometric methods
Complex cos(const Complex & c)
```

```
    {
    Complex result;

    result.Real =  cos(c.Real) * cosh(c.Imag);
    result.Imag = -sin(c.Real) * sinh(c.Imag);

    return result;
    }

Complex sin(const Complex & c)
    {
    Complex result;

    result.Real = sin(c.Real) * cosh(c.Imag);
    result.Imag = cos(c.Real) * sinh(c.Imag);

    return result;
    }

Complex tan(const Complex & c)
    {
    Complex result = sin(c) / cos(c);

    return result;
    }

Complex cosh(const Complex & c)
    {
    Complex result;

    result.Real = cos(c.Imag) * cosh(c.Real);
    result.Imag = sin(c.Imag) * sinh(c.Real);

    return result;
    }

Complex sinh(const Complex & c)
    {
    Complex result;

    result.Real = cos(c.Imag) * sinh(c.Real);
    result.Imag = sin(c.Imag) * cosh(c.Real);

    return result;
    }

Complex tanh(const Complex & c)
    {
    Complex result = sinh(c) / cosh(c);

    return result;
    }
```

cp_log.cpp

```
//  Module:     Cp_log
//  Version:    2.20
//
//  Language:   C++ 2.0
//  Environ:    Any
//
//  Purpose:    Logarithmic functions for Complex class
//
//  Written by: Scott Robert Ladd

#include "Complex.hpp"

extern "C"
    {
    #include "math.h"
    #include "stdlib.h"
    }

// logarithmic methods
Complex exp(const Complex & c)
    {
    double X = exp(c.Real);

    Complex result;

    result.Real = X * cos(c.Imag);
    result.Imag = X * sin(c.Imag);

    return result;
    }

Complex log(const Complex & c)
    {
    double hypot = abs(c);

    Complex result;

    if (hypot > 0.0)
        {
        result.Real = log(hypot);
        result.Imag = atan2(c.Imag, c.Real);
        }
    else
        Complex::ErrorHandler();

    return result;
    }
```

cp_pow.cpp

```
//  Module:     Cp_Pow
//  Version:    2.20
//
//  Language:   C++ 2.0
//  Environ:    Any
//
//  Purpose:    Power function for Complex class
//
//  Written by: Scott Robert Ladd

#include "Complex.hpp"

extern "C"
    {
    #include "math.h"
    #include "stdlib.h"
    }

// "power" methods
Complex pow(const Complex & c, const Complex & power)
    {
    Complex result;

    if (power.Real == 0.0 && power.Imag == 0.0)
        {
        result.Real = 1.0;
        result.Imag = 0.0;
        }
    else
        {
        if (c.Real != 0.0 || c.Imag != 0.0)
            result = exp(log(c) * power);
        else
            Complex::ErrorHandler();
        }

    return result;
    }

Complex sqrt(const Complex & c)
    {
    return pow(c,Complex(0.5,0.0));
    }
```

cp_misc.cpp

```
//   Module:     Cp_Misc
//   Version:    2.20
//
//   Language:   C++ 2.0
//   Environ:    Any
//
//   Purpose:    Miscellaneous methods for Complex class
//
//   Written by: Scott Robert Ladd

#include "Complex.hpp"

extern "C"
    {
    #include "math.h"
    #include "stdio.h"
    #include "stdlib.h"
    }

// polar coordinate methods
Complex polar(const double radius, const double theta)
    {
    Complex result;

    result.Real = radius * cos(theta);
    result.Imag = radius * sin(theta);

    return result;
    }

Complex conj(const Complex & c)
    {
    Complex result;

    result.Real =  c.Real;
    result.Imag = -c.Imag;

    return result;
    }

// output method
int Complex::Print() const
    {
    int out_len;

    out_len = printf("(%g", Real);

    if (Imag >= 0.0)
```

```
          {
          ++out_len;
          putchar('+');
          }

     out_len += printf("%g)", Imag);

     return out_len;
     }
```

Chapter 8

containr.hpp

```
//  Header:     Containr (Abstract Base Class for Containers)
//  Version:    3.20
//
//  Language:   C++ 2.0
//  Environ:    Any
//
//  Purpose:    Provides an abstract base class for container classes.
//
//  Written by: Scott Robert Ladd

#if !defined(__CONTAINR_HPP)
#define __CONTAINR_HPP 1

class Container
    {
    protected:
        // number of items in this list
        unsigned long Count;

        // pointer to exception handler
        void (* ErrorHandler)();

    public:
        // constructor
        Container();

        // copy constructor
        Container(const Container & c);
```

```
        // assignment opeartor
        void operator = (const Container & c);

        // store an item
        virtual int Store(void * item) = 0;

        // examine an item
        virtual void * Examine() = 0;

        // retrieve an item
        virtual void * Retrieve() = 0;

        // eliminate contents
        virtual void Empty() = 0;

        // return number of items in a container
        unsigned long GetCount()
            {
            return Count;
            }

        // set function for exception handler
        void AssignHandler(void (* userHandler)())
            {
            ErrorHandler = userHandler;
            }
    };

#endif
```

containr.cpp

```
//  Module:     Containr (Abstract Base Class for Containers)
//  Version:    3.20
//
//  Language:   C++ 2.0
//  Environ:    Any
//
//  Purpose:    Provides an abstract base class for container classes.
//
//  Written by: Scott Robert Ladd

#include "Containr.hpp"

extern "C"
    {
    #include "stdio.h"
    }
```

```
// prototypes
static void DefaultHandler();

// default exception handler
static void DefaultHandler()
    {
    puts("\aContainer Error: memory allocation failure!");
    }

// constructor
Container::Container()
    {
    Count = 0;
    ErrorHandler = DefaultHandler;
    }

// copy constructor
Container::Container(const Container & c)
    {
    Count = c.Count;
    ErrorHandler = c.ErrorHandler;
    }

// assignment opeartor
void Container::operator = (const Container & c)
    {
    Count = c.Count;
    ErrorHandler = c.ErrorHandler;
    }
```

singlist.hpp

```
//   Header:    SingList (Singly-Linked Lists)
//   Version:   3.20
//
//   Language:  C++ 2.0
//   Environ:   Any
//
//   Purpose:   Provides a general set of singly-linked list classes
//
//   Written by: Scott Robert Ladd

#if !defined(__SINGLIST_HPP)
#define __SINGLIST_HPP 1

#include "Containr.hpp"
```

```
class SinglyLinkedList : public Container
    {
    protected:
        // structure of a node in a list
        struct ListNode
            {
            ListNode  *  Next;
            void      *  DataPtr;
            };

        ListNode * Head;  // pointer to first node
        ListNode * Tail;  // pointer to the last node

        // duplication method
        void Copy(const SinglyLinkedList & sl);

    public:
        // constructor
        SinglyLinkedList();

        // copy contructor
        SinglyLinkedList(const SinglyLinkedList & sl);

        // assignment operator
        void operator = (const SinglyLinkedList & sl);

        // destructor
        ~SinglyLinkedList();

        // store an item
        virtual int Store(void * item) = 0;

        // examine an item
        virtual void * Examine() = 0;

        // retrieve an item
        virtual void * Retrieve() = 0;

        // remove all items from a list
        virtual void Empty();
    };

#endif
```

singlist.cpp

```cpp
//  Module:      SingList (Singly-Linked Lists)
//  Version:     3.20
//
//  Language:    C++ 2.0
//  Environ:     Any
//
//  Purpose:     Provides a general set of singly-linked list classes
//
//  Written by: Scott Robert Ladd

#include "SingList.hpp"

extern "C"
    {
    #include "stddef.h"
    }

// duplication method
void SinglyLinkedList::Copy(const SinglyLinkedList & sl)
    {
    Head = NULL;
    Tail = NULL;

    ListNode * temp = sl.Head;

    while (temp != NULL)
        {
        if (Tail == NULL)
            {
            Tail = new ListNode;

            if (Tail == NULL)
                ErrorHandler();

            Head = Tail;

            Tail->Next    = NULL;
            Tail->DataPtr = temp->DataPtr;
            }
        else
            {
            Tail->Next = new ListNode;

            if (Tail->Next == NULL)
                ErrorHandler();

            Tail->Next->Next    = NULL;
            Tail->Next->DataPtr = temp->DataPtr;
```

```
                Tail = Tail->Next;
                }

        temp = temp->Next;
        }
    }

// constructor
SinglyLinkedList::SinglyLinkedList() : Container()
    {
    Head  = NULL;
    Tail  = NULL;
    }

// copy contructor
SinglyLinkedList::SinglyLinkedList(const SinglyLinkedList & sl) : Container(sl)
    {
    Copy(sl);
    }

// assignment operator
void SinglyLinkedList::operator = (const SinglyLinkedList & sl)
    {
    this->Empty();

    Count = sl.Count;

    Copy(sl);
    }

// destructor
SinglyLinkedList::~SinglyLinkedList ()
    {
    this->Empty();
    }

// remove all items from a list
void SinglyLinkedList::Empty()
    {
    ListNode * temp, * hold;

    temp = Head;

    while (temp != NULL)
        {
        hold = temp->Next;
        delete temp;
        temp = hold;
        }
    }
```

C++ Techniques and Applications

stack.hpp

```
//  Header:     Stack     (A stack class)
//  Version:    3.20
//
//  Language:   C++ 2.0
//  Environ:    Any
//
//  Purpose:    Provides a a stack class for C++
//
//  Written by: Scott Robert Ladd

#if !defined(__STACK_HPP)
#define __STACK_HPP 1

#include "SingList.hpp"

class Stack : public SinglyLinkedList
    {
    public:
        // constructor
        Stack();

        // copy constructor
        Stack(const Stack & st);

        // assignment operator
        void operator = (const Stack & st);

        // store an item in a stack
        virtual int Store(void * item);

        // examine the top item in the stack
        virtual void * Examine();

        // retrieve the top item in a stack (and remove it)
        virtual void * Retrieve();
    };

#endif
```

362

stack.cpp

```
//  Module:      Stack    (A stack class)
//  Version:     3.20
//
//  Language:    C++ 2.0
//  Environ:     Any
//
//  Purpose:     Provides a a stack class for C++
//
//  Written by: Scott Robert Ladd

#include "Stack.hpp"

extern "C"
    {
    #include "stddef.h"
    }

// constructor
Stack::Stack() : SinglyLinkedList()
    {}

// copy constructor
Stack::Stack(const Stack & st) : SinglyLinkedList(st)
    {}

// assignment operator
void Stack::operator = (const Stack & st)
    {
    this->SinglyLinkedList::operator = (st);
    }

// add new item
int Stack::Store(void * item)
    {
    ListNode * new_node;

    new_node = new ListNode;

    if (NULL == new_node)
        return 1;

    new_node->Next    = Head;
    new_node->DataPtr = item;

    Head = new_node;

    if (Tail == NULL)
        Tail = new_node;

    ++Count;

    return 0;
    }
```

```
// examine the top item on the stack
void * Stack::Examine()
    {
    if (Count == 0)
        return NULL;

    return Head->DataPtr;
    }

// read and remove the top item on the stack
void * Stack::Retrieve()
    {
    ListNode * temp;
    void *     value;

    if (Count == 0)
        return NULL;

    value = Head->DataPtr;
    temp  = Head->Next;

    delete Head;

    Head = temp;

    --Count;

    return value;
    }
```

queue.hpp

```
//  Header:     Queue     (A queue class)
//  Version:    3.20
//
//  Language:   C++ 2.0
//  Environ:    Any
//
//  Purpose:    Provides a general-purpose queue class
//
//  Written by: Scott Robert Ladd

#if !defined(__QUEUE_HPP)
#define __QUEUE_HPP 1

#include "Stack.hpp"

class Queue : public Stack
    {
    public:
        // constructor
```

```
        Queue();

        // copy constructor
        Queue(const Queue & q);

        // assignment constructor
        void operator = (const Queue & q);

        // store an item in a queue
        virtual int Store(void * item);
    };

#endif
```

queue.cpp

```
// Header:     Queue      (A queue class)
// Version:    3.20
//
// Language:   C++ 2.0
// Environ:    Any
//
// Purpose:    Provides a general-purpose queue class
//
// Written by: Scott Robert Ladd

#include "Queue.hpp"

extern "C"
    {
    #include "stddef.h"
    }

// constructor
Queue::Queue() : Stack()
    {}

// copy constructor
Queue::Queue(const Queue & q) : Stack(q)
    {}

// assignment constructor
void Queue::operator = (const Queue & q)
    {
    this->Stack::operator = (q);
    }

// add new item
```

```
int Queue::Store(void * item)
    {
    ListNode * new_node;

    new_node = new ListNode;

    if (NULL == new_node)
        return 1;

    new_node->Next    = NULL;
    new_node->DataPtr = item;

    if (Count > 0)
        {
        Tail->Next = new_node;
        Tail       = new_node;
        }
    else
        {
        Head = new_node;
        Tail = new_node;
        }

    ++Count;

    return 0;
    }
```

dbllist.hpp

```
//  Header:     DblList  (Doubly-Linked Lists)
//  Version:    3.20
//
//  Language:   C++ 2.0
//  Environ:    Any
//
//  Purpose:    Provides a general doubly-linked list class
//
//  Written by: Scott Robert Ladd

#if !defined(__DBLLIST_HPP)
#define __DBLLIST_HPP 1

#include "Containr.hpp"

class DoublyLinkedList : public Container
    {
    protected:
```

```
        // structure of a node in a list
        struct DListNode
            {
            DListNode * Prev;
            DListNode * Next;
            void      * DataPtr;
            };

        // pointers to first and last nodes in list
        DListNode * Head;
        DListNode * Tail;

        // duplication method
        void Copy(const DoublyLinkedList & sl);

    public:
        // constructor
        DoublyLinkedList();

        // copy contructor
        DoublyLinkedList(const DoublyLinkedList & sl);

        // assignment operator
        void operator = (const DoublyLinkedList & sl);

        // destructor
        ~DoublyLinkedList();

        // store an item
        virtual int Store(void * item) = 0;

        // examine an item
        virtual void * Examine() = 0;

        // retrieve an item
        virtual void * Retrieve() = 0;

        // remove all items from a list
        virtual void Empty();
    };

#endif
```

dbllist.cpp

```
//  Header:    DblList  (Doubly-Linked Lists)
//  Version:   3.20
//
```

```
//  Language:    C++ 2.0
//  Environ:     Any
//
//  Purpose:     Provides a general doubly-linked list class
//
//  Written by: Scott Robert Ladd

#include "DblList.hpp"

extern "C"
    {
    #include "stddef.h"
    }

// duplication method
void DoublyLinkedList::Copy(const DoublyLinkedList & dl)
    {
    Head = NULL;
    Tail = NULL;

    DListNode * temp = dl.Head;

    while (temp != NULL)
        {
        if (Tail == NULL)
            {
            Tail = new DListNode;

            if (Tail == NULL)
                ErrorHandler();

            Head = Tail;

            Tail->Next    = NULL;
            Tail->Prev    = NULL;
            Tail->DataPtr = temp->DataPtr;
            }
        else
            {
            Tail->Next = new DListNode;

            if (Tail->Next == NULL)
                ErrorHandler();

            Tail->Next->Next    = NULL;
            Tail->Next->Prev    = Tail;
            Tail->Next->DataPtr = temp->DataPtr;

            Tail = Tail->Next;
            }
```

```
        temp = temp->Next;
        }
    }

// constructor
DoublyLinkedList::DoublyLinkedList() : Container()
    {
    Head  = NULL;
    Tail  = NULL;
    }

// copy contructor
DoublyLinkedList::DoublyLinkedList(const DoublyLinkedList & dl)
    {
    Copy(dl);
    }

// assignment operator
void DoublyLinkedList::operator = (const DoublyLinkedList & dl)
    {
    this->Empty();

    Count = dl.Count;

    Copy(dl);
    }

// destructor
DoublyLinkedList::~DoublyLinkedList()
    {
    this->Empty();
    }

// remove all items from a list
void DoublyLinkedList::Empty()
    {
    DListNode * temp, * hold;

    temp = Head;

    while (temp != NULL)
        {
        hold = temp->Next;
        delete temp;
        temp = hold;
        }
    }
```

C++ Techniques and Applications

worklist.hpp

```
//   Header:      WorkList (A Useful Kind of Doubly-Linked List)
//   Version:     3.20
//
//   Language:    C++ 2.0
//   Environ:     Any
//
//   Purpose:     I'm not sure what to call this kind of doubly-linked list;
//                it's been so useful, I needed to create a class for it. So,
//                WorkList is what it's called!
//
//   Written by: Scott Robert Ladd

#if !defined(__WORKLIST_HPP)
#define __WORKLIST_HPP 1

#include "DblList.hpp"

class WorkList : public DoublyLinkedList
    {
    protected:
        DListNode * Current; // currently selected node in the list

    public:
        // constructor
        WorkList();

        // copy constructor
        WorkList(const WorkList & wl);

        // assignment operator
        void operator = (const WorkList & wl);

        // store an item
        virtual int Store(void * item);

        // examine an item
        virtual void * Examine();

        // read and remove an item
        virtual void * Retrieve();

        // delete an item from the list
        virtual int Delete(void * item);

        // go to head of list
        virtual void GoToHead();

        // go to end of list
        virtual void GoToTail();
```

370

```
        // go to next item in list
        virtual void GoNext();

        // go to previous item in list
        virtual void GoPrev();
    };

#endif
```

worklist.cpp

```
// Module:      WorkList (A Useful Kind of Doubly-Linked List)
// Version:     3.20
//
// Language:    C++ 2.0
// Environ:     Any
//
// Purpose:     I'm not sure what to call this kind of doubly-linked list;
//              it's been so useful, I needed to create a class for it. So,
//              WorkList is what it's called!
//
// Written by:  Scott Robert Ladd

#include "WorkList.hpp"

extern "C"
    {
    #include "stddef.h"
    }

// constructor
WorkList::WorkList() : DoublyLinkedList()
    {
    Current = NULL;
    }

// copy constructor
WorkList::WorkList(const WorkList & wl) : DoublyLinkedList(wl)
    {}

// assignment operator
void WorkList::operator = (const WorkList & wl)
    {
    DoublyLinkedList::operator = (wl);

    Current = Head;
    }
```

```
// store an item
int WorkList::Store(void * item)
    {
    DListNode * new_item;

    new_item = new DListNode;

    if (item == NULL)
        return 1;

    new_item->Prev    = NULL;
    new_item->Next    = NULL;
    new_item->DataPtr = item;

    if (Head == NULL)
        {
        Head    = new_item;
        Tail    = new_item;
        Current = new_item;
        }
    else
        {
        Head->Prev = new_item;
        new_item->Next = Head;
        Head = new_item;
        }

    ++Count;

    return 0;
    }

// examine an item
void * WorkList::Examine()
    {
    if (Current == NULL)
        return NULL;
    else
        return Current->DataPtr;
    }

// read and remove an item
void * WorkList::Retrieve()
    {
    void * value = Examine();

    Delete(value);

    return value;
    }
```

```
// delete an item from the list
int WorkList::Delete(void * item)
    {
    DListNode * temp;

    temp = Head;

    while (temp != NULL)
        {
        if (temp->DataPtr == item)
            {
            if (temp == Current)
                Current = temp->Next;

            if (temp->Prev == NULL)
                {
                Head = temp->Next;

                if (Head != NULL)
                    Head->Prev = NULL;

                if (temp->Next == NULL)
                    Tail = NULL;
                }
            else
                {
                temp->Prev->Next = temp->Next;

                if (temp->Next == NULL)
                    Tail = temp->Prev;
                else
                    temp->Next->Prev = temp->Prev;
                }

            delete temp;

            --Count;

            return 0;
            }

        temp = temp->Next;
        }

    return 1;
    }

// go to head of list
void WorkList::GoToHead()
    {
```

```
    Current = Head;
    }

// go to end of list
void WorkList::GoToTail()
    {
    Current = Tail;
    }

// go to next item in list
void WorkList::GoNext()
    {
    if (Current != NULL)
        Current = Current->Next;
    }

// go to next item in list
void WorkList::GoPrev()
    {
    if (Current != NULL)
        Current = Current->Prev;
    }
```

Chapter 9

sort.hpp

```
//   Header:     Sort
//   Version:    1.00
//
//   Language:   C++ 2.0
//   Environ:    Any
//
//   Purpose:    A generic array sorting class
//
//   Written by: Scott Robert Ladd

#if !defined(__SORT_HPP)
#define __SORT_HPP 1

class SortArray
    {
    protected:
        void * Array;
        int    Size;
```

```
        int (* Compare)(void *, void *);

        void * ItemPtr(int item)
            {
            return (void *)((char *)Array + (Size * (item - 1)));
            }

    public:
        virtual void Sort(void * arrayPtr, int arrayLen, int itemSize,
                          int (* CompareFunc)(void * item1, void * item2))
            {
            Array = arrayPtr;
            Size  = itemSize;

            Compare = CompareFunc;
            }
    };

#endif
```

qsort.hpp

```
//  Header:     QSort
//  Version:    1.00
//
//  Language:   C++ 2.0
//  Environ:    Any
//
//  Purpose:    A QuickSort for arrays
//
//  Written by: Scott Robert Ladd

#if !defined(__QSORT_HPP)
#define __QSORT_HPP 1

#include "Sort.hpp"

class QuickSortArray : public SortArray
    {
    private:
        void * temp;

        void QSRecursive(int l, int r);

    public:
        virtual void Sort(void * arrayPtr, int arrayLen, int itemSize,
                          int (* CompareFunc)(void * item1, void * item2));
    };

#endif
```

qsort.cpp

```
//  Module:     QSort
//  Version:    1.00
//
//  Language:   C++ 2.0
//  Environ:    Any
//
//  Purpose:    A QuickSort for arrays
//
//  Written by: Scott Robert Ladd

#include "QSort.hpp"

extern "C"
    {
    #include "string.h"
    }

void QuickSortArray::Sort(void * arrayPtr, int arrayLen, int itemSize,
                          int (* CompareFunc)(void * item1, void * item2))
    {
    SortArray::Sort(arrayPtr, arrayLen, itemSize, CompareFunc);

    temp = new char [Size];

    QSRecursive(1,arrayLen);

    delete temp;
    }

void QuickSortArray::QSRecursive(int l, int r)
    {
    int i, j;
    void * x, * y;

    i = l;
    j = r;
    x = ItemPtr((l + r) / 2);

    do  {
        while (Compare(ItemPtr(i), x))
            ++i;

        while (Compare(x, ItemPtr(j)))
```

```
                --j;

        if (i <= j)
            {
            x = ItemPtr(i);
            y = ItemPtr(j);

            memcpy(temp,x,Size);
            memcpy(x,y,Size);
            memcpy(y,temp,Size);

            ++i;
            --j;
            }

        if (l < j)
            QSRecursive(l,j);

        if (i < r)
            QSRecursive(i,r);
        }
    while (i <= j);
    }
```

hsort.hpp

```
//  Header:     HSort
//  Version:    1.00
//
//  Language:   C++ 2.0
//  Environ:    Any
//
//  Purpose:    A HeapSort for arrays
//
//  Written by: Scott Robert Ladd

#if !defined(__HSORT_HPP)
#define __HSORT_HPP 1

#include "Sort.hpp"

class HeapSortArray : public SortArray
    {
    private:
        int  l, r;
        void * temp, * src, * dest;

        void Sift();
```

```
    public:
        virtual void Sort(void * arrayPtr, int arrayLen, int itemSize,
                          int (* CompareFunc)(void * item1, void * item2));
    };

#endif
```

hsort.cpp

```
//  Module:      HSort
//  Version:     1.00
//
//  Language:    C++ 2.0
//  Environ:     Any
//
//  Purpose:     A HeapSort for arrays
//
//  Written by: Scott Robert Ladd

#include "HSort.hpp"

extern "C"
    {
    #include "string.h"
    }


void HeapSortArray::Sift()
    {
    int i, j;

    i = 1;
    j = 2 * 1;

    src = ItemPtr(i);
    memcpy(temp,src,Size);

    while (j <= r)
        {
        if (j < r)
            if (Compare(ItemPtr(j),ItemPtr(j + 1)))
                ++j;

        if (Compare(ItemPtr(j),temp))
            goto done;

        src  = ItemPtr(j);
```

```
        dest = ItemPtr(i);

        memcpy(dest,src,Size);

        i = j;
        j = 2 * i;
        }

    done:

    dest = ItemPtr(i);

    memcpy(dest,temp,Size);
    }

void HeapSortArray::Sort(void * arrayPtr, int arrayLen, int itemSize,
                    int (* CompareFunc)(void * item1, void * item2))
    {
    SortArray::Sort(arrayPtr, arrayLen, itemSize, CompareFunc);

    temp = new char [Size];

    l = (arrayLen / 2) + 1;
    r = arrayLen;

    while (l > 1)
        {
        --l;
        Sift();
        }

    while (r > 1)
        {
        src  = ItemPtr(l);
        dest = ItemPtr(r);

        memcpy(temp,src,Size);
        memcpy(src,dest,Size);
        memcpy(dest,temp,Size);

        --r;
        Sift();
        }

    delete temp;
    }
```

Chapter 10

dynamic.hpp

```
//  Header:     Dynamic      (Improved Dynamic Memory Allocation)
//  Version:    1.01
//
//  Language:   C++ 2.0
//  Environ:    Any
//
//  Purpose:    Implements a template for replacing C++'s default memory
//              allocation operators
//
//  Written by: Scott Robert Ladd

extern "C"
    {
    #include "stddef.h"
    }

void * operator new (size_t size);

void operator delete (void * ptr);

extern "C" {
    void * _vec_new (
        void *        aptr,
        unsigned int  num,
        size_t        size,
        void *        (*ctor)(void *));

    void _vec_delete (
        void *        aptr,
        unsigned int  num,
        size_t        size,
        int           (*dtor)(int, void *),
        int           freeup);
    }
```

dynamic.cpp

```
//  Module:     Dynamic      (Improved Dynamic Memory Allocation)
//  Version:    1.00
//
//  Language:   C++ 2.0
//  Environ:    Any
```

```
//
//  Purpose:     Implements an improved memory allocation scheme for C++ by
//               overloading the built-in new and delete operators.
//
//  Written by: Scott Robert Ladd

#include "Dynamic.hpp"

extern "C"
    {
    #include "stdlib.h"
    }

void * operator new (unsigned int size)
    {
    void * temp = malloc(size);

    return temp;
    }

void operator delete (void * ptr)
    {
    free(ptr);
    }

void * _vec_new(
    void *        aptr,
    unsigned int num,
    size_t        size,
    void *        (* ctor)(void *))
    {
    aptr = malloc(num * size);

    if ((ctor != NULL) && (aptr != NULL))
        {
        for (unsigned int n = 0; n < num; ++n)
            ctor((char *)aptr + n * size);
        }

    return aptr;
    }

void _vec_delete(
    void *        aptr,
    unsigned int num,
    size_t        size,
    int           (*dtor)(int, void *),
    int           freeup)
    {
    if (aptr == NULL)
        return;
```

```
    if (dtor != NULL)
        {
        for (unsigned int n = 0; n < num; ++n)
            dtor(2,(char *)aptr + n * size);
        }

    if (freeup)
        free(aptr);
    }
```

Chapter 11

bitset.hpp

```
//   BitSet
//       2.10     25-Mar-1990
//       C++ 2.0
//
//       Defines a set of bits
//
//       Written by Scott Robert Ladd

#if !defined(_BitSet_HPP)
#define _BitSet_HPP 1

extern "C"
    {
    #include "stddef.h"
    #include "string.h"
    }

class BitSet
    {
    protected:
        unsigned long   Length;
        unsigned char * Data;

        BitSet()
            {
            Length = 0L;
            Data   = NULL;
            }

    public:
        // constructors
```

```
BitSet(unsigned long size);

BitSet(BitSet & bs);

// destructor
~BitSet(void);

// assignment operator
void operator = (BitSet & bs);

// Get number of bits in set
unsigned long Size()
    {
    return Length;
    }

// operation methods
void Include(unsigned long bit)
    {
    if (bit < Length)
        Data[bit / 8] |= (unsigned char)(1 << (bit & 7));
    }

void Exclude(unsigned long bit)
    {
    if (bit < Length)
        Data[bit / 8] &= ~(unsigned char)(1 << (bit & 7));
    }

// turn all bits in set on
void AllOn()
    {
    memset(Data,'\xFF',(Length + 7) / 8);
    }

// turn all bits in set off
void AllOff()
    {
    memset(Data,'\x00',(Length + 7) / 8);
    }

// union operators
BitSet operator & (BitSet & bs);
BitSet operator &= (BitSet & bs);

// synonyms for union operators
BitSet operator +  (BitSet & bs);
BitSet operator += (BitSet & bs);

// intersection operators
BitSet operator |  (BitSet & bs);
```

```
        BitSet operator |= (BitSet & bs);

        // difference operators
        BitSet operator -  (BitSet & bs);
        BitSet operator -= (BitSet & bs);

        // complement operator
        BitSet operator ~ ();

        // comparison operator
        int operator == (BitSet & bs);
        int operator != (BitSet & bs);

        // value retrieval method
        int operator [] (unsigned long bit)
            {
            if (bit < Length)
                return (Data[bit / 8] & (1 << (bit & 7)));
            else
                return 0;
            }
    };

#endif
```

bitset.cpp

```
//   BitSet
//       2.10     25-Mar-1990
//       C++ 2.0
//
//       Defines a set of bits
//
//       Written by Scott Robert Ladd

#include "BitSet.hpp"

extern "C"
    {
    #include "stddef.h"
    #include "string.h"
    }

// constructors
BitSet::BitSet(unsigned long size)
    {
    unsigned long alloc;
```

```
    Length = size;

    alloc = (size + 7) / 8;

    Data = new unsigned char[(unsigned int)alloc];

    memset(Data,'\x00',(unsigned int)alloc);
    }

BitSet::BitSet(BitSet & bs)
    {
    unsigned long alloc;

    Length = bs.Length;

    alloc = (bs.Length + 7) / 8;

    Data = new unsigned char[(unsigned int)alloc];

    memcpy(Data,bs.Data,(unsigned int)alloc);
    }

// destructor
BitSet::~BitSet(void)
    {
    if (Data != NULL)
        delete Data;
    }

// assignment operator
void BitSet::operator = (BitSet & bs)
    {
    unsigned long alloc;

    if (Length != bs.Length)
        {
        Length = bs.Length;

        alloc = (bs.Length + 7) / 8;

        if (Data != NULL)
            delete Data;

        Data = new unsigned char[(unsigned int)alloc];

        memcpy(Data,bs.Data,(unsigned int)alloc);
        }
    else
        memcpy(Data,bs.Data,(unsigned int)((Length + 7) / 8));
    }
```

```
// union operators
BitSet BitSet::operator & (BitSet & bs)
    {
    BitSet result;

    unsigned long bit;

    if (Length < bs.Length)
        {
        result = bs;

        for (bit = 0; bit < Length; ++bit)
            if ((*this)[bit])
                result.Include(bit);
        }
    else
        {
        result = *this;

        for (bit = 0; bit < bs.Length; ++bit)
            if (bs[bit])
                result.Include(bit);
        }

    return result;
    }

BitSet BitSet::operator &= (BitSet & bs)
    {
    *this = *this & bs;

    return *this;
    }

// synonyms for union operators
BitSet BitSet::operator + (BitSet & bs)
    {
    BitSet result = *this & bs;

    return result;
    }

BitSet BitSet::operator += (BitSet & bs)
    {
    BitSet result = *this &= bs;

    return result;
    }

// intersection operators
BitSet BitSet::operator | (BitSet & bs)
```

```
    {
    BitSet result;

    unsigned long max;

    if (Length > bs.Length)
        {
        result = BitSet(Length);
        max    = bs.Length;
        }
    else
        {
        result = BitSet(bs.Length);
        max    = Length;
        }

    for (unsigned long bit = 0; bit < max; ++bit)
        if ((*this)[bit] & bs[bit])
            result.Include(bit);

    return result;
    }

BitSet BitSet::operator |= (BitSet & bs)
    {
    *this = *this | bs;

    return *this;
    }

// difference operators
BitSet BitSet::operator - (BitSet & bs)
    {
    BitSet result = *this;

    unsigned long stop = (Length < bs.Length) ? Length : bs.Length;

    for (unsigned long bit = 0; bit < stop; ++bit)
        if (bs[bit])
            result.Exclude(bit);

    return result;
    }

BitSet BitSet::operator -= (BitSet & bs)
    {
    *this = *this - bs;

    return *this;
    }
```

```
// complement operator
BitSet BitSet::operator ~ ()
    {
    BitSet result(Length);

    for (unsigned long bit = 0; bit < Length; ++bit)
        if ((*this)[bit])
            result.Exclude(bit);
        else
            result.Include(bit);

    return result;
    }

// comparison operators
int BitSet::operator == (BitSet & bs)
    {
    if (Length != bs.Length)
        return 0;

    for (unsigned long bit = 0; bit < Length; ++bit)
        if ((*this)[bit] != bs[bit])
            return 0;

    return 1;
    }

int BitSet::operator != (BitSet & bs)
    {
    if (Length != bs.Length)
        return 1;

    unsigned long bit = 0;

    while (bit < Length)
        if ((*this)[bit] == bs[bit])
            ++bit;
        else
            return 1;

    return 0;
    }
```

chrset.hpp

```
//  Header:     CharSet
//  Version:    2.00
//
```

```
//  Language:   C++ 2.0
//  Environ:    Any
//
//  Purpose:    Provides the equivalent of Pascal's SET OF CHAR.
//
//  Written by: Scott Robert Ladd

#if !defined(__CHARSET_HPP)
#define __CHARSET_HPP 1

#include "BitSet.hpp"

class CharSet : public BitSet
    {
    public:
        // constructors
        CharSet() : BitSet(256)
            {}

        CharSet(CharSet & cs) : BitSet(cs)
            {}

        CharSet(char * Values);

        // assignment operator
        void operator = (CharSet & cs)
            {
            BitSet::operator = (cs);
            }
    };

#endif
```

charset.cpp

```
//  Module:     CharSet
//  Version:    2.00
//
//  Language:   C++ 2.0
//  Environ:    Any
//
//  Purpose:    Provides the equivalent of Pascal's SET OF CHAR.
//
//  Written by: Scott Robert Ladd

#include "CharSet.hpp"

CharSet::CharSet(char * Values) : BitSet(256)
```

```
        {
    while (*Values != '\x00')
        {
        Include(*Values);
        ++Values;
        }
    }
```

bitgrid.hpp

```
//   Header:     BitGrid
//   Version:    2.00
//
//   Language:   C++ 2.0
//   Environ:    Any
//
//   Purpose:    A class for a two-dimensional array of bits. Only those methods
//               defined in this file should be used on a BitGrid.
//
//   Written by: Scott Robert Ladd

#if !defined(__BITGRID_HPP)
#define __BITGRID_HPP 1

#include "BitSet.hpp"

class BitGrid : public BitSet
    {
    private:
        unsigned long Width;

    public:
        // constructor
        BitGrid(unsigned long x_dim, unsigned long y_dim)
            : BitSet(x_dim * y_dim)
            {
            Width = x_dim;
            }

        // include a bit
        void Include(unsigned long x_pos, unsigned long y_pos)
            {
            BitSet::Include(y_pos * Width + x_pos);
            }

        // exclude a bit
        void Exclude(unsigned long x_pos, unsigned long y_pos)
            {
```

```
        BitSet::Exclude(y_pos * Width + x_pos);
        }

    //
    int IsSet(unsigned long x_pos, unsigned long y_pos)
        {
        return BitSet::operator [] (y_pos * Width + x_pos);
        }
    };

#endif
```

Chapter 12

str.hpp

```
//  Header:     Str  (Dynamic Strings)
//  Version:    3.10
//
//  Language:   C++ 2.0
//  Environ:    Any
//
//  Purpose:    Provides a general dynamic string class.
//
//  Written by: Scott Robert Ladd

#if !defined(__STRING_HPP)
#define __STRING_HPP 1

enum StrCompVal  {SC_LESS, SC_EQUAL, SC_GREATER, SC_ERROR};
enum StrCompMode {SM_SENSITIVE, SM_IGNORE};
enum StrError    {SE_ALLOC, SE_TOO_LONG};

class String
    {
    private:
        // instance variables
        unsigned int Siz;     // allocated size
        unsigned int Len;     // current length
        char * Txt;           // pointer to text

        // class constant
        static unsigned int AllocIncr;

        // pointer to exception handler
        static void (*ErrorHandler)(StrError err);
```

```
        // private method used to shrink string to minimum allocation
        void Shrink();

    public:
        // constructor
        String();
        String(const String & str);
        String(const char * cstr);
        String(char fillCh, unsigned int count);

        // destructor
        ~String();

        // value return methods
        unsigned int Length();
        unsigned int Size();

        // Assign an exception handler
        static void SetErrorHandler(void (* userHandler)(StrError));

        // create a c-string from String method
        operator const char * ();

        // assignment method
        void operator = (const String & str);

        // concatenation methods
        friend String operator + (const String & str1, const String & str2);
        void operator += (const String & str);

        // comparison methods
        int operator <  (const String & str);
        int operator >  (const String & str);
        int operator <= (const String & str);
        int operator >= (const String & str);
        int operator == (const String & str);
        int operator != (const String & str);

        StrCompVal Compare(const String & str, StrCompMode caseChk= SM_IGNORE);

        // substring search methods
        int Find(const String & str, unsigned int & pos,
                StrCompMode caseChk = SM_IGNORE);

        // substring deletion method
        void Delete(unsigned int pos, unsigned int count);

        // substring insertion methods
        void Insert(unsigned int pos, char ch);
        void Insert(unsigned int pos, const String & str);
```

```
        // substring retrieval method
        String SubStr(unsigned int start, unsigned int count);

        // character retrieval method
        char operator [] (unsigned int pos);

        // case-modification methods
        String ToUpper();
        String ToLower();
    };

// value return methods
inline unsigned int String::Length()
    {
    return Len;
    }

inline unsigned int String::Size()
    {
    return Siz;
    }

// comparison methods
inline int String::operator <  (const String & str)
    {
    return (Compare(str) == SC_LESS);
    }

inline int String::operator >  (const String & str)
    {
    return (Compare(str) == SC_GREATER);
    }

inline int String::operator <= (const String & str)
    {
    return (Compare(str) != SC_GREATER);
    }

inline int String::operator >= (const String & str)
    {
    return (Compare(str) != SC_LESS);
    }

inline int String::operator == (const String & str)
    {
    return (Compare(str) == SC_EQUAL);
    }

inline int String::operator != (const String & str)
    {
```

```
    return (Compare(str) != SC_EQUAL);
    }

// character retrieval method
inline char String::operator [] (unsigned int pos)
    {
    if (pos >= Len)
        return '\x00';
    else
        return Txt[pos];
    }

#endif
```

str.cpp

```
// Module:     Str  (Dynamic Strings)
// Version:    3.10
//
// Language:   C++ 2.0
// Environ:    Any
//
// Purpose:    Provides a general dynamic string class.
//
// Written by: Scott Robert Ladd

#include "Str.hpp"

extern "C"
    {
    #include "string.h"
    #include "stdio.h"
    #include "stdlib.h"
    #include "ctype.h"
    #include "limits.h"
    }

// prototype for default error handler
static void DefaultHandler(StrError err);

// class-global constant intialization
unsigned int String::AllocIncr = 8;
void (*(String::ErrorHandler))(StrError) = DefaultHandler;

// default exception handler
static void DefaultHandler(StrError err)
    {
    printf("\aERROR in String object: ");
```

```
    switch (err)
        {
        case SE_ALLOC :
            printf("memory allocation failure");
            break;
        case SE_TOO_LONG :
            printf("exceeded %d character limit",UINT_MAX);
        }

    printf("\n");

    exit(1);
    }

// private function to shrink the size of an allocated string
void String::Shrink()
    {
    char * temp;

    if ((Siz - Len) > AllocIncr)
        {
        Siz  = ((Len + AllocIncr) / AllocIncr) * AllocIncr;

        temp = new char [Siz];

        if (temp != NULL)
            {
            strcpy(temp,Txt);
            delete Txt;
            Txt  = temp;
            }
        else
            ErrorHandler(SE_ALLOC);
        }
    }

// constructor
String::String()
    {
    Len = 0;
    Siz = AllocIncr;

    Txt = new char[Siz];

    if (Txt == NULL)
        ErrorHandler(SE_ALLOC);

    Txt[0] = '\x00';
    }
```

```
String::String(const String & str)
    {
    Len = str.Len;
    Siz = str.Siz;

    Txt = new char[Siz];

    if (Txt == NULL)
        ErrorHandler(SE_ALLOC);

    strcpy(Txt,str.Txt);
    }

String::String(const char * cstr)
    {
    if ((cstr == NULL) || (cstr[0] == '\x00'))
        {
        Len = 0;
        Siz = AllocIncr;
        }
    else
        {
        Len = strlen(cstr);
        Siz = ((Len + AllocIncr) / AllocIncr) * AllocIncr;
        }

    Txt = new char [Siz];

    if (Txt == NULL)
        ErrorHandler(SE_ALLOC);

    if (Len > 0)
        strcpy(Txt,cstr);
    else
        Txt[0] = '\x00';
    }

String::String(char fillCh, unsigned int count)
    {
    Siz = ((count + AllocIncr) / AllocIncr) * AllocIncr;
    Len = Siz;

    Txt = new char[Siz];

    if (Txt == NULL)
        ErrorHandler(SE_ALLOC);

    memset(Txt,fillCh,count);

    Txt[count] = '\x00';
    }
```

```
// destructor
String::~String()
    {
    delete Txt;
    }

// Assign an exception handler
void String::SetErrorHandler(void (* userHandler)(StrError))
    {
    ErrorHandler = userHandler;
    }

// create a c-string from String method
String::operator const char * ()
    {
    return Txt;
    }

// assignment method
void String::operator = (const String & str)
    {
    Len = str.Len;
    Siz = str.Siz;

    delete Txt;

    Txt = new char[Siz];

    if (Txt == NULL)
        ErrorHandler(SE_ALLOC);

    strcpy(Txt,str.Txt);
    }

// concatenation methods
String operator + (const String & str1, const String & str2)
    {
    unsigned long totalLen;
    unsigned int newLen, newSiz;
    String tempStr;
    char * temp;

    totalLen = str1.Len + str2.Len;

    if (totalLen > UINT_MAX)
        String::ErrorHandler(SE_TOO_LONG);

    newLen  = (unsigned int)totalLen;

    newSiz  = str1.Siz + str2.Siz;
```

```
        temp = new char[newSiz];

        if (temp == NULL)
            String::ErrorHandler(SE_ALLOC);

        strcpy(temp,str1.Txt);

        strcpy(&temp[str1.Len],str2.Txt);

        tempStr = temp;

        return tempStr;
        }

void String::operator += (const String & str)
        {
        unsigned long totalLen;
        unsigned int newLen, newSiz;
        char * temp;

        totalLen = str.Len + Len;

        if (totalLen > UINT_MAX)
            ErrorHandler(SE_TOO_LONG);

        newLen  = (unsigned int)totalLen;
        newSiz  = Siz + str.Siz;

        temp = new char[newSiz];

        if (temp == NULL)
            ErrorHandler(SE_ALLOC);

        strcpy(temp,Txt);

        delete Txt;

        Txt = temp;

        strcpy(&Txt[Len],str.Txt);

        Len = newLen;
        Siz = newSiz;

        Shrink();
        }

StrCompVal String::Compare(const String & str, StrCompMode caseChk)
        {
        char * tempStr1, * tempStr2;
```

```
    StrCompVal compVal;

    tempStr1 = strdup(Txt);

    if (tempStr1 == NULL)
        ErrorHandler(SE_ALLOC);

    tempStr2 = strdup(str.Txt);

    if (tempStr2 == NULL)
        ErrorHandler(SE_ALLOC);

    if (caseChk == SM_IGNORE)
        {
        strupr(tempStr1);
        strupr(tempStr2);
        }

    switch (strcmp(tempStr1,tempStr2))
        {
        case -1:
            compVal = SC_LESS;
            break;
        case 0:
            compVal = SC_EQUAL;
            break;
        case 1:
            compVal = SC_GREATER;
            break;
        default:
            compVal = SC_ERROR;
        }

    delete tempStr1;
    delete tempStr2;

    return compVal;
    }

// substring search methods
int String::Find(const String & str, unsigned int & pos, StrCompMode caseChk)
    {
    char * tempStr1, * tempStr2;
    unsigned int lastPos, searchLen, tempPos;
    int found;

    tempStr1 = strdup(Txt);

    if (tempStr1 == NULL)
        ErrorHandler(SE_ALLOC);
```

```
    tempStr2 = strdup(str.Txt);

    if (tempStr2 == NULL)
        ErrorHandler(SE_ALLOC);

    if (caseChk == SM_IGNORE)
        {
        strupr(tempStr1);
        strupr(tempStr2);
        }

    pos     = 0;
    tempPos = 0;
    found   = 0;

    searchLen = str.Len;
    lastPos   = Len - searchLen;

    while ((tempPos <= lastPos) && !found)
        {
        if (0 == strncmp(&tempStr1[tempPos],tempStr2,searchLen))
            {
            pos   = tempPos;
            found = 1;
            }
        else
            ++tempPos;
        }

    delete tempStr1;
    delete tempStr2;

    return found;
    }
// substring deletion method
void String::Delete(unsigned int pos, unsigned int count)
    {
    unsigned int copyPos;

    if (pos > Len)
        return;

    copyPos = pos + count;

    if (copyPos >= Len)
        Txt[pos] = 0;
    else
        while (copyPos <= Len + 1)
            {
            Txt[pos] = Txt[copyPos];
```

```
                ++pos;
                ++copyPos;
                }

        Len -= count;

        Shrink();
        }

// substring insertion methods
void String::Insert(unsigned int pos, char ch)
    {
    char * temp;

    if (pos > Len)
        return;

    if (Len + 1 == Siz)
        {
        Siz  += AllocIncr;
        temp  = new char[Siz];

        if (temp == NULL)
            ErrorHandler(SE_ALLOC);

        strcpy(temp,Txt);

        delete Txt;

        Txt = temp;
        }

    for (unsigned int col = Len + 1; col > pos; --col)
        Txt[col] = Txt[col-1];

    Txt[pos] = ch;

    ++Len;

    Txt[Len + 1] = '\x00';
    }

void String::Insert(unsigned int pos, const String & str)
    {
    unsigned long totalLen = str.Len + Len;

    if (totalLen > UINT_MAX)
        ErrorHandler(SE_TOO_LONG);

    unsigned int SLen = str.Len;
```

```
    if (SLen > 0)
        for (unsigned int i = 0; i < SLen; ++i)
            {
            Insert(pos,str.Txt[i]);
            ++pos;
            }
    }

// substring retrieval method
String String::SubStr(unsigned int start, unsigned int count)
    {
    String tempStr;
    char * temp;

    if ((start < Len) && (count > 0))
        {
        temp = new char [count + 1];

        memcpy(temp,&Txt[start],count);

        temp[count] = '\x00';
        }
    else
        temp = "";

    tempStr = temp;

    delete temp;

    return tempStr;
    }

// case-modification methods
String String::ToUpper()
    {
    String tempStr = *this;

    strupr(tempStr.Txt);

    return tempStr;
    }

String String::ToLower()
    {
    String tempStr = *this;

    strlwr(tempStr.Txt);

    return tempStr;
    }
```

Chapter 13

screen.hpp

```
//   Header:      Screen   (MS-DOS Text Video Display Class)
//   Version:     1.10
//
//   Language:    C++ 2.0
//   Environ:     MS-DOS w/monochrome or color text display
//
//   Purpose:     Provides a class for manipulating a text display.
//
//   WARNING!     To drastically improve the speed of this class, NO RANGE
//                CHECKING is done! Invalid line/column values may cause
//                portions of non-video memory to be corrupted!
//
//   Written by: Scott Robert Ladd

#if !defined(__SCREEN_HPP)
#define __SCREEN_HPP 1

#include "Str.hpp"

extern "C"
    {
    #include "peekpoke.h"
    #include "stddef.h"
    }

enum BoxType {BT_NONE, BT_SINGLE, BT_DOUBLE, BT_SOLID};

class Screen
    {
    protected:
        static unsigned int  Width;         // width of the screen in characters
        static unsigned int  Length;        // length of the screen in characters

        static unsigned int  BaseAdr;       // base address of character memory

        static unsigned int  CursorShape;   // stored shape of the cursor
        static int           CursorHidden;  // non-zero if cursor has been hidden

        static unsigned int  HowMany;       // How many screens instantiated?

    public:
```

```
        // constructor
        Screen();

        // destructor
        ~Screen();

        // retrieve screen size method
        static void Dimensions(unsigned int & wid, unsigned int & len);

        // cursor methods
        static void CursorHide();
        static void CursorUnhide();

        static void CursorSetPos(unsigned int line, unsigned int col);
        static void CursorGetPos(unsigned int & line, unsigned int & col);

        // data display methods
        static void PutChar(unsigned int line, unsigned int col,
                            unsigned char attr, char ch);

        static void PutStr(unsigned int line, unsigned int col,
                           unsigned char attr, String & str);

        // data retrieval methods
        static void GetChar(unsigned int line, unsigned int col,
                            unsigned char & attr, char & ch);

        // box display method
        static void DrawBox(unsigned int topLine, unsigned int leftCol,
                            unsigned int btmLine, unsigned int rightCol,
                            unsigned char attr, BoxType typeBox);

        // screen clearing methods
        static void Clear();
        static void ClearLine(unsigned int line, unsigned int col = 0);
    };

// character display method
inline void Screen::PutChar(unsigned int line, unsigned int col,
                            unsigned char attr, char ch)
    {
    unsigned int v = ((unsigned int)attr << 8) | (unsigned char)ch;

    Poke(BaseAdr, (line * Width * 2) + (2 * col), v);
    }

// data retrieval methods
inline void Screen::GetChar(unsigned int line, unsigned int col,
                            unsigned char & attr, char & ch)
    {
    unsigned int v = Peek(BaseAdr, (line * Width * 2) + (2 * col));
```

```
        attr = v >> 8;
        ch   = v & 0xFF;
        }

extern Screen Display;

#endif
```

screen.cpp

```
//  Module:      Screen   (MS-DOS Text Video Display Class)
//  Version:     1.10
//
//  Language:    C++ 2.0
//  Environ:     MS-DOS w/monochrome or color text display
//
//  Purpose:     Provides a class for manipulating a text display.
//
//  WARNING!     To drastically improve the speed of this class, NO RANGE
//               CHECKING is done! Invalid line/column values may cause
//               portions of non-video memory to be corrupted!
//
//  Written by: Scott Robert Ladd

#include "Screen.hpp"
#include "Str.hpp"

extern "C"
    {
    #include "dos.h"
    }

// assign values to static class members
unsigned int  Screen::Width        = 0;
unsigned int  Screen::Length       = 0;
unsigned int  Screen::BaseAdr      = 0;
unsigned int  Screen::CursorShape  = 0;
int           Screen::CursorHidden = 0;

Screen Display;

// constructor
Screen::Screen()
    {
    ++HowMany;

    if (HowMany > 1)
```

```
        return;

    union REGS regs;

    regs.h.ah = 0x0f;

    int86(0x10,&regs,&regs);

    if (regs.h.al == 0x07)
        BaseAdr = 0xB000;
    else
        BaseAdr = 0xB800;

    Width = (int) regs.h.ah;

    regs.x.ax = 0x1130;
    regs.h.bh = 0;
    regs.x.dx = 0;

    int86(0x10,&regs,&regs);

    Length = regs.x.dx + 1;

    if (Length == 1)
        Length = 25;

    Clear();

    CursorHidden = 0;
    }

// destructor
Screen::~Screen()
    {
    --HowMany;

    if (HowMany > 0)
        return;

    Clear();

    CursorSetPos(0,0);
    }

// access methods
void Screen::Dimensions(unsigned int & wid, unsigned int & len)
    {
    wid = Width;
    len = Length;
    }
```

```
// cursor methods
void Screen::CursorHide()
    {
    if (CursorHidden)
        return;

    union REGS regs;

    regs.h.ah = 3;
    regs.h.bh = 0;

    int86(0x10,&regs,&regs);

    CursorShape = regs.x.cx;

    regs.h.ah = 1;
    regs.x.cx = 0x2000;

    int86(0x10,&regs,&regs);

    CursorHidden = 1;
    }

void Screen::CursorUnhide()
    {
    if (!CursorHidden)
        return;

    union REGS regs;

    regs.h.ah = 1;
    regs.x.cx = CursorShape;

    int86(0x10,&regs,&regs);

    CursorHidden = 0;
    }

void Screen::CursorSetPos(unsigned int line, unsigned int col)
    {
    union REGS regs;

    regs.h.ah = 2;
    regs.h.bh = 0;
    regs.h.dh = line;
    regs.h.dl = col;

    int86(0x10,&regs,&regs);
    }

void Screen::CursorGetPos(unsigned int & line, unsigned int & col)
```

```
    {
    union REGS regs;

    regs.h.ah = 3;
    regs.h.bh = 0;

    int86(0x10,&regs,&regs);

    line = regs.h.dh;
    col  = regs.h.dl;
    }

// display a text string method
void Screen::PutStr(unsigned int line, unsigned int col,
                    unsigned char attr, String & str)
    {
    for (unsigned int i = 0; str[i] != '\000'; ++i)
        PutChar(line, col + i, attr, str[i]);
    }




// box display methods
void Screen::DrawBox(unsigned int topLine, unsigned int leftCol,
                     unsigned int btmLine, unsigned int rightCol,
                     unsigned char attr, BoxType typeBox)
    {
    if ((typeBox == BT_NONE) || (leftCol >= rightCol) || (topLine >= btmLine))
        return;

    char v, h;

    switch (typeBox)
        {
        case BT_SINGLE:
            v = '\xB3';
            h = '\xC4';
            PutChar(topLine, leftCol,  attr, '\xDA');
            PutChar(topLine, rightCol, attr, '\xBF');
            PutChar(btmLine, leftCol,  attr, '\xC0');
            PutChar(btmLine, rightCol, attr, '\xD9');
            break;
        case BT_DOUBLE:
            v = '\xBA';
            h = '\xCD';
            PutChar(topLine, leftCol,  attr, '\xC9');
            PutChar(topLine, rightCol, attr, '\xBB');
            PutChar(btmLine, leftCol,  attr, '\xC8');
            PutChar(btmLine, rightCol, attr, '\xBC');
            break;
        case BT_SOLID:
```

```
                    v = '\xDB';
                    h = '\xDB';
                    PutChar(topLine, leftCol,  attr, '\xDB');
                    PutChar(topLine, rightCol,  attr, '\xDB');
                    PutChar(btmLine, leftCol,  attr, '\xDB');
                    PutChar(btmLine, rightCol,  attr, '\xDB');
                }

        for (int c = leftCol + 1; c < rightCol; ++c)
            {
            PutChar(topLine, c, attr, h);
            PutChar(btmLine, c, attr, h);
            }

        for (int l = topLine + 1; l < btmLine; ++l)
            {
            PutChar(l, leftCol,  attr, v);
            PutChar(l, rightCol,  attr, v);
            }
        }


// screen clearing methods
void Screen::Clear()
    {
    for (int l = 0; l < Length; ++l)
        {
        for (int c = 0; c < Width; ++c)
            PutChar(l,c,7,' ');
        }
    }

void Screen::ClearLine(unsigned int line, unsigned int col)
    {
    for (int c = col; c < Width; ++c)
        PutChar(line,c,7,' ');
    }
```

peekpoke.h

```
/*
    Header:    PeekPoke
    Version:   1.01

    Language:  Intel 80x86 Macro Assembler
    Environ:   IBM-PC compatible

    Purpose:   Provides functions to peek and poke values into specific
```

```
                    memory locations.

    Written by: Scott Robert Ladd
*/

/* prototypes */

void Poke(unsigned int segm, unsigned int offs, unsigned int value);

unsigned int Peek(unsigned int segm, unsigned int offs);
```

peekpoke.asm

```
;    Module:     PeekPoke
;    Version:    1.01
;
;    Language:   Intel 80x86 Macro Assembler
;    Environ:    IBM-PC compatible
;
;    Purpose:    Provides functions to peek and poke values into specific
;                memory locations.
;
;    Written by: Scott Robert Ladd

.8086

IFDEF MML
    .MODEL LARGE,C
    %OUT "Large Model"
ELSE
    .MODEL SMALL,C
    %OUT "Small Model"
ENDIF

.CODE

PUBLIC Peek
PUBLIC Poke

Peek        PROC    segm:WORD, offs:WORD

            push    es
            push    si

            mov     ax,segm
            mov     es,ax

            mov     si,offs
```

```
        mov     ax, es:[si]

        pop     si
        pop     es

        ret

Peek    ENDP


Poke    PROC    segm:WORD, offs:WORD, value:WORD

        push    es
        push    di

        mov     ax,segm
        mov     es,ax

        mov     di,offs

        mov     cx,value

        mov     es:[di], cx

        pop     di
        pop     es

        ret

Poke    ENDP


END
```

window.hpp

```
//  Header:     Window  (Window Class)
//  Version:    2.11
//
//  Language:   C++ 2.0
//  Environ:    IBM-PC MS-DOS
//
//  Purpose:    Provides the definition of the stacked Windows module
//
//  Written by: Scott Robert Ladd

#if !defined(__WINDOW_HPP)
```

```
#define __WINDOW_HPP 1

#include "Screen.hpp"
#include "Str.hpp"
#include "WorkList.hpp"

extern "C"
    {
    #include "stddef.h"
    }

class Window
    {
    protected:
        static WorkList  WdwList;
        static Window ** ScrnOwner;
        static int       Initialized;
        static Window *  TopWindow;

        static unsigned int MaxLength;
        static unsigned int MaxWidth;

        unsigned int HomeLine;
        unsigned int HomeCol;
        unsigned int Length;
        unsigned int Width;
        unsigned int CrsLine;
        unsigned int CrsCol;

        unsigned char InsideColor;
        unsigned char BorderColor;

        BoxType Border;

        // header text
        String Header;

        // flags
        int Wrapped;
        int Concealed;

        // buffer for this window
        struct WindowWord
            {
            unsigned char Attribute;
            char Symbol;
            };

        WindowWord * BufferSW;

        // private methods
```

```
    static void FirstTime();

    void Display(int line, int col,
             unsigned char attr, char ch);

    static void Restack();

    void PlotOwnership();

    static void (* ErrorHandler)();

public:
    // constructor
    Window(unsigned int  line, unsigned int  col,
           unsigned int  len,  unsigned int  wid,
           unsigned char iattr, unsigned char battr,
           BoxType bord,
           String & heading, int wrapMode = 0);

    // copy constructor
    Window(const Window & w);

    // assignment operator
    void operator = (const Window & w);

    // destructor
    ~Window();

    // assign an exception handler
    static void SetErrorHandler(void (* userHandler)());

    // paint a window
    void Paint();

    // paint a line
    void PaintLine(unsigned int line);

    // change position
    void Move(unsigned int line, unsigned int col);

    // make this the top window
    void Hoist();

    // conceal this window
    void Conceal();

    // reveal this window
    void Reveal();

    // turn wrap on
    void WrapOn();
```

```
        // turn wrap off
        void WrapOff();

        // change headings
        void SetHead(String & heading);

        // set the cursor position
        void SetCursor(unsigned int line, unsigned int col);

        // get the cursor position
        void GetCursor(unsigned int & line, unsigned int & col);

        // store a character
        void PutChar(unsigned int  line, unsigned int col,
                  unsigned char attr, char c);

        // store a string
        void PutStr(unsigned int line, unsigned int col,
                  unsigned char attr, String & s);

        // clear entire window
        void ClearAll();

        // clear one line of window
        void ClearLine(unsigned int line, unsigned int col = 0);
    };

#endif
```

wdw_main.cpp

```
//   Module:    Wdw_Main  (Window Class main routines)
//   Version:   2.11
//
//   Language:  C++ 2.0
//   Environ:   IBM-PC MS-DOS
//
//   Purpose:   Static member initialization, utility functions and other.
//
//   Written by: Scott Robert Ladd

#include "Screen.hpp"
#include "Str.hpp"
#include "Window.hpp"

extern "C"
```

```
    {
#include "string.h"
#include "stddef.h"
#include "dos.h"
    }

// internal prototype
static void DefaultHandler();

// initialize static class members!

WorkList      Window::WdwList;

Window **     Window::ScrnOwner   = NULL;
int           Window::Initialized = 0;
Window *      Window::TopWindow    = NULL;
unsigned int Window::MaxLength    = 0;
unsigned int Window::MaxWidth     = 0;


// actually display a character
void Window::Display(int line, int col,
                     unsigned char attr, char ch)
    {
    unsigned int rl = line + HomeLine;
    unsigned int rc = col  + HomeCol;

    if ((rl >= MaxLength) || (rc >= MaxWidth))
        return;

    if (this == ScrnOwner[rl * MaxWidth + rc])
        Screen::PutChar(rl,rc,attr,ch);
    }

// restack all windows
void Window::Restack()
    {
    Screen::Clear();

    // clear screen ownership grid
    for (unsigned int l = 0; l < MaxLength; ++l)
        {
        for (unsigned int c = 0; c < MaxWidth; ++c)
            ScrnOwner[l * MaxWidth + c] = NULL;
        }


    // start with the "lowest" window in the list
    WdwList.GoToTail();

    Window * curWdw = (Window *)WdwList.Examine();
```

415

```
    while (curWdw != NULL)
        {
        // plot what a Window owns
        curWdw->PlotOwnership();

        // the paint it
        curWdw->Paint();

        // get the next window
        WdwList.GoPrev();

        curWdw = (Window *)WdwList.Examine();
        }
    }

// plot which screen locations belong to this window
void Window::PlotOwnership()
    {
    unsigned int l, c;

    if (Concealed)
        return;

    // mark locations own by display area of window
    if ((Length == MaxLength) && (Width == MaxWidth))
        {
        for (l = 0; l < Length; ++l)
            for (c = 0; c < Width; ++c)
                ScrnOwner[l * MaxWidth + c] = this;
        }
    else
        {
        for (l = HomeLine; l < HomeLine + Length; ++l)
            for (c = HomeCol; c < HomeCol + Width; ++c)
                if ((l < MaxLength) && (c < MaxWidth))
                    ScrnOwner[l * MaxWidth + c] = this;
        }

    // mark border locations
    if (Border != BT_NONE)
        {
        if (HomeCol > 0)
            {
            if (HomeLine > 0)
                ScrnOwner[(HomeLine - 1) * MaxWidth + (HomeCol - 1)] = this;

            if (Length < MaxLength)
                ScrnOwner[(Length + HomeLine) * MaxWidth + (HomeCol - 1)] = this;
            }
```

```
    if (Width < MaxWidth)
        {
        if (HomeLine > 0)
            ScrnOwner[(HomeLine - 1) * MaxWidth + (Width + HomeCol)] = this;

        if (Length < MaxLength)
            ScrnOwner[(Length + HomeLine) * MaxWidth + (Width + HomeCol)]
                = this;
        }

    if ((HomeLine + Length) < MaxLength)
        {
        for (c = HomeCol; c <= HomeCol + Width; ++c)
            ScrnOwner[(Length + HomeLine) * MaxWidth + c] = this;
        }

    if (HomeLine > 0)
        {
        for (c = HomeCol; c <= HomeCol + Width; ++c)
            ScrnOwner[(HomeLine - 1) * MaxWidth + c] = this;
        }

    if ((HomeCol + Width) < MaxWidth)
        {
        for (l = HomeLine; l <= HomeLine + Length; ++l)
            ScrnOwner[l * MaxWidth + Width + HomeCol] = this;
        }

    if (HomeCol > 0)
        {
        for (l = HomeLine; l <= HomeLine + Length; ++l)
            ScrnOwner[l * MaxWidth + HomeCol - 1] = this;
        }
    }
}
```

wdw_ctdt.cpp

```
// Module:    Wdw_ctdt  (Window Class)
// Version:   2.11
//
// Language:  C++ 2.0
// Environ:   IBM-PC MS-DOS
//
// Purpose:   Constructor / destructor
//
// Written by: Scott Robert Ladd

#include "Str.hpp"
```

```
#include "Window.hpp"

extern "C"
    {
    #include "string.h"
    #include "stddef.h"
    }

// constructor
Window::Window(unsigned int line, unsigned int col,
                unsigned int len,  unsigned int wid,
                unsigned char iattr, unsigned char battr,
                BoxType bord, String & heading, int wrapMode)
    : Header(heading)
    {
    if (!Initialized)
        FirstTime();

    // make sure window is created on the scree
    if ((line > MaxLength) || (col > MaxWidth))
        {
        line = 0;
        col  = 0;
        }

    // set instance variables
    HomeLine = line;
    HomeCol  = col;
    Length   = len;
    Width    = wid;
    CrsLine  = 0;
    CrsCol   = 0;

    InsideColor = iattr;
    BorderColor = battr;

    Border = bord;

    Wrapped   = wrapMode;
    Concealed = 0;

    // no border, no heading
    if (Border == BT_NONE)
        Header = "";

    // add the window to the list
    WdwList.Store(this);

    // allocate buffer to store window contents
    BufferSW = new WindowWord [Length * Width];
```

```
    if (BufferSW == NULL)
        ErrorHandler();

    // make the new window the top window
    TopWindow = this;

    PlotOwnership();

    // clear the window
    ClearAll();

    // and display it
    Paint();
    }

// destructor
Window::~Window()
    {
    // remove window from list
    WdwList.Delete(this);

    // get a new top window
    WdwList.GoToHead();

    TopWindow = (Window *)WdwList.Examine();

    // free buffer space
    delete BufferSW;

    // restack all windows
    Restack();
    return;
    }
```

wdw_copy.cpp

```
// Module:     Wdw_Copy  (Window Class)
// Version:    2.11
//
// Language:   C++ 2.0
// Environ:    IBM-PC MS-DOS
//
// Purpose:    Copy constructor / assignment operator
//
// Written by: Scott Robert Ladd

#include "Str.hpp"
#include "Window.hpp"
```

```
extern "C"
    {
    #include "string.h"
    #include "stdio.h"
    #include "stddef.h"
    #include "dos.h"
    }

// copy constructor
Window::Window(const Window & w) : Header(w.Header)
    {
    // duplicate instance variables
    HomeLine = w.HomeLine;
    HomeCol  = w.HomeCol;
    Length   = w.Length;
    Width    = w.Width;
    CrsLine  = w.CrsLine;
    CrsCol   = w.CrsCol;

    InsideColor = w.InsideColor;
    BorderColor = w.BorderColor;

    Border = w.Border;

    Wrapped   = w.Wrapped;
    Concealed = w.Concealed;

    // allocate a buffer

    BufferSW = new WindowWord [Length * Width];

    if (BufferSW == NULL)
        ErrorHandler();

    // copy existing buffer into new buffer
    for (unsigned int l = 0; l < Length; ++l)
        {
        for (unsigned int c = 0; c < Width; ++c)
            BufferSW[l * Width + c] = w.BufferSW[l * Width + c];
        }

    // add window to list
    WdwList.Store(this);

    // make this the top window
    TopWindow = this;

    // plot what it owns
    PlotOwnership();
```

```
        // display it
        Paint();
        }

// assignment operator
void Window::operator = (const Window & w)
        {
        // free old buffer
        delete BufferSW;

        // copy instance variables
        HomeLine = w.HomeLine;
        HomeCol  = w.HomeCol;
        Length   = w.Length;
        Width    = w.Width;
        CrsLine  = w.CrsLine;
        CrsCol   = w.CrsCol;

        InsideColor = w.InsideColor;
        BorderColor = w.BorderColor;

        Border = w.Border;

        Wrapped   = w.Wrapped;
        Concealed = w.Concealed;

        Header = w.Header;

        // allocate new buffer
        BufferSW = new WindowWord [Length * Width];

        if (BufferSW == NULL)
            ErrorHandler();

        // copy buffer from existing window
        for (unsigned int l = 0; l < Length; ++l)
            {
            for (unsigned int c = 0; c < Width; ++c)
                BufferSW[l * Width + c] = w.BufferSW[l * Width + c];
            }

        // plot what this window owns
        PlotOwnership();

        // paint all windows
        Restack();
        }
```

wdw_disp.cpp

```
//  Module:      Wdw_Disp  (Window Class)
//  Version:     2.11
//
//  Language:    C++ 2.0
//  Environ:     IBM-PC MS-DOS
//
//  Purpose:     Display methods
//
//  Written by: Scott Robert Ladd

#include "Str.hpp"
#include "Window.hpp"

extern "C"
    {
    #include "string.h"
    #include "stdio.h"
    #include "stddef.h"
    #include "dos.h"
    }

// paint entire window
void Window::Paint()
    {
    if (Concealed)
        return;

    unsigned int l, c, hpos;

    // draw border
    switch (Border)
        {
        case BT_SINGLE :
            Display(-1,-1,BorderColor,'\xDA');
            Display(Length,-1,BorderColor,'\xC0');
            Display(Length,Width,BorderColor,'\xD9');
            Display(-1,Width,BorderColor,'\xBF');

            if (Header.Length() == 0)
                for (c = 0; c < Width; ++c)
                    {
                    Display(-1,c,BorderColor,'\xC4');
                    Display(Length,c,BorderColor,'\xC4');
                    }
            else
                {
                hpos = 0;

                for (c = 0; c < Width; ++c)
```

```
            {
            if (hpos < Header.Length())
                {
                Display(-1,c,BorderColor,Header[hpos]);
                ++hpos;
                }
            else
                Display(-1,c,BorderColor,'\xC4');

            Display(Length,c,BorderColor,'\xC4');
            }
        }

    for (l = 0; l < Length; ++l)
        {
        Display(l,-1,BorderColor,'\xB3');
        Display(l,Width,BorderColor,'\xB3');
        }

    break;

case BT_DOUBLE :
    Display(-1,-1,BorderColor,'\xC9');
    Display(Length,-1,BorderColor,'\xC8');
    Display(Length,Width,BorderColor,'\xBC');
    Display(-1,Width,BorderColor,'\xBB');

    if (Header.Length() == 0)
        for (c = 0; c < Width; ++c)
            {
            Display(-1,c,BorderColor,'\xCD');
            Display(Length,c,BorderColor,'\xCD');
            }
    else
        {
        hpos = 0;

        for (c = 0; c < Width; ++c)
            {
            if (hpos < Header.Length())
                {
                Display(-1,c,BorderColor,Header[hpos]);
                ++hpos;
                }
            else
                Display(-1,c,BorderColor,'\xCD');

            Display(Length,c,BorderColor,'\xCD');
            }
        }
```

```
                for (1 = 0; 1 < Length; ++1)
                        {
                        Display(1,-1,BorderColor,'\xBA');
                        Display(1,Width,BorderColor,'\xBA');
                        }
            }

    unsigned int pos;

    // display each character in buffer
    for (1 = 0; 1 < Length; ++1)
        for (c = 0; c < Width; ++c)
            {
            pos = 1 * Width + c;
            Display(1, c, BufferSW[pos].Attribute, BufferSW[pos].Symbol);
            }

    // set the cursor position
    SetCursor(CrsLine, CrsCol);
    }

// paint one line
void Window::PaintLine(unsigned int line)
    {
    if ((Concealed) || (line > Length))
        return;

    unsigned int pos;

    // draw just one line of contents
    for (unsigned int c = 0; c < Width; ++c)
        {
        pos = line * Width + c;
        Display(line, c, BufferSW[pos].Attribute, BufferSW[pos].Symbol);
        }
    }

// store a character in the window
void Window::PutChar(unsigned int line, unsigned int col,
                    unsigned char attr, char ch)
    {
    if ((line >= Length) || (col >= Width))
        return;

    unsigned int pos = line * Width + col;

    // store the character...
    BufferSW[pos].Symbol = ch;

    // ... and its attribute
    if (attr != 0)
```

```
        BufferSW[pos].Attribute = attr;
    else
        BufferSW[pos].Attribute = InsideColor;
    }

// store a string in the window
void Window::PutStr(unsigned int line, unsigned int col,
                    unsigned char attr, String & s)
    {
    if ((line >= Length) || (col >= Width))
        return;

    if (attr == 0)
        attr = InsideColor;

    unsigned char l = line;
    unsigned char c = col;

    unsigned int spos = 0;
    unsigned int wpos;

    // display text
    while (s[spos] != '\x00')
        {
        wpos = l * Width + c;

        BufferSW[wpos].Symbol    = s[spos];
        BufferSW[wpos].Attribute = attr;

        if (c == (Width - 1))
            {
            if (!Wrapped)
                return;

            if (l < Length)
                {
                c = 0;
                ++l;
                }
            else
                return;
            }
        else
            ++c;

        ++spos;
        }
    }
```

wdw_misc.cpp

```
//  Module:      Wdw_Misc  (Window Class)
//  Version:     2.11
//
//  Language:    C++ 2.0
//  Environ:     IBM-PC MS-DOS
//
//  Purpose:     Miscellaneous methods
//
//  Written by:  Scott Robert Ladd

#include "Screen.hpp"
#include "Str.hpp"
#include "Window.hpp"

extern "C"
    {
    #include "string.h"
    #include "stddef.h"
    #include "dos.h"
    }

// change position
void Window::Move(unsigned int line, unsigned int col)
    {
    if ((line > MaxLength) || (col > MaxWidth))
        return;

    // set new window position
    HomeLine = line;
    HomeCol  = col;

    // redisplay all windows
    Restack();
    }

// make this the top window
void Window::Hoist()
    {
    // delete window from list
    WdwList.Delete(this);

    // add it to the list (making it the top window)!
    WdwList.Store(this);

    TopWindow = this;

    // redisplay all windows
    Restack();
    }
```

```
// conceal this window
void Window::Conceal()
    {
    Concealed = 0;

    Restack();
    }

// reveal this window
void Window::Reveal()
    {
    Concealed = 0;

    Restack();
    }

// turn wrap on
void Window::WrapOn()
    {
    Wrapped = 1;
    }

// turn wrap off
void Window::WrapOff()
    {
    Wrapped = 0;
    }

// set the heading
void Window::SetHead(String & heading)
    {
    if (Border == BT_NONE)
        return;

    unsigned int c, hpos;
    char bordchar;

    // pick border charatater
    if (Border == BT_SINGLE)
        bordchar = 0xC4;
    else
        bordchar = 0xCD;

    Header = heading;

    // no header, fill in border
    if (Header.Length() == 0)
        {
        for (c = 0; c < Width; ++c)
```

```
            Display(-1,c,BorderColor,bordchar);

        return;
        }

    hpos = 0;

    // display header and border fragment
    for (c = 0; c < Width; ++c)
        if (hpos < Header.Length())
            {
            Display(-1,c,BorderColor,Header[hpos]);
            ++hpos;
            }
        else
            Display(-1,c,BorderColor,bordchar);
    }

// set the cursor position
void Window::SetCursor(unsigned int line, unsigned int col)
    {
    // cursor can only be positioned within top window
    if ((line > Length) || (col > Width) || (this != TopWindow))
        return;

    unsigned char newl = line + HomeLine;
    unsigned char newc = col  + HomeCol;

    if ((newl > MaxLength) || (newc > MaxWidth))
        return;

    CrsLine = line;
    CrsCol  = col;

    // physically set cursor position
    Screen::CursorSetPos(newl, newc);
    }

// get the cursor position
void Window::GetCursor(unsigned int & line, unsigned int & col)
    {
    line = CrsLine;
    col  = CrsCol;
    }

// clear the entire window
void Window::ClearAll()
    {
    unsigned int pos = 0;

    for (unsigned char l = 0; l < Length; ++l)
```

```
        {
        for (unsigned char c = 0; c < Width; ++c)
            {
            BufferSW[pos].Symbol    = ' ';
            BufferSW[pos].Attribute = InsideColor;

            ++pos;
            }
        }
    }

// clear one line of the window
void Window::ClearLine(unsigned int line, unsigned int col)
    {
    unsigned int pos;

    for (unsigned char c = col; c < Width; ++c)
        {
        pos = line * Width + c;

        BufferSW[pos].Symbol    = ' ';
        BufferSW[pos].Attribute = InsideColor;
        }
    }
```

wdw_err.cpp

```
//  Module:     Wdw_Err  (Window Class main routines)
//  Version:    2.11
//
//  Language:   C++ 2.0
//  Environ:    IBM-PC MS-DOS
//
//  Purpose:    Error handler and first-time initialization
//
//  Written by: Scott Robert Ladd

#include "Screen.hpp"
#include "Window.hpp"

extern "C"
    {
    #include "stdio.h"
    #include "stdlib.h"
    }

// internal prototype
static void DefaultHandler();
```

```
void (* Window::ErrorHandler)() = DefaultHandler;

// default exception handler
static void DefaultHandler()
    {
    puts("\aWindow Error: allocation failure\n");
    }

// assign an exception handler
void Window::SetErrorHandler(void (* userHandler)())
    {
    ErrorHandler = userHandler;
    }

// first time initialization function
void Window::FirstTime()
    {
    Initialized = 1;

    // obtain screen dimensions
    Screen::Dimensions(MaxWidth, MaxLength);

    unsigned int area = MaxLength * MaxWidth;

    // using malloc due to bug in cfront
    ScrnOwner = (Window **)malloc(area * sizeof(Window *));

    if (ScrnOwner == NULL)
        ErrorHandler();

    // clear the ownership array
    for (unsigned int l = 0; l < MaxLength; ++l)
        {
        for (unsigned int c = 0; c < MaxWidth; ++c)
            ScrnOwner[l * MaxWidth + c] = NULL;
        }
    }
```

Chapter 14

creature.hpp

```
// Header:      Creature
// Version:     2.00
//
// Language:    C++ 2.0
// Environ:     MS-DOS, Zortech C++ v2.0x
//
// Purpose:     SIMECO Creature class definition
//
// Written by: Scott Robert Ladd

#if !defined(__CREATURE_HPP)
#define __CREATURE_HPP 1

#include "WorkList.hpp"

class Creature
    {
    protected:
        unsigned char Color;      // this Creature's color

        int Energy;               // current energy level
        int Age;                  // current age
        int AgeRep;               // age since last reproduction

        int PosX, PosY;           // horizontal position on screen

    public:
        // public list of all creatures
        static WorkList CList;    // list of all creatures in existence

        // constructor
        Creature(unsigned char c, int e, int x, int y);

        // ask creature to perform an action
        virtual int Move() = 0;

        // tell creature to draw itself
        virtual void Draw() = 0;

        // tell creature to erase itself
        virtual void Erase() = 0;
    };

#endif
```

creature.cpp

```
//  Program:     Creature
//  Version:     2.00
//
//  Language:    C++ 2.0
//  Environ:     MS-DOS, Zortech C++ v2.0x
//
//  Purpose:     SIMECO Creature class definition
//
//  Written by: Scott Robert Ladd

extern "C"
    {
    #include "stdio.h"
    #include "stdlib.h"
    }

#include "Creature.hpp"

// initialize static members
WorkList Creature::CList;

// constructor
Creature::Creature(unsigned char c, int e, int x, int y)
    {
    // set values of members
    Color  = c;
    Energy = e;
    Age    = 0;
    AgeRep = 0;
    PosX   = x;
    PosY   = y;

    // add creature to creature list
    if (CList.Store(this))
        {
        printf("Error: Creature cannot be added to list\n");
        exit(0);
        }
    }
```

grazer.hpp

```
//  Header:     Grazer
//  Version:    2.00
//
//  Language:   C++ 2.0
//  Environ:    MS-DOS, Zortech C++ v2.0x
//
//  Purpose:    SIMECO Grazer class definition
//
//  Written by: Scott Robert Ladd

#if !defined(__GRAZER_HPP)
#define __GRAZER_HPP 1

#include "Creature.hpp"
#include "BitGrid.hpp"

class Grazer : public Creature
    {
    protected:
        unsigned char Movement[8];  // chance of movement in a given direction
        unsigned char MoveCount;    // sum of values in Movement[]

        unsigned char Sense;        // distance at which food is sensed

        static int Count;           // number of living grazers

        static int MaxEnergy;       // maximum energy
        static int MaxAge;          // maximum age
        static int MaxSense;        // maximum sense value
        static int ReproAge;        // age at which a Grazer can reproduce
        static int RepEnergy;       // energy required for reproduction
        static int FoodValue;       // energy obtained from eating food

        static int NoMoveGenes;     // number of movement genes

        static int MoveTable[8][2]; // class-global table of movements

        static BitGrid *FoodSupply; // pointer to supply of food for grazers

        static int MaxX;            // maximum X dimension for Grazer
        static int MaxY;            // maximum Y dimension for Grazer

    public:
        // basic constructor
        Grazer(int x, int y);

        // copy constructor (used in birth of a new Grazer)
        Grazer(const Grazer & G);

        // destructor
        ~Grazer();

        // retrieve number of living grazers
        static int Population()
```

```
            {
            return Count;
            }

        // set food supply and area dimensions
        static void SetRegion(BitGrid * food, int xmax, int ymax);

        // ask grazer to do something
        virtual int Move();

        // tell grazer to draw itself
        virtual void Draw();

        // tell grazer to erase itself
        virtual void Erase();
    };

#endif
```

grazer.cpp

```
//  Header:      Grazer
//  Version:     2.00
//
//  Language:    C++ 2.0
//  Environ:     MS-DOS, Zortech C++ v2.0x
//
//  Purpose:     SIMECO Grazer class definition
//
//  Written by:  Scott Robert Ladd

// include class definition
#include "Grazer.hpp"

// include C library headers
extern "C"
    {
    #include "stdio.h"
    #include "stdlib.h"
    #include "graphvga.h"
    }

// this macro returns a random number between 1 and n
#define RandVal(n) ((rand() % n) + 1)

// initialize the static members of Grazer class
int Grazer::Count       =    0;
int Grazer::MaxEnergy   = 3000;
int Grazer::MaxAge      =  300;
int Grazer::MaxSense    =    3;
int Grazer::ReproAge    =  100;
```

```
int Grazer::RepEnergy   = 2000;
int Grazer::FoodValue   =  150;
int Grazer::NoMoveGenes =    8;

int Grazer::MoveTable[8][2] =
    { {-3, -3}, { 0, -3}, { 3, -3},
      {-3,  0},           { 3,  0},
      {-3,  3}, { 0,  3}, { 3,  3} };

// globals defining area which grazers live in
BitGrid * Grazer::FoodSupply = NULL;

int Grazer::MaxX = 0;
int Grazer::MaxY = 0;

// basic constructor for a new creature
Grazer::Grazer(int x, int y)
    : Creature(15,1500,x,y)
    {
    for (int i = 0; i < NoMoveGenes; ++ i)
        Movement[i] = 1;

    MoveCount = NoMoveGenes;

    Sense = 0;

    ++Count;

    Draw();
    }

// copy constructor
Grazer::Grazer(const Grazer & G)
    : Creature(15,G.Energy,G.PosX,G.PosY)
    {
    for (int i = 0; i < NoMoveGenes; ++i)
        Movement[i] = G.Movement[i];

    MoveCount = G.MoveCount;

    Sense = G.Sense;

    int choice = RandVal(10);

    switch (choice)
        {
        case 1: // modify movement genes
        case 2:
        case 3:
            int move = RandVal(NoMoveGenes) - 1;
```

```
                if (1 == RandVal(2))
                    {
                    if (Movement[move] == 1)
                        {
                        ++Movement[move];
                        ++MoveCount;
                        }
                    }
                else
                    {
                    if (Movement[move] == 2)
                        {
                        --Movement[move];
                        --MoveCount;
                        }
                    }
                break;

            case 4: // modify sense value
                if (1 == RandVal(2))
                    {
                    if (Sense < MaxSense)
                        ++Sense;
                    }
                else
                    {
                    if (Sense > 0)
                        --Sense;
                    }
            }

    ++Count;

    Draw();
    }

// destructor
Grazer::~Grazer()
    {
    if (CList.Delete(this))
        {
        printf("Error: Creature cannot be deleted from list\n");
        exit(0);
        }

    Erase();

    --Count;
    }

// set food supply and area dimensions
```

```
void Grazer::SetRegion(BitGrid * food, int xmax, int ymax)
    {
    FoodSupply = food;

    MaxX = xmax;
    MaxY = ymax;
    }

// ask grazer to do something
int Grazer::Move()
    {
    ++Age;
    ++AgeRep;

    if ((AgeRep >= ReproAge) && (Energy >= RepEnergy))
        {
        AgeRep = 0;

        Energy /= 2;

        Grazer * newG = new Grazer(*this);

        if (newG == NULL)
            {
            printf("Error! Grazer Repro\n");
            exit(1);
            }
        }

    int i, x, y, newx, newy, m, weight, move;

    if (Sense > 0)
        {
        int move_value, j, ix, iy;

        int hi_value = -1;

        move = 0;

        for (i = 0; i < NoMoveGenes; ++i)
            {
            move_value = 0;

            x = PosX;
            y = PosY;

            for (j = 0; j < Sense; ++j)
                {
                x += MoveTable[i][0];
                y += MoveTable[i][1];
```

```
            if (x < 1) x = MaxX;
            if (x > MaxX) x = 1;
            if (y < 1) y = MaxY;
            if (y > MaxY) y = 1;

            for (ix = x - 1; ix <= x + 1; ++ix)
                for (iy = y - 1; iy <= y + 1; ++iy)
                    if (FoodSupply->IsSet(ix,iy))
                        ++move_value;
            }

        if (move_value > hi_value)
            {
            hi_value = move_value;
            move = i;
            }
        else
            if ((move_value == hi_value) && (Movement[i] >= Movement[move]))
                if ((Movement[i] > Movement[move]) || (RandVal(2) == 1))
                    move = i;
        }
    }
else
    {
    weight = Movement[0];
    m      = RandVal(MoveCount);

    move =  0;

    while (m > weight)
        {
        ++move;
        weight += Movement[move];
        }
    }

if ((move == 0) || (move == 2) || (move == 5) || (move == 7))
    Energy -= 5;
else
    Energy -= 3;

// did it die?
if ((Age == MaxAge) || (Energy <= 0))
    return 1;

newx = PosX + MoveTable[move][0];
newy = PosY + MoveTable[move][1];

Erase();

PosX = newx;
```

```
    PosY = newy;

    if (PosX < 1) PosX = MaxX;
    if (PosX > MaxX) PosX = 1;
    if (PosY < 1) PosY = MaxY;
    if (PosY > MaxY) PosY = 1;

    for (x = PosX - 1; x <= PosX + 1; ++x)
        for (y = PosY - 1; y <= PosY + 1; ++y)
            if (FoodSupply->IsSet(x,y))
                {
                Energy += FoodValue;
                FoodSupply->Exclude(x,y);
                }

    Draw();

    return 0;
    }

// tell grazer to draw itself
void Grazer::Draw()
    {
    for (int x = PosX - 1; x <= PosX + 1; ++x)
        for (int y = PosY - 1; y <= PosY + 1; ++y)
            PlotPixel(x,y,Color);
    }

// tell grazer to erase itself
void Grazer::Erase()
    {
    for (int x = PosX - 1; x <= PosX + 1; ++x)
        for (int y = PosY - 1; y <= PosY + 1; ++y)
            PlotPixel(x,y,0);
    }
```

ecosys.cpp

```
//    Program:    SimEco    (Simulated Ecosystem)
//    Version:    2.00
//
//    Language:   C++ 2.0
//    Environ:    MS-DOS, Zortech C++ v2.0x
//
//    Purpose:    This program simulates a primitive ecosystem.
//
//    Written by: Scott Robert Ladd
```

```
// include standard C libraries
extern "C"
    {
    #include "conio.h"
    #include "time.h"
    #include "stdio.h"
    #include "stdlib.h"
    #include "graphvga.h"
    }

// this macro returns a random number between 1 and n
#define RandVal(n) ((rand() % n) + 1)

// include C++ classes
#include "Creature.hpp"
#include "Grazer.hpp"
#include "BitGrid.hpp"

// These definitions change how food is distributed
// #define GARDEN 1
#define NORMAL_FOOD 1
#define NEW_FOOD 2

// constants which define the size of the grid array
const int MaxX = 630;
const int MaxY = 450;

// global data items
BitGrid * GrazerFood;

// function prototypes
int  Initialize();
void LifeCycle();
void cdecl Finish();
int  main();

int Initialize()
    {
    GraphInit();

    // set function to be called at exit
    if (atexit(Finish))
        return 1;

    srand(unsigned(time(NULL)));

    GrazerFood = new BitGrid (630, 450);

    Grazer::SetRegion(GrazerFood, MaxX, MaxY);

    Grazer * G;
```

```
    int i, x, y;

    for (i = 0; i < 40; ++i)
        {
        x = RandVal(MaxX);
        y = RandVal(MaxY);

        G = new Grazer(x,y);

        if (G == NULL)
            {
            printf("Error: Init Grazers\n");
            return 2;
            }
        }

    for (i = 0; i < 4000; ++i)
        {
        do {
            x = RandVal(MaxX);
            y = RandVal(MaxY);
            }
        while (GrazerFood->IsSet(x,y));

        GrazerFood->Include(x,y);

        PlotPixel(x,y,14);
        }

    return 0;
    }

void LifeCycle()
    {
    Creature * C;
    unsigned long move;
    char stat_line[20];
    int x, y, i;

    move = 0L;

    while ((Grazer::Population() > 0) && !kbhit())
        {
        Creature::CList.GoToHead();

        while (1)
            {
            C = Creature::CList.Examine();

            if (NULL == C)
                break;
```

```
            Creature::CList.GoNext();

            if (C->Move())
                delete (Grazer *)C;
            }

        for (i = 0; i < NEW_FOOD; ++i)
            {
            #if defined(GARDEN)
                do  {
                    x = RandVal(100) + 270;
                    y = RandVal(100) + 175;
                    }
                while (GrazerFood->IsSet(x,y));

                GrazerFood->Include(x,y);

                PlotPixel(x,y,14);
            #endif

            #if defined(NORMAL_FOOD)
                do  {
                    x = RandVal(MaxX);
                    y = RandVal(MaxY);
                    }
                while (GrazerFood->IsSet(x,y));

                GrazerFood->Include(x,y);

                PlotPixel(x,y,14);
            #endif
            }

        ++move;

        sprintf(stat_line,"M: %6ld, C: %3d",move,Grazer::Population());

        PutGraphString(465,10,stat_line,15,0);
        }
    }

void cdecl Finish()
    {
    while (!kbhit()) ;

    if (!getch()) getch();

    GraphDone();
    }
```

```
int main()
    {
    if (Initialize())
        return 1;

    LifeCycle();

    return 0;
    }
```

The GraphVGA Library

The *GraphVGA* library provides simple graphics routines for working with IBM-compatible VGA displays in 640 by 480 mode (with 16 colors). *GraphVGA* is written in C, and it can be linked to C++ programs if type-safe linkage (see Chapter 3) is employed. The *EcoSys* program described in Chapter Fourteen uses the *GraphVGA* library.

Since the focus of this book is on C++ programming, and not on VGA graphics, I won't be giving a complete description of how *GraphVGA* works. If you need to convert *GraphVGA* to work with a non-VGA display and video adapter, or you simply wish to better understand how *GraphVGA* works, I'd suggest that you purchase *Graphics Programming in C* (M&T Books, 1989).

Listing 1 is *graphvga.h*, and Listing 2 is *graphvga.c*. Type-safe linkage instructions are already built-in to *graphvga.h*. These files were designed to be compiled with Zortech C++ 2.07; if you have another C++ compiler, you may need to make some changes. In particular, the *outport* and *outportb* functions are named *outpw* and *outp* in Microsoft C (which is used by many MS-DOS C++ translators).

Listing 1

```
/*
    Header:     GraphVGA
    Version     2.00

    Language:   ANSI C w/MS-DOS extensions
    Environ:    IBM-PC compatibles w/VGA

    Purpose:    A library of routines for use with VGA cards in 640 by 480
                16 color mode.

    Written by: Scott Robert Ladd
*/

#if !defined(__GRAPHVGA_H)
#define __GRAPHVGA_H 1

#define PXL_SET  0
#define PXL_AND  1
#define PXL_OR   2
#define PXL_XOR  3

void GraphInit(void);
void GraphDone(void);

int  SetPixelMode(int PixMode);

void PlotPixel(int x, int y, int color);
int  ReadPixel(int x, int y);

void PutGraphChar(int X, int Y, char Ch, int ColorF, int ColorB);

void PutGraphString(int X, int Y, char * Str, int ColorF, int ColorB);

#endif
```

Listing 2

```
/*
    Header:     GraphVGA
    Version     2.00

    Language:   ANSI C w/MS-DOS extensions
    Environ:    IBM-PC compatibles w/VGA

    Purpose:    A library of routines for use with VGA cards in 640 by 480
                16 color mode.

    Written by: Scott Robert Ladd
*/

#include "conio.h"
#include "dos.h"
#include "graphvga.h"

static const unsigned int VideoSeg = 0xA000;

static unsigned char OriginalMode = 0;

static int PixelMode = PXL_SET;

static int Inited = 0;

/* define the character set being used */
unsigned char CharSet[128][8] =
    {
    0, 0, 0, 0, 0, 0, 0, 0,
    0, 126, 129, 165, 129, 165, 153, 126,
    0, 0, 0, 0, 0, 0, 0, 0,
    0, 0, 0, 0, 0, 0, 0, 0,
    0, 0, 0, 0, 0, 0, 0, 0,
    0, 0, 0, 0, 0, 0, 0, 0,
    0, 0, 0, 0, 0, 0, 0, 0,
    0, 0, 0, 0, 0, 0, 0, 0,
    0, 0, 0, 0, 0, 0, 0, 0,
    0, 0, 0, 0, 0, 0, 0, 0,
    0, 0, 0, 0, 0, 0, 0, 0,
    0, 0, 0, 0, 0, 0, 0, 0,
    0, 0, 0, 0, 0, 0, 0, 0,
    0, 64, 64, 68, 66, 127, 2, 4,
    0, 0, 0, 0, 0, 0, 0, 0,
    0, 0, 0, 0, 0, 0, 0, 0,
    0, 0, 0, 0, 0, 0, 0, 0,
    0, 0, 0, 0, 0, 0, 0, 0,
    0, 0, 0, 0, 0, 0, 0, 0,
    0, 0, 0, 0, 0, 0, 0, 0,
```

```
0, 0, 0, 0, 0, 0, 0, 0,
0, 0, 0, 0, 0, 0, 0, 0,
0, 0, 0, 0, 0, 0, 0, 0,
0, 0, 0, 0, 0, 0, 0, 0,
0, 0, 0, 0, 0, 0, 0, 0,
0, 0, 0, 0, 0, 0, 0, 0,
0, 0, 0, 0, 0, 0, 0, 0,
0, 0, 0, 0, 0, 0, 0, 0,
0, 0, 0, 0, 0, 0, 0, 0,
0, 0, 0, 0, 0, 0, 0, 0,
0, 0, 0, 0, 0, 0, 0, 0,
0, 0, 0, 0, 0, 0, 0, 0,
0, 0, 0, 0, 0, 0, 0, 0,
0, 8, 8, 8, 8, 8, 0, 8,
0, 54, 54, 36, 0, 0, 0, 0,
0, 0, 36, 126, 36, 126, 36, 0,
0, 8, 62, 9, 62, 72, 62, 8,
0, 67, 35, 16, 8, 4, 98, 97,
0, 0, 0, 0, 0, 0, 0, 0,
0, 48, 32, 16, 0, 0, 0, 0,
0, 32, 16, 8, 8, 8, 16, 32,
0, 4, 8, 16, 16, 16, 8, 4,
0, 0, 42, 28, 127, 28, 42, 0,
0, 0, 8, 8, 127, 8, 8, 0,
0, 0, 0, 0, 0, 24, 16, 8,
0, 0, 0, 0, 126, 0, 0, 0,
0, 0, 0, 0, 0, 0, 24, 24,
0, 64, 32, 16, 8, 4, 2, 1,
0, 126, 97, 81, 73, 69, 67, 63,
0, 8, 12, 10, 8, 8, 8, 62,
0, 62, 65, 64, 48, 12, 2, 127,
0, 62, 65, 64, 60, 64, 65, 62,
0, 56, 36, 34, 33, 127, 32, 32,
0, 127, 1, 1, 63, 64, 64, 63,
0, 62, 65, 1, 63, 65, 65, 62,
0, 127, 64, 32, 16, 8, 8, 8,
0, 62, 65, 65, 62, 65, 65, 62,
0, 62, 65, 65, 126, 64, 65, 62,
0, 0, 0, 24, 24, 0, 24, 24,
0, 0, 24, 24, 0, 24, 16, 8,
0, 48, 8, 4, 2, 4, 8, 48,
0, 0, 0, 126, 0, 126, 0, 0,
0, 6, 8, 16, 32, 16, 8, 6,
0, 62, 65, 32, 16, 8, 0, 8,
0, 62, 64, 95, 81, 81, 81, 126,
0, 8, 20, 34, 65, 127, 65, 65,
0, 63, 65, 65, 63, 65, 65, 63,
0, 62, 65, 1, 1, 1, 65, 62,
0, 63, 65, 65, 65, 65, 65, 63,
0, 127, 1, 1, 31, 1, 1, 127,
0, 127, 1, 1, 31, 1, 1, 1,
```

```
0, 62, 65, 1, 1, 121, 65, 62,
0, 65, 65, 65, 127, 65, 65, 65,
0, 62, 8, 8, 8, 8, 8, 62,
0, 64, 64, 64, 64, 65, 65, 62,
0, 33, 17, 9, 15, 17, 33, 65,
0, 1, 1, 1, 1, 1, 1, 127,
0, 65, 99, 85, 73, 65, 65, 65,
0, 65, 67, 69, 73, 81, 97, 65,
0, 62, 65, 65, 65, 65, 65, 62,
0, 63, 65, 65, 63, 1, 1, 1,
0, 62, 65, 65, 65, 81, 97, 126,
0, 63, 65, 65, 63, 17, 33, 65,
0, 62, 65, 1, 62, 64, 65, 62,
0, 127, 8, 8, 8, 8, 8, 8,
0, 65, 65, 65, 65, 65, 65, 62,
0, 65, 65, 65, 65, 34, 20, 8,
0, 65, 65, 65, 65, 73, 85, 34,
0, 65, 34, 20, 8, 20, 34, 65,
0, 65, 34, 20, 8, 8, 8, 8,
0, 127, 32, 16, 8, 4, 2, 127,
0, 62, 2, 2, 2, 2, 2, 62,
0, 1, 2, 4, 8, 16, 32, 64,
0, 62, 32, 32, 32, 32, 32, 62,
0, 8, 20, 34, 0, 0, 0, 0,
0, 0, 0, 0, 0, 0, 0, 255,
0, 12, 4, 8, 0, 0, 0, 0,
0, 0, 0, 8, 20, 34, 127, 65,
0, 0, 0, 63, 65, 63, 65, 63,
0, 0, 0, 62, 65, 1, 65, 62,
0, 0, 0, 63, 65, 65, 65, 63,
0, 0, 0, 127, 1, 31, 1, 127,
0, 0, 0, 127, 1, 31, 1, 1,
0, 0, 0, 126, 1, 113, 65, 126,
0, 0, 0, 65, 65, 127, 65, 65,
0, 0, 0, 62, 8, 8, 8, 62,
0, 0, 0, 224, 64, 65, 65, 62,
0, 0, 0, 33, 17, 15, 17, 33,
0, 0, 0, 1, 1, 1, 1, 127,
0, 0, 0, 65, 99, 85, 73, 65,
0, 0, 0, 67, 69, 73, 81, 97,
0, 0, 0, 62, 65, 65, 65, 62,
0, 0, 0, 63, 65, 63, 1, 1,
0, 0, 0, 62, 65, 81, 97, 126,
0, 0, 0, 63, 65, 63, 17, 33,
0, 0, 0, 62, 1, 62, 64, 62,
0, 0, 0, 127, 8, 8, 8, 8,
0, 0, 0, 65, 65, 65, 65, 62,
0, 0, 0, 65, 65, 34, 20, 8,
0, 0, 0, 65, 65, 73, 85, 34,
0, 0, 0, 65, 34, 28, 34, 65,
0, 0, 0, 65, 34, 20, 8, 8,
```

```
    0, 0, 0, 126, 32, 24, 4, 126,
    0, 0, 0, 0, 0, 0, 0, 0,
    0, 8, 8, 8, 0, 8, 8, 8,
    0, 0, 0, 0, 0, 0, 0, 0,
    0, 0, 76, 50, 0, 0, 0, 0,
    0, 0, 0, 0, 0, 0, 0, 0
    };

void GraphInit(void)
    {
    union REGS regs;

    regs.h.ah = 0x0F;
    int86(0x10,&regs,&regs);
    OriginalMode = regs.h.al;

    regs.h.ah = 0;
    regs.h.al = 0x12;
    int86(0x10,&regs,&regs);

    Inited = 1;
    }


void GraphDone(void)
    {
    union REGS regs;

    if (!Inited)
        return;

    regs.h.ah = 0;
    regs.h.al = OriginalMode;
    int86(0x10,&regs,&regs);
    }

int SetPixelMode(int pixMode)
    {
    if ((pixMode < PXL_SET) || (pixMode > PXL_XOR))
        return 1;

    PixelMode = pixMode;

    return 0;
    }

void PlotPixel(int x, int y, int color)
    {
    unsigned char pixel_mask;
    volatile unsigned char dummy;
    unsigned char far * pixel_byte;
```

```
    /* find the byte containing our pixel */
    pixel_byte = MK_FP(VideoSeg, (y * 80) + (x >> 3));

    /* set up mask */
    pixel_mask = (char)(0x80 >> (x & 7));

    /* set-up video controller */
    outp(0x03CE, 8);
    outp(0x03CF, pixel_mask);

    outp(0x03CE, 3);
    outp(0x03CF, (char)(PixelMode << 3));

    outp(0x03C4, 2);
    outp(0x03C5, 0x0F);

    /* do a dummy read to load latches */
    dummy = *pixel_byte;

    /* clear latches */
    *pixel_byte = 0;

    /* set bit planes */
    outp(0x03C4, 2);
    outp(0x03C5, (char)color);

    *pixel_byte = 0xFF;

    /* finish up */
    outp(0x03C4, 2);
    outp(0x03C5, 0x0F);

    outp(0x03CE, 3);
    outp(0x03CF, 0);

    outp(0x03CE, 8);
    outp(0x03CF, 0xFF);
    }

int ReadPixel(int x, int y)
    {
    char i;
    int color = 0;
    unsigned int pixel_mask;
    unsigned char far * pixel_byte;

    /* find the byte containing our pixel */
    pixel_byte = MK_FP(VideoSeg, (y * 80 + (x >> 3)));

    /* set up mask */
```

```
    pixel_mask = 0x80 >> (x & 7);

    /* read the color bits */
    for (i = 0; i < 4; ++i)
        {
        outp(0x3CE, 4);
        outp(0x3CF, i);

        outp(0x3CE, 5);
        outp(0x3CF, 0);

        if (*pixel_byte & pixel_mask)
            color |= 1 << i;
        }

    return color;
    }

void PutGraphChar(int x, int y, char ch, int colorF, int colorB)
    {
    int xi, yi;

    if (ch < 0) return;

    for (xi = 0; xi < 8; ++xi)
        for (yi = 0; yi < 8; ++yi)
            if (CharSet[ch][xi] & (1 << yi))
                PlotPixel(y + yi, x + xi, colorF);
            else
                PlotPixel(y + yi, x + xi, colorB);
    }

void PutGraphString(int x, int y, char * str, int colorF, int colorB)
    {
    char * ch = str;

    while (*ch)
        {
        PutGraphChar(x, y, *ch, colorF, colorB);
            ++ch;
        y += 8;
        }
    }
```

Other Object-Oriented Programming Languages

C++ isn't the only object-oriented programming language available. While you may never work with any of these other languages, it can be helpful to know that alternatives exist. I'll begin by discussing the different types of object-oriented programming languages.

Object-Oriented Language Types

There are two approaches to creating an object-oriented programming language. A pure object-oriented language is designed as object-oriented from the keel up. These languages tend to have lexical and logical constructs very different from those found in traditional structured languages. The other approach is the hybrid approach, which adds object-oriented capabilities to an existing language. The first truly object-oriented language, Simula, was a hybrid based on Algol.

There is heated debate as to which approach, pure or hybrid, is best. Many object-oriented purists frown upon hybrid languages as "kludges" which do not enforce the object-oriented paradigm. Advocates of hybrid languages point out that pure languages take longer to learn and have performance problems. From an open-minded standpoint, both types of languages have their pluses and minuses.

The pure languages tend to be interpreted, which makes them more flexible than their hybrid cousins, which usually compile programs into native machine code. You can play with an interpreted language, watching to see what happens as you test ideas and their variants. Late binding (essential to polymorphism) is easier to implement in an interpreted language than it is in a hybrid one, although the reverse is true of early binding.

Interpreted programs are easy to debug; when a problem shows up, you merely fix the problem and start over again. On the other hand, interpreted programs are slower than compiled ones. Also, interpreted programs must be distributed in source code format; compiled programs can be sent out as executable code. In a competitive marketplace, it is not a good idea to distribute the source code for your applications.

Pure languages force the programmer to use object-oriented techniques; hybrid languages allow other paradigms to be used. The greater conceptual scope of hybrid languages tends to make them popular with power programmers. Supporters of the pure approach, however, can validly point out that the hybrid capability dilutes the effectiveness of the object-oriented paradigm. Programs written in hybrid languages often fail to use object-oriented capabilities to their fullest. And many hybrid languages have non-object-oriented features which can confuse someone new to the paradigm.

Smalltalk

Smalltalk is the premiere object-oriented language. Designed at Xerox's Palo Alto Research Center (PARC), Smalltalk epitomizes the object-oriented paradigm. It is not just a programming language; it is an entire environment. This environment has had an important impact on the computing industry. For example, the Macintosh interface is loosely based on ideas Steve Jobs picked up while at PARC.

The Smalltalk environment itself is object-oriented, with windows, pull-down and pop-up menus, and dozens of other facilities designed in. The syntax of Smalltalk expresses object-oriented concepts very clearly. In addition, the source for the classes which make up the environment is included. This not only provides excellent examples of how to program in an object-oriented way, it also gives the programmer a set of pre-designed classes from which programs can be built.

As with most pure object-oriented languages, Smalltalk programs are interpreted. This makes the language very flexible, but also limits its utility for commercial projects. A Smalltalk program must be run from within the environment, and therefore the portability of a Smalltalk application is limited to those hardware platforms for which a Smalltalk environment has been implemented. This is not always a disadvantage; the Smalltalk environment is available on many current platforms. With graphic interfaces becoming more prominent, Smalltalk may well find its way to being the utility language of the 1990s.

Turbo/Quick Pascal

In early 1989, Borland International and Microsoft simultaneously released object-oriented versions of Pascal. Borland used a C++-like approach in their *Turbo Pascal* product, while Microsoft opted for a Smalltalk-like object implementation in *QuickPascal*.

These are what I call "minimalist" object-oriented languages. They support the creation of classes, inheritance, and polymorphism -- the bare necessities for any object-oriented language. Alas, neither implements scope control for object members, operator/function overloading, or other sophisticated features found in languages like Smalltalk and C++.

Turbo Pascal's implementation of objects is more robust than *QuickPascal*'s, although both are equally limited in scope. In some ways, *QuickPascal* is easier to learn than *Turbo Pascal*, because it implements object in a simpler manner. For professional development, though, *Turbo Pascal* is the better of the two.

Either of these products makes for an excellent introduction to object-oriented programming. For the beginning C++ programmer, *Turbo Pascal* can serve as a "tutorial" to show how to use objects. Being simpler then C++, *Turbo Pascal* cen help you learn about objects without getting you mired down in complex details.

Actor

Actor is a very specialized programming language -- as of this writing, it is the only programming language specifically design to be used with Microsoft *Windows* for creating *Windows* applications.

Actor is a cross between Pascal and Smalltalk. Unlike *QuickPascal*, though, *Actor* is very functional and powerful. For instance, *Actor* includes a Smalltalk-like selection of built-in classes. *Actor*'s object-oriented features provide an abstract shell for working with the complex *Windows* programming environment. In many ways, *Actor* is the easiest programming language to use if you're building *Windows* programs

Glossary of Object-Oriented Programming Terms

Abstract Class — A class which is used to define the common characteristics of a set of classes. An abstract class is usually used as a
template which defines a series of related, polymorphic classes.
In C++, an the term "abstract class" is used specifically to refer
to any class which defines *pure virtual methods*.

Abstraction — The ability to look at something as a whole, without
being concerned with its details. The purpose of abstraction is to
allow a person understand something without having a complete
comprehension of its internal structure or function. Object-oriented
programming involves both data and functional abstraction.

Base Class — The class a derived class inherits from. See also *Parent
Class*.

Child Class — A class which is a descendant of another class. See
also *Derived Class*.

Class — The definition of an object type. A class describes both the
instance variables and methods of an object.

Class Hierarchy — A hierarchy exists when classes inherit from each other. You can think of a class hierarchy as a family tree, with derived classes as the children of their base (or parent) classes. Classes inherit the features of all of their direct ancestor classes.

Data Abstraction — This is the ability to "hide" the specific implementation details of a data type. For instance, very few programmers are concerned with the exact implementation of REAL values, so long as operations on those values work correctly. An object-oriented programming language like QuickPascal allows the programmer to create their own abstract data types via classes.

Derived Class — A class which inherits from another class. See also *Child Class.*

Encapsulation — The ability to place all of the data and functionality of a data type in a controlled and abstract structure. Classes are designed to give the programmer the freedom to encapsulate instance variables and methods within a single structure.

Functional Abstraction — Functional abstraction allows a programmer to look at a function, procedure, or method without concern for the actual algorithms used. If an operation is performed correctly, it is often unnecessary to know the specifics of how that operation is implemented. In your car, you aren't particularly aware of whether you have drum or disc brakes when you press on the brake pedal; your assume car will stop regardless of the actual type of the braking mechanism.

Inheritance — A class can inherit the instance variables and methods of any other class. The new class, called a derived or child class, has all of the characteristics of the class it is inheriting from, and can add new instance variables and methods of its own.

Instance — An object for which memory space has been allocated.

Instance Variable — A variable unique to a specific object. When an object is created, space is allocated for the variables defined in the object's class definition. The instance variables of one object have no affect on the instance variables of another object.

Instantiation — This refers to the process of creating an object.

Member — All objects which are declared to be of a specific class are termed members of that class. Members of a derived class are also members of the base class — but not vice versa. Classes have both data and function members.

Message — The term used for a method when its is applied to an object. Methods define the messages which can be sent to a class of objects. In most ways, the invocation of message is similar to a standard function or procedure call.

Method — An implementation of a message for a class. When a message is sent to an object, the method defined for the object's class (with the same name as the message) is executed.

Object — A variable defined to be a member of a class.

Parent Class — The class from which a child class inherits. See also *Base Class*.

Polymorphism — The ability of a message to modify its implementation based on the specific class of the object it is being sent to. When a derived class is created, it can replace the implementations of any methods it inherits from its base class. A message sent to a base class object uses the method defined for that message in the base class. If a derived class overrides a method inherited from its base class, a message of the same name as the

—

overridden method sent to an object of the derived class will invoke the method defined for the derived class.

Sending a Message — The act of calling a method for an object.

About the Author

Scott Robert Ladd is a full-time programmer and writer. His articles, benchmarks, and reviews have appeared in various technical publications, including *Dr. Dobb's Journal, BYTE, PC World, Micro Cornucopia, Computer Language Magazine,* and *The C User's Journal.*

Index

More Programming Tools from M&T Books

Graphics Programming in C

by Roger T. Stevens

All the information you need to program graphics in C, including source code, is presented. You'll find complete discussions of ROM BIOS, VGA, EGA, and CGA inherent capabilities; methods of displaying points on a screen; improved, faster algorithms for drawing and filling lines, rectangles, rounded polygons, ovals, circles, and arcs; graphics cursors; and much more! A complete description of how to print hard copies of graphics display screens is included. Both Turbo C and Microsoft C are supported.

Book & Disk (MS-DOS)	*Item #019-4*	*$36.95*
Book only	*Item #018-4*	*$26.95*

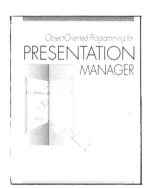

Object-Oriented Programming for Presentation Manager

by William G.Wong

Written for programmers and developers interested in OS/2 Presentation Manager (PM), as well as DOS programmers who are just beginning to explore Object-Oriented Programming and PM. Topics include a thorough overview of Presentation Manager and Object-Oriented Programming, Object-Oriented Programming lanuages and techniques, developing Presentation Manager applications using C and OOP techniques, and more.

Book and Disk (MS-DOS)	*Item #079-6*	*$39.95*
Book only	*Item #074-5*	*$29.95*

C++ Techniques and Applications

by Scott Robert Ladd

  This book guides the professional into the practical use of the C++ programming language—an object-oriented enhancement of the popular C programming language. The book contains three major sections. Part One introduces programmers tothe syntax and general usage of C++ features; Part Two covers object-oriented programming goals and techniques; and Part Three focuses on the creation of applications.

Book & Disk (MS-DOS)   *Item #076-1*   *$39.95*
Book only   *Item #075-3*   *$29.95*

To Order: Return this form with your payment to **M&T Books**, 501 Galveston Drive, Redwood City, CA 94063 or **CALL TOLL-FREE 1-800-533-4372** (in California, call 1-800-356-2002). Ask for Operator 7086.

☐ **YES!** Please send me the following: ☐ Check enclosed, payable to **M&T Books**.

Item#	Description	Qty	Price

Charge my ☐ Visa ☐ MC ☐ AmEx
Card No. _____ Exp. Date _____
Signature _____

Subtotal _____

CA residents add sales tax __%_____

Add $3.50 per item for shipping
and handling _____

TOTAL _____

Name _____
Address _____
City _____
State _____ Zip_____

Note: Prices subject to change without notice. Disks may be returned for exchange only if damaged in transit.

M&T BOOKS

7086